journalism***NEXT***

third edition

journalism*NEXT*
third edition

A Practical Guide to
Digital Reporting and Publishing

*mark*BRIGGS

With a foreword by Jennifer Preston

Los Angeles | London | New Delhi
Singapore | Washington DC

Los Angeles | London | New Delhi
Singapore | Washington DC

FOR INFORMATION:

CQ Press

An Imprint of SAGE Publications, Inc.

2455 Teller Road

Thousand Oaks, California 91320

E-mail: order@sagepub.com

SAGE Publications Ltd.

1 Oliver's Yard

55 City Road

London EC1Y 1SP

United Kingdom

SAGE Publications India Pvt. Ltd.

B 1/I 1 Mohan Cooperative Industrial Area

Mathura Road, New Delhi 110 044

India

SAGE Publications Asia-Pacific Pte. Ltd.

3 Church Street

#10-04 Samsung Hub

Singapore 049483

Copyright © 2016 Mark Briggs

Printed in the United States of America

ISBN 978-1-4833-5685-3

This book is printed on acid-free paper.

Executive Editor: Matthew Byrnie

Editorial Assistant: Janae Masnovi

Production Editor: David C. Felts

Copy Editor: Judy Selhorst

Typesetter: C&M Digitals (P) Ltd.

Proofreader: Scott Oney

Indexer: Sylvia Coates

Cover Designer: Scott Van Atta

Marketing Manager: Ashlee Blunk

Certified Chain of Custody
SUSTAINABLE Promoting Sustainable Forestry
FORESTRY www.sfiprogram.org
INITIATIVE SFI-01268

SFI label applies to text stock

15 16 17 18 19 10 9 8 7 6 5 4 3 2 1

CONTENTS

UNIT TWO: MULTIMEDIA

UNIT THREE: EDITING AND DECISION MAKING

FOREWORD

By Jennifer Preston, vice president, journalism,
The John S. and James L. Knight Foundation

When Mark Briggs wrote his first book, "Journalism 2.0: How to Survive and Thrive in the Digital Age," it was published online as a PDF by American University's J-Lab and the Knight Citizen News Network. It was downloaded more than 200,000 times in English, Spanish and Portuguese.

That was in 2007. I not only downloaded it, I also printed it out. At the time, I was an editor at The New York Times, overseeing a team that produced four Sunday metropolitan sections. I was eager to learn about technology and new digital media storytelling techniques, but there were few formal training opportunities inside the newsroom. The print and digital newsrooms had yet to be fully integrated.

I found that Mark's primer answered questions I didn't even know to ask. With a yellow highlighter, I marked up passages about RSS and CSS, along with tips on video storytelling and audio slide shows. I finally understood the difference between bits and bytes and why one browser was better than another. Once I understood the language of the technology, what all of those acronyms actually meant, I was able to more easily have conversations with Web producers, developers and multimedia editors about doing more than just posting our Sunday section stories and photos online.

Mark knew what journalists needed to know because he had run two newspaper Web sites. Two years later, he published an updated version of the PDF as a book, "Journalism Next: A Practical Guide to Digital Reporting and Publishing." Again, I found myself using the update as a guide in my new role as the first social media editor at The New York Times.

In this new edition of "Journalism Next," Mark clearly explains how to combine the values of journalism with the latest storytelling, engagement and distribution tools we have today. He draws on his experience inside a television newsroom as the digital director of KING 5 Television in Seattle, as well as on his network of people experimenting with new ways to tell stories all over the world.

Much has changed inside and outside newsrooms in the eight years since Mark first presented his easy-to-consume PDF digital journalism guide. A huge proportion of traffic for news and information is mobile. BuzzFeed, Upworthy, Vox and Quartz have developed enviable distribution models. CNN, ESPN and National Geographic are now delivering news and information through Snapchat's Discover feature. A Facebook page created in the aftermath of Hurricane Sandy to deliver updates for residents along the Jersey Shore is filling the information gaps left by the closure of newspaper bureaus there.

The Des Moines Register and Gannett Digital made a first attempt at creating a journalism feature for Oculus Rift, the first truly immersive virtual reality headset for video games. The New York Times "Innovation" report changed the way the newsroom, along with newsrooms around the world, embraces audience development efforts. The Seattle Times is experimenting with a new model called Solutions Journalism to increase engagement with local residents around its education coverage. Some of the most important journalism continues to be produced from not-for-profit news sites, from the Voice of San Diego to the Texas Tribune to Pro Publica and the Marshall Project, a single-topic online news site that focuses on criminal justice.

In this ever-evolving world, journalists continuously learn how to leverage technology—not just to produce stronger journalism with data, curated video and involving users in the creative process, but to use the powerful tools available today and engage and build an audience around quality journalism.

Some news organizations are helping their journalists keep up with all of the changes by delivering digital media training. Unfortunately, many have not been providing the level of digital training—or the leadership and content-management systems—needed to transform their newsrooms into truly digital and mobile-first operations.

But there are signs that this is changing. In my new role as vice president of journalism at the John S. and James L. Knight Foundation, I am visiting newsrooms around the country and meeting journalists committed to embracing change.

And in a recent Poynter survey, funded by the Knight Foundation, two-thirds of journalists said they had received some kind of training in the past 12 months. The most heartening news is that the more the respondents learned, the more they wanted to know, especially on topics with a digital focus.

Seven out of the top 10 topics they identified to Poynter involved digital training, with social media, the use of digital tools and video skills as the top three areas where journalists thought that training could help them in their profession during the coming year. Other items in the top 10 included audience development, data, mobile, managing change, Web analytics, Web design and writing skills.

Where does a journalist hungry for this kind of information find low-cost, convenient training and support to keep learning and remain abreast of the changes taking place in our industry?

A few thoughts:

Explore online resources, like Poynter's NewsU or the high-quality MOOCS by the Knight Center for Journalism in the Americas at the University of Texas.

Keep up with changes in the industry by reading Nieman Lab, MediaLab or Poynter every day. Create a Twitter list of journalists using social media in smart ways and sharing valuable information. Make sure Brian Stelter of CNN's "Reliable Sources" is on it. Follow journalism organizations and journalists who post tips.

Consider joining the Online News Association. Attend a local Online News Association meetup. There you will find not only people sharing best digital journalism practices but also a community of like-minded people who want to learn and share. If there isn't a local meetup group, create one.

Sign up for Hacks and Hackers. Is there a tech meetup in your community? Go to a meeting. Find out what classes you can audit at a local college with a journalism program. Perhaps you may be able to mentor students about journalism in exchange for learning new digital skills. It was as an adjunct for Sree Sreenivasan, former dean of students at Columbia University's Graduate School of Journalism, that I first learned how to use Google Docs in 2007 and later learned about new social media curation tools.

Attend a conference held by Investigative Reporters and Editors or the National Institute for Computer-Assisted Reporting. If your news organization won't pay for you to go, use vacation days to attend and offer to volunteer at the conference to defray costs. Investing in your continuous learning is the best way to ensure you will always know how to report, present and distribute important journalism.

Most important, this edition of "Journalism Next" will get you started.

PREFACE

By Mark Briggs

Much has changed since the first edition of this book became available in 2009, when the world had not yet heard of Instagram, Pinterest or Snapchat. But the core concept of this guidebook—to leverage digital technology to do better journalism—has not changed at all.

What is coming "next" in journalism? No one knows for sure, but we can all agree that it will be digital. Social networks will always come and go, and digital technology will continue to evolve at a dizzying pace. The pursuit of harnessing it to do better journalism will never end.

Learning about new technology is nice, but it's not enough. What makes this book essential reading for students, professors and working journalists is the connection it makes between new technology and emerging concepts with the core principles of journalism.

To help you get your arms around the limitless possibilities, the book starts with basic concepts like Web design, blogging and crowdsourcing. Once you have a sufficient digital foundation, you'll explore specialized skills in multimedia, including audio, video and photography. The final section takes you through more advanced concepts, including data-driven journalism and building an online audience.

It's important to first understand the concepts and techniques, so each is defined (see "What is it?" subheads), then explored and then applied to journalism (see "What's Next?" subheads).

The goal is to get you going with a new skill or concept right away. After all, there's no time to waste. The summary checklists at the ends of the chapters spell out specifically how you can do just that.

The format also makes it convenient for you to select the specific skills you need to explore today. While there is a logical sequence to the material, it's also organized so that you can bounce around and hit the areas you need most right now. Have an idea for a podcast? Jump to the chapter on audio. Need help with your blog? See chapter 2 for tips and suggestions from some of the best in the business.

There are many different layers to the complex topic of technology. Some readers will be experiencing certain concepts for the first time, while they are already familiar with others. That's why you'll see "Drilling Down" boxes throughout the text—each gives more experienced readers a window into an advanced skill or tool.

Since this is a practical guide, each chapter features a "Newsroom Innovator." These sections offer tips and suggestions from working professionals who are subject-matter experts in their field—in their own words.

Getting started with new technology can be intimidating. Making sense of it and finding the right opportunities with regard to journalism are additional challenges that have kept many smart news professionals on the digital sidelines. Don't let that happen to you. Jump in, get going and help build what's "next" in journalism.

ACKNOWLEDGMENTS

I don't consider myself an expert, but, thankfully, I know a lot of them.

The generosity of dozens of experts in various fields made the practical guidance contained in this text possible. They responded to e-mails and phone calls and took time out of their busy schedules to contribute to this project.

I also drew from countless conference presentations (and conversations in the hallways), insightful blog posts and articles from dedicated professionals helping journalism adapt to the digital age.

While their names appear in the text where they directly contributed expertise, here's a tip of my hat to each of them (in alphabetical order, of course):

Ellyn Angelotti	Jennifer Carroll	John Henrikson
David Ardia	Tom Chester	Burt Herman
Patrick Beeson	John Cook	Richard Hernandez
Cory Bergman	Deb Cram	Val Hoeppner
Charles Bertram	Adam Davidson	Karin Høgh
Paul Bradshaw	Nicola Dowling	Etan Horowitz
Shirley Brady	Cory Haik	Jeff Jarvis

Scott Karp

Jonathan Kern

Chris Krewson

Jack Lail

Solana Larsen

Greg Linch

Mark Luckie

Mark Maley

Oscar Martinez

Michele McLellan

Misty Montano

Shawn Montano

Angela Morris

Matt Mrozinski

Colin Mulvaney

Naka Nathaniel

Marissa Nelson

Sona Patel

Tim Peek

Meghan Peters

Ryan Pitts

Lauren Rabaino

Tim Repsher

Jeremy Rue

Mike Sando

Ken Sands

Mara Schiavocampo

Ryan Sholin

Ivan Sigal

Dwight Silverman

Jason Silverstein

Jennifer Sizemore

Robert Smith

Lauren Spuhler

Dale Steinke

Jim Stovall

Ron Sylvester

Alana Taylor

Josh Trujillo

Linda Thomas

Matt Thompson

Patrick Thornton

Derek Willis

As well, I'd like to thank the professors and journalists who reviewed this third edition for CQ Press: Wasim Ahmad, Stony Brook University; Karin Becker, University of North Dakota; Kris Boyle, Creighton University; Patrick Howe, California Polytechnic State University; Marsha Little Matthews, The University of Texas at Tyler; Chris Snider, Drake University; and Mary Williams, University of Portsmouth. Thanks also to those professionals and academics who contributed thoughtful reviews on earlier editions: Lee Becker, Jon Glass, Alfred Hermida, Michelle Johnson, Scott Maier, Nikhil Moro, Nikki Schwab, Michael Schwartz, Dave Sennerud, Julie Shirley and Lisa Rose Weaver.

In addition, I would like to thank:

Jennifer Preston, who wrote an inspiring foreword and is one of the true leaders in digital journalism.

For the first edition, a couple of people who made the foundation that we built in 2009 rock solid: Charisse Kiino, for guidance and inspiration; Jane Harrigan, my tireless development editor; and Christina Mueller, who kept the trains running on time. The book would be nowhere near as good as it is without their effort and expertise, and the good work of everyone else at CQ Press who has touched my project, including Matthew Byrnie, Janae Masnovi, David Felts, Astrid Virding and Judy Selhorst, whose masterful copyediting on this edition is so appreciated.

Jan Schaffer, the hardest-working woman in journalism innovation, who came up with the idea for my first book, "Journalism 2.0." This book—in its third edition—wouldn't have been possible without the first one, so I owe Jan a great deal of thanks and appreciation.

Separately, I would be remiss if I didn't recognize all of the smart, dedicated co-workers I've collaborated with at KING-TV, The News Tribune and The Herald, as well as my colleagues from news organizations throughout Gannett, Belo, McClatchy and The Washington Post Co. Thanks for influencing my journalism career and helping me along the way.

INTRODUCTION

> **Journalism Is About People, Not Technology**

"The future is already here. It's just not very evenly distributed yet."

When William Gibson made that observation in 1993, there was no Facebook, no Google, no iPhones or iPads. It is among the most prescient observations I've heard, and it still rings true today.

People often ask about the future of journalism. As Gibson noted, it's already here.

To survive and thrive in the digital age, I argued in my first book, "Journalism 2.0," journalists must adopt a new way of thinking and approaching their craft. Learning the skills and technology is actually the easy part. Recognizing you are part of a new information ecosystem, aka "the future," is the steeper hill to climb.

That perspective, at least the latter part, now almost seems quaint. When "Journalism 2.0" was published (in 2007), most journalists in the United States were ambivalent (at best) toward the new digital information ecosystem. Then social media happened, driven largely by Facebook and Twitter, and it became difficult to find anyone in journalism who didn't believe the landscape has been significantly altered.

I wrote that book for working journalists: those who had spent years or decades doing one form of journalism and were now being asked to evolve. Thanks to funding from the Knight Foundation, the book was made available as a free downloadable e-book, and more than 200,000 people have taken advantage. (Many of those downloads have been in Spanish or Portuguese.) Surprising to me, many colleges and universities adopted the book, despite the fact it is more like a pamphlet than a textbook. (I think they liked the price.)

A revised, updated and expanded version of the book, titled "Journalism Next," was published in 2009 by CQ Press. It was aimed at those getting started in journalism or digital publishing, whether students or midcareer professionals looking for a new direction.

Regardless, the message is the same for both students and practitioners: "The future is now."

Though it is not the only industry to be upended in recent years, the pace of disruption for mainstream media—daily newspapers, local TV stations and magazines—is certainly in full force. As a result, the evolution of the business model is (finally) receiving the focus it deserves, meaning we have already begun to glimpse what the next incarnation of sustainable journalism looks like. (My other book, "Entrepreneurial Journalism," covers this area.) The disruption of the traditional business model has led many in journalism, especially those who have worked at newspapers, to question the future for journalism. Don't be one of them.

"The future of journalism can and will be better than its past," says Richard Gingras, the former CEO of Salon.com, who is now head of news products at Google. "[But] we need to rethink every facet of what we do. There's a large amount of transformation to get from here to there."

WELCOME TO THE AGE OF TRANSFORMATION

The news business, and all business really, will be forever changing. The dizzying pace of technological innovation will ensure it. There is no magical switch to flip that will move us all from one model to another.

"The culture of innovation is not a luxury," says Google's Gingras. "It can't be intermittent. It must of part of an organization's DNA."

When "Journalism 2.0" was first published, the first iPhone had just been released. There is no mention in the book of Twitter. The iPad? Android? Tumblr? All (and many more) were still in development and mostly just ideas.

We are living in the age of digital Darwinism. This affects any business using digital technology to publish content, whether it's journalism, music, movies or funny cat videos.

Unfortunately, many of the people running news companies today still remember the best of times during the 1970s, '80s and '90s. Given that experience, it can be difficult not to hope that the current state of flux is only temporary. Those decades were a golden period for publishers, where organizations grew large and consolidated, pushing profit margins up and supporting publicly traded companies.

Remember, however, that mainstream news organizations, the commercial enterprises that have supported journalism in the United States, haven't always been like this. Prior to 1970, journalism was practiced by many more organizations of differing sizes. And looking forward, the state of news, media and journalism will probably look a lot more like it did at the beginning of the 20th century, when far more news organizations were competing for audience. Each was tiny compared with the behemoths of the 1990s and 2000s, but there were many more of them. Instead of a daily newspaper with 50 journalists, a midsize city might have 10 digital news operations with about five journalists each, each operation covering a topical or geographic niche. Another operation might combine editors and programmers to aggregate the journalism available in all these locations and deliver a cohesive package to a different audience.

WHAT JOB CAN I GET IN JOURNALISM?

My last three jobs in journalism did not exist when I was in college.

If you're a student reading this, think about what that means for your future. How do you prepare yourself today for a job that doesn't currently exist? If you're an educator reading this, how do you prepare your students for jobs that don't currently exist? (And jobs that didn't exist while you were working in the profession?)

I can tell you what worked for me:

- **Use a wide-angle lens when viewing the world:** Journalism, especially newspaper and broadcast television journalism, is an extremely insular industry. To prepare yourself for what's coming next you must be aware of the wide range of innovation, from technology to entertainment and new consumer products. Read business magazines and Web sites. Follow smart people on social media who have nothing to do with news. Attend events that are not related to journalism.

- **Feed your journalistic curiosity, starve your journalistic skepticism:** Curiosity is inherent in journalists. Most of the people who end up in journalism are there because they want to answer questions, for themselves and their audience. Apply that curiosity to new products, software tools, gadgets and apps. Become an early adopter.

- **Collaborate:** Whenever possible, collaborate with people outside your regular team. Mixing with people from other disciplines or interests will teach you new ways of thinking and approaching problems.

It is uncertain where your next career opportunity will come from. It may come from a traditional news company in a newly created role. Or it could come from a start-up news blog or a new enterprise you launch yourself. "Journalism will survive its institutions," says entrepreneurial journalist David Cohn. But only if a new generation of journalists with an entrepreneurial spirit hit the ground running.

Here's why it's a good time to go into journalism:

▶ 1. Journalism has a bright future

Experimental news operations have popped up all over the Web since "Journalism 2.0" was first published. Some have become sustainable businesses in a very short time. Others are still searching for viability while finding new ways to cover issues and communities.

In short, the demand for journalism from its audience hasn't diminished. But the models are starting to look very different.

A more narrow focus is required. Think of it as "bottom-up" journalism instead of "top-down." Technology and political and hyperlocal news sites have been the first to find success by starting small and concentrating on very specific topics. This, of course, is counter to the course of the more general audience publications that dominated when printing and distribution monopolies ruled the day.

Now that anyone can become a publisher with a few clicks, trying to be everything to everyone is a recipe for failure.

The future of journalism will be fueled by these independent trailblazers—Huffington Post, Vox Media, BuzzFeed, Vice, Texas Tribune, West Seattle Blog, Mic—and many others yet to be created.

Unleashed from corporate-run organizations sweating out the quarterly profit margin, the journalists powering these new sites have infused them with a level of energy, commitment and passion that can be found only in start-up companies. It's easy to see how these sites will pave the way for the true digital transformation of mainstream news companies, by finding successful new methods to inform and connect communities online.

Or, in some cases, they will replace mainstream news companies.

"Make it awesome," is how Vox CEO Jim Bankoff explained his company's strategy to an audience at the 2014 International Symposium for Online Journalism at the University of Texas. Bankoff encouraged media leaders to "enable quality storytelling, production and design" and to embrace talent and technology.

▶ 2. That future is in your hands

Journalism needs you. It needs someone who can bring a fresh approach without the baggage that burdened earlier generations.

As the institutions that perform journalism struggled economically through the past decade, it became increasingly apparent that the people in charge did not have what it takes to oversee a digital transformation that would secure a viable future. Harsh words, I know. But their inability to put the audience first and use new technology to do better journalism—instead of copying the existing model and pasting it online—created a world where every newspaper and local TV news Web site is immediately identifiable. Most are disjointed repositories of what a news organization has always produced, with some new twists thrown in for good measure, instead of rich, vibrant information sources their communities want and need.

That's where you come in. Whether you end up working for a newspaper, magazine, TV station or Internet start-up, you will have the opportunity—make that responsibility—to do things differently. My first job in journalism (part-time sports clerk) was mostly answering phones and doing grunt work where no one asked me about my ideas. Your first job is likely to be much different.

In fact, I'd venture a guess that you won't get a first job *without* your ideas, in addition to your skills and experience.

▶ 3. Journalism will be better than it was before

Transformation and evolution are messy, emotional processes. When they produce advancement for society and business, they are seen as healthy and worthwhile, but not necessarily to those on the front lines.

After all, change is inevitable, but progress is optional.

The transformation to digital started more than 15 years ago for news companies and the Web. If you're just getting started in journalism, you benefit by having missed the early mess.

The game isn't over—it's just getting started. And, since tomorrow's journalists inherently "get" the Internet because they grew up with it, they have the opportunity to shape the future of journalism online as no generation has before.

If you didn't grow up with the Internet, don't despair. I didn't either. My first newspaper reporting job had me sending stories back to the office on a Radio Shack computer device dubbed the "Trash-80" using cups over the receiver at a pay phone. (It only worked about half the time, so there was a lot of dictation.) Now, digital information and communication are like the air I breathe: I don't even notice they're there.

Interactive, transparent, collaborative journalism works. Digital technologies, some that have yet to be invented, will aid you. But they can't replace a thoughtful, skilled professional with an entrepreneurial spirit. You will be ready to try, fail and try again. Thankfully, you will find a more experimental culture at news organizations today (and tomorrow) to test those new ideas.

You don't need to confine yourself to the road traveled before you—the opportunity to chart your own course is not only available: it's mandatory.

SUMMARY

While journalism isn't the only industry caught in the middle of a massive upheaval, I would argue it's an industry that stands a great chance of making it to the other side and dramatically improving along the way.

"I think in the long run," author Steven Berlin Johnson said, "we're going to look back at many facets of old media and realize that we were living in a desert disguised as a rain forest."

Here's the new deal: You probably won't get to travel a well-marked, established career path as those who came before you did. But you will have a say in how the fourth estate evolves and how citizens are informed and engaged in the decades to come. And you will have the chance to be part of something bigger and better than it's ever been before.

Sounds like a pretty good deal to me. So, let's get started.

We Are All Web Workers Now

How much time do you spend on the Internet each day? If not on a laptop, then chances are you use a tablet or a smartphone many times every day. Whether you're a digital native or a digital immigrant, some basic terms and concepts probably remain a mystery. This chapter will briefly explain the essential building blocks of online work that will be used throughout other chapters—and throughout your career, whether it's in journalism or some other form of communication.

One of the barriers to more deeply understanding how the Internet and other technologies work is the endless sea of acronyms and jargon. This chapter will break those apart and define the basic concepts of online technology that are such a significant part of your daily life.

We're all Web workers now. Previous generations of journalists—and other workers in all industries—had the luxury of expecting some supergeeks in their organizations to take care of the digital duties for them. For better or worse, those days are gone.

It has been said that technology can become effective only when we start taking it for granted. Our society has reached that point with e-mail and Web browsing, which enable us to connect with one another and connect with information easily and constantly. But if we take online technology for granted, we can miss some important opportunities to leverage it to gather information better, to communicate better and to create better journalism.

Let's take a step back and break down the most basic Web technologies so you can learn how to get the most out of your online existence. After all, the Web is simply a way to send and receive digital information. Each of these building blocks serves a different need or offers a unique opportunity to do that:

- How Web browsers work

- How FTP transfers large files over the Web

- How HTML, CSS and XML work

- How to create a basic Web site using WordPress

DIGITAL INFORMATION

In the ensuing chapters, you will learn to create several types of digital files: text files, audio files, photo files and video files. It is important that you understand how to "weigh" these files, because the larger the file size, the longer it takes to download over the Internet.

The digital revolution can be explained in bits and bytes. A byte is a unit of measure for digital information. A single byte contains eight consecutive bits and is capable of storing a single ASCII (pronounced as-kee) character.

The American Standard Code for Information Interchange (ASCII) first published a standard in 1967. It defines the 95 printable characters that create the text in computers and communications devices. Essentially, it's everything on your keyboard: letters, numbers and basic symbols such as % and &.

To make it easier to talk about a lot of bytes, we use prefixes like kilo, mega and giga, as in kilobyte, megabyte and gigabyte (also shortened to K, M and G, as in KB, MB and GB). Table 1.1 shows the number of bytes contained in each.

You can see in this table that kilo is about a thousand, mega is about a million, giga is about a billion and so on. So, when someone says, "This computer has an 80-gig hard drive," that means the hard drive stores 80 gigabytes, or approximately 80 billion bytes. How could you possibly need 80 gigabytes of space? Well, one CD holds 650 megabytes, so it won't take long to fill the whole thing, especially if you have a lot of music and digital photographs. Petabyte databases are actually common these days, from the Pentagon to major retailers like Sears who use them to store customer data. And a consumer can pick up a terabyte hard drive at a big-box store or an electronics store for about $150.

Knowing the relative size of computer data is important for many reasons. For starters, you should never send an e-mail with an attachment larger than 1 MB, especially to someone with a company e-mail address, or you will clog your server and the recipient's server. And you should especially never send

| Table 1.1 | "HOW BITS AND BYTES WORK" |

Name	Abbreviation	Size
Kilo	K	1,024
Mega	M	1,048,576
Giga	G	1,073,741,824
Tera	T	1,099,511,627,776
Peta	P	1,125,899,906,842,624
Exa	E	1,152,921,504,606,846,976
Zetta	Z	1,180,591,620,717,411,303,424
Yotta	Y	1,208,925,819,614,629,174,706,176

Source: Adapted from Marshall Brain, "How Bits and Bytes Work," HowStuffWorks, April 1, 2000. www.howstuffworks.com/bytes.htm/printable.

an e-mail with a large attachment, such as a photo, to a group list. The server will have to make copies of your large file for everyone on the distribution list.

You should also begin to recognize the size of the files (PDFs or video clips) that you download from the Web. Note how long it takes to download a file that is 500K versus one that is 5MB. Knowing the difference between large and small computer files is part of a basic digital literacy you need today.

Recognizing the difference between file sizes is important for online publishing because the speed of an Internet connection plus the size of the file to be downloaded determines how fast someone can download your content. If it's just text, like a news story, it's probably only a few KB, which will download quickly, even over a slow mobile connection on a cell phone.

What is it? | What's Next? | Summary

⍰ HOW THE INTERNET WORKS

As you know, the Internet is a network of connected computers that share information. Contrary to popular belief, *Internet* is not synonymous with *World Wide Web*. The Web is not the computer network but rather a way of accessing information through the network, using hypertext transfer protocol (HTTP) and Web browsers. The Web does not include other protocols such as e-mail, instant messaging (IM) and file transfer (FTP).

How Web servers work

A Web server is a special type of computer that stores and distributes information over the Internet. You will probably never work directly with a Web server, but understanding how servers power the information you consume over the Internet every day will give you a better foundation for working online. (Knowing how to fix a car isn't necessary for driving one, but you have to know when it needs gas and an oil change.)

But how does the server know which information to serve? The URL (uniform resource locator), or Web address, is the key, and it works much the way your home address does. Although you recognize a Web address such as www.yahoo.com, Web servers know that location as http://209.131.36.158. That's the IP address (IP = Internet protocol), which is a unique numeric identity of a Web-server location. All Web addresses have corresponding IP addresses that computers recognize but people never would. Registering a domain name secures a human-readable Web address and associates it with a numeric and computer-friendly IP address.

DRILLING DOWN

Web Browsers   If you haven't tried a new Web browser lately, you should. These programs, which are all free downloads, are constantly updated and improved. Even old favorites, such as **Safari**, offer new versions that work much faster. Serious Web geeks prefer the **Chrome** browser, which is made by Google and is now the dominant browser on the Internet, with more than 60 percent of the market. Also try **Firefox**, which was developed as an open-source project and has been the second most popular browser for years.

[*Note:* Information on Chrome usage from "Browser Statistics," W3Schools, October 2014. www.w3schools.com/browsers/browsers_stats.asp.]

How Web browsers work

The Web browser is the tool that you use to access over the Internet information that is published as part of the World Wide Web. It is software that you know as Internet Explorer, Chrome, Safari or Firefox, and it does three important things:

1. It searches for and finds information on Web servers.

2. It retrieves the information and brings it back to you.

3. It renders the information for display on your computer or mobile device.

When a browser retrieves a Web page and brings it back to you, it makes a copy of the various components of that particular Web page and stores those files on your computer. This copy is called the cache.

The cache is a temporary storage of all the files you download while you're browsing the Web. You can adjust the settings on your browser's cache to store a few or a lot of these temporary files. Clearing your cache regularly is a good idea—it helps your browser run efficiently, and it deletes unneeded temporary files from your computer, which helps your entire system run better.

▶▶ *Your browser's cache*
How to clear your cache depends on which browser you use:

- Chrome: To clear the cache, select CLEAR BROWSER DATA from the top Chrome menu item. Once on the settings page, select CLEAR BROWSING DATA.

- Firefox: To clear the cache, select HISTORY, then Clear RECENT HISTORY.

- Safari: Click on HISTORY in the top menu, then select CLEAR HISTORY AND WEBSITE DATA.

- Internet Explorer: To clear the cache, select Tools, then Internet Options. Click the Advanced tab. Scroll down to Security and check the Empty Temporary Internet Files folder when the browser is closed.

To make sure the browser is showing the most updated files for a Web page, use the **REFRESH** button (or hit F5 on your keyboard if using Windows, **APPLE-R** if using a Mac). This tells the browser to go back to the Web server and get new copies of all the files that make up that particular Web page.

▶▶ *Plug-ins and extensions*
Modern Web browsers can display more than just text and graphics, but most need the aid of plug-ins or extensions. A couple of these popular add-ons are Adobe Acrobat Reader (for reading PDFs) and Flash. The makers of the Firefox browser opened up their software to the outside development of plug-ins and add-ons, a decision that changed the way users think about browser technology, much as applications for the iPhone have changed the way users think about cell phones.

Firefox and Chrome developers have made available dozens of cool plug-ins and add-ons. Popular add-ons block pop-up ads or unwanted scripts, manage downloads and translate text from Web pages into different languages.

For Chrome extensions, go to **WINDOW** in the top menu and select **EXTENSIONS**. You can search for new extensions by selecting "Get More Extensions" at the bottom of the page. For Firefox extensions, go to https://addons.mozilla.org/en-US/firefox.

What is it? | What's Next? | Summary

⚡ SYNDICATED CONTENT WITH RSS

RSS stands for Really Simple Syndication, which is a great name because the concept is just that: really simple. RSS enables you to subscribe to an information feed that gets delivered directly to an RSS reader or Web browser. So, instead of visiting several different Web pages each day or performing the same Web searches over and over, you can set up RSS feeds to do that for you.

RSS is still an underrated tool for Internet users, more than 15 years after it became widely available. Because subscribing is free, Web publishers—news sites especially—love RSS for the consistent delivery of content. But, for whatever reason, RSS has never caught on with a critical mass of users and, when Google shut down its Reader product in 2013, the still-fledgling technology was dealt a significant blow.

Some RSS feeds give the reader only the first paragraph of an article and require a user to visit the host's Web page for the rest. This protects a Web site's traffic numbers and ad-serving opportunities. But this practice runs counter to the idea of helping your audience access content easily. Publishers are experimenting with ways to include advertising in RSS feeds, too.

As a journalist, you are a merchant of information. You acquire and exchange information to do your job. And you are an information seeker and a naturally curious person, so learning to use a Web browser to gather and report information didn't require a giant leap. But a Web browser by itself is limited in its ability to handle the massive amount of information available online.

Thankfully, you can use RSS feeds to dramatically increase the amount, and improve the quality, of information that interests you. In fact, acquiring a daily RSS habit is the best way for you to increase your knowledge of any subject.

RSS is essential. The bottom line is that using RSS is the most efficient way to consume massive amounts of information in a structured and organized way. And who doesn't want to learn more while saving time?

"RSS is an important way of tracking what multiple people are saying about a certain subject," said John Cook, a former business reporter for the Seattle Post-Intelligencer who is now executive editor for GeekWire, a site he co-founded. "Also, a number of the companies I track keep blogs, so putting their feeds into my RSS reader is one way to stay up on what they are doing. With so much being written these days, this is one way to track what is going on."

If you've ever received an e-mail news alert from Google or Yahoo on a search term that you set up, you understand the amount of information available on the Web and the need for smart technology to help you track it. E-mail, however, is not an efficient tool for tracking dozens or even hundreds of topics. RSS can do that and help you track many topics with the click of a mouse.

What is it? | **What's *Next?*** | Summary

⬇ SET UP AN RSS READER AND SUBSCRIBE TO FEEDS

When you subscribe to RSS feeds, you create a convenient, one-stop information shop tailored to your needs and interests. Setting up a feed is similar to bookmarking a Web site, but a feed is much more efficient and powerful. And getting started is really easy. Here's how:

1. Select a reader.
2. Find a feed.
3. Add it to your reader.

▶ Select a reader

You can choose from two types of RSS readers: Web-based readers that you access by logging in to a specific Web page, or apps for your tablet or smartphone.

Cover Stories ⌄   Q

Flipboard

Is Instagram Really Worth More Than These Companies?
[H] Shared by Huffington Post

huffingtonpost.com • Facebook could have bought *The New York Times* for less.

That's right, the $1 billion in cash and stock that Facebook paid for Instagram Monday values the two-year old mobile photo-sharing app more than *The New York Times*.

Knight Digital Media Center Weblog
Shared by AdamWestbrook

multimedia.journalism.berkeley.ed u • *This is a guest post by David Beriain, José Carlos Castaño, Sergio Caro and Ernesto Villalba. They are members of* Once Upon a Time *and* En Pie de Guerra, *multimedia ...*

The Knight-Mozilla Fellowships
Shared by Joshua Hatch

mozillaopennews.org • The centerpiece of the Open-News program, the Knight-Mozilla Fellow-ships embed developers and technologists in newsrooms around the world to spend a year

writing code in collaboration with reporters, designers, and newsroom developers. Fellows work in the open by sharing their code and their discoveries on the web, helping to ...

6 Reasons Twitter is Becoming My New E-mail
Shared by Mich Sineath

forbes.com • In the busy world of real-time business and push information, browsing my e-mail inbox almost seems like a relaxing ...

Latest   ◦ ◦ ◾ ◦ ◦   Sunday   ✎

> *Screenshot of content displayed in Flipboard.* <

DRILLING DOWN ▲▼

Twitter Instead of RSS   For many people, Twitter has replaced an RSS reader. The ability to follow news organizations *and* individual journalists is a powerful combination that allows users to keep track of news and information. You can organize large amounts of content efficiently by using a Twitter client such as Hootsuite or TweetDeck. You can set up separate columns for separate topics, making it easy to consume the information you want on a particular session.

Apps for your tablet or smartphone: One of the reasons that RSS probably never caught on as a "killer app" was because it was just technical enough to intimidate users. These days, people use RSS every day without even knowing it. Mainstream apps like Flipboard, Readly and Feedly use RSS technology to allow users to subscribe to news feeds without ever realizing they are using RSS.

Visit the iTunes Store or Google Play Store, depending on what kind of mobile device you have,

→ *Columns of Twitter feeds displayed on Hootsuite or TweetDeck.* ←

and search for news apps. Choose an app to download and start subscribing to news content that interests you. This will allow you to explore new content on multiple sites efficiently with a single app.

▶ Find a feed and subscribe

Locate a link to RSS on a Web site with content you want to receive automatically. Usually a little orange icon will signal the availability of RSS. Most news Web sites have index pages with dozens of feeds available. To the left is a partial list of feeds available on washingtonpost.com.

Click on the link of the feed to which you want to subscribe. Modern Web browsers such as Chrome, Firefox and Safari will recognize a URL that ends with

Politics

Blogs

- Post Politics
- The Fact Checker
- The Federal Eye
- Govbeat
- In the Loop
- The Fix
- Monkey Cage

Opinions

Blogs

- Alyssa Rosenberg's' 'Act Four'
- Ask the Post

Credit: The Washington Post

> RSS feeds offered on washingtonpost.com.

"xml" and automatically take you to a page that allows you to quickly add the feed to a Web-based reader such as Yahoo or AOL.

▶ Determine what is best to subscribe to

- Sections on news Web sites that are targeted to your interest or beat

- Blogs that discuss a topic of interest

- Blogs by companies or people you cover

- Web searches such as Google news alerts on terms, names of people and companies

- Content from your own Web site that is worth tracking, such as most popular stories

▶ Subscribe to news alerts and searches

Instead of performing several—even dozens of—Web searches every day, most journalists have learned to rely on e-mail news alerts from Google or Yahoo to keep them posted when new items are published. Even though your e-mail inbox is probably full enough, and e-mail is not as efficient at tracking news alerts as an RSS reader, Google discontinued its simple feature of adding alerts and searches to an RSS reader when it shuttered Google Reader.

DRILLING DOWN ▲▼

Organize Your RSS Use the folders of your RSS reader to organize your feeds and track information efficiently. It's a good idea to group feeds by topic or priority. For example, create a "Priority 1" or "A-list" folder with the feeds that you want to read every day even if you have only 10 minutes. You can also create a folder for news searches so you don't have to clutter your e-mail inbox.

The difference between a Web search and an alert is like the difference between going to the business section of The New York Times to look for an article about Microsoft and going to Google or Yahoo News and entering "Microsoft." If you are very interested in a topic and want to find information from many sources, with an alert your computer will perform the search for you.

Here's how to set it up:

1. Perform the news search (in Google News or Yahoo News).
2. Click on the "Create Alert" link on the first results page.
3. Enter your e-mail address and submit.

Do you want to be smarter tomorrow than you are today? Adopting a daily RSS habit is the easiest way to make that happen.

What is it? | What's *Next?* Summary

⬆ FTP (FILE TRANSFER PROTOCOL)

File transfer protocol is a simple process for moving those big files between computers that e-mail can't handle.

Credit: Google

Screenshot of creating an alert from a Google News search.

The Internet uses several different protocols, or methods, to transfer data. Web pages work on the hypertext transfer protocol (which explains the http:// in the address bar of your Web browser), while e-mail works with the simple mail transfer protocol (SMTP).

Although those methods do more than transfer data—Web sites and e-mail programs also display the information—FTP is a one-trick pony. It simply moves a file from one computer to another.

When would you use FTP? You'd use it if you have captured some photos or video or recorded some audio and want to publish this material online with the story you are working on.

Digital audio and video—and some PDF and PowerPoint files—can exceed 1 MB in size. Some video files exceed even 1 GB. Transferring files larger than 1 MB by e-mail is not a good idea because most network servers are not capable of handling them. (Third-party e-mail programs such as Gmail handle them pretty well, however.)

FTP is also the primary method for uploading Web pages onto a Web server to publish them online.

What is it? | **What's *Next*?** | Summary

⬇ SET UP AN FTP PROGRAM

There are dozens of FTP software programs available to execute the task, and most are free. FileZilla and Free FTP are FTP programs I've used successfully on the Windows platform. For the Mac, Fetch, Cute FTP or Cyberduck will do the trick.

You can also add an extension like sFTP or FreeFTP to the Chrome browser. Or, if Firefox is your browser, you can download the FireFTP plug-in and add FTP capability to your current browser.

Note: To find any of the services here, simply run a Web search on Google or Yahoo for the name.

Transferring files: All you need to transfer a large file (or files) over the Internet, besides some free software, is the account information of the server where you want to send the file. Get the account information from your Internet hosting service or, if you're working within an organization, from the company's technical staff. It will look like this:

Account name: Newspaper FTP (*this is optional—something you create for yourself*)

Host: ftp.newspaper.com

Login: crazyfiles

Password: !secretstuff%

Most FTP programs save the information the first time you enter it so you'll be able to easily return and send additional files with one or two clicks.

Setup: The setup for most FTP programs is the same: a folder layout on the left side of the interface that reflects the file structure of your computer (aka local site) and a folder layout on the right side that reflects the file structure of the server (aka remote site). Navigate to the folder where you want to copy the target file (if that folder is not already visible), then find the file in your file structure, click on it and drag it across. It's that easy.

Transfer large files over the Internet with free software like FireFTP.

WEB-DESIGN BASICS

Actual computer code can be scary stuff. I've met too many veteran journalists who grimace when faced with even the smallest amount of computer code.

"I'm not a programmer!" they shriek. "I can't do this!"

Many younger journalists who grew up with YouTube and Facebook, whom one might expect to be much more code savvy, have yet to get their hands dirty with code. I've met countless college journalism students in the past few years who have no experience with—or interest in—modifying a Web page with code, yet they have their own blogs, Facebook pages and more.

Even though it's possible to lead a digital life without learning basic coding skills, a journalist's ability to execute ideas and be a better journalist will be limited without such skills. Learning to code opens up opportunities; when you have an idea for something new on your Web site, you don't want to wait until the "Web person" can get around to it. That's like having to go through a specialist to get a news article written.

And besides, coding is pretty easy to learn.

"If you're an aspiring journalist who knows how to code really well, you are in a very hot market," says Nate Silver, who founded the news Web site FiveThirtyEight (which ESPN acquired in 2014) after a successful stint at The New York Times blogging about politics based on data analysis. "Realize that you only get better by learning."[1]

So, let's get started with some building blocks. HTML, CSS and XML are markup languages—not programming languages—that control how information is displayed and distributed on the Web. Once you're familiar with how they work, you'll be ready to tackle some basic programming languages such as PhP or Javascript.

What is it?   What's Next?   Summary

⁈ HOW WEB PAGES WORK

A basic Web page is a document created with HTML code stored on a computer that is running as a Web server. The code tells a Web browser how

---

[1]Taylor Soper, "Nate Silver's Advice to Young Journalists: Learn to Code Now," GeekWire, April 25, 2014. www.geekwire.com/2014/nate-silver.

to display the text and where to include the graphics (or audio or video). The images and graphics are not included in the main HTML document but are stored somewhere on a server that is also accessible on the Internet.

When a Web browser finds the right Web page on the right server, it then makes a copy of the HTML document (and any images that are included) on your computer and builds the Web page based on the instructions in the code.

Here's how it works:

1. Web browser finds Web page on Web server.

2. Web browser retrieves Web page from Web server, makes a copy on local computer.

3. Web browser displays Web page on local computer.

HTML is a collection of tags that tell a Web browser how to display information on a Web page. True, you can create Web pages with online services like WordPress or Blogger or Facebook, or create new Web pages from scratch, with software like Dreamweaver, without knowing any HTML. But mastering the basics of HTML will enable you to troubleshoot and customize your Web pages in a way that is not otherwise possible.

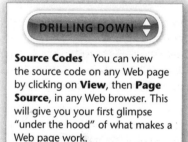

DRILLING DOWN

Source Codes You can view the source code on any Web page by clicking on **View**, then **Page Source**, in any Web browser. This will give you your first glimpse "under the hood" of what makes a Web page work.

Most of the tags in HTML are used in pairs, with an opening and a closing tag. For example, the HTML tag to begin a new paragraph is <p>, and the tag to end the paragraph is </p>. Notice the addition of a slash in the closing tag; the slash in effect turns off the command in the first tag of the pair. To present a word in bold type, for example, you'd enter this: word.

What is it?   **What's *Next?***   Summary

⬇ BUILD AN HTML PAGE QUICKLY

In 1995, I was the editor and general manager of a weekly newspaper in a community of small towns outside Seattle. I was intrigued by this newfangled Internet and decided to build a Web site for the newspaper. So I searched the Web for "html tutorial" and got going. I created a four-page Web site by typing out every individual bit of code. The end result wasn't pretty, but it gave me a solid understanding of how Web browsers interpret HTML code to display Web pages.

Now it's your turn. Let's create a simple HTML page and name it "simple.html."

1. Open a text editor on your computer; for example, Notepad (Windows) or TextEdit (Mac).

2. Create a new document and save your file with an .html extension on the end (for example, simple.html).

3. Type the following code and then save the page:

```
<html>
<head>
<title>HTML Tutorials</title>
</head>
<body>
<table style="text-align: left; width: 300px;" border="1"
cellpadding="2" cellspacing="2">
<tbody>
<tr>
<td style="vertical-align: top;"> <h1>About HTML</h1>
<p>There is a lot more you can learn about HTML. And the best place to
turn for complete information on any topic related to Web design is, of
course, the Web. The following sites offer helpful tutorials so you can learn
more about HTML. </p> </td>
</tr>
<tr>
<td style="vertical-align: top;"><br>
<b>HTML Tutorials</b><br>
<ul>
<li><a href="http://www.w3.org/MarkUp/Guide/">http://www.w3.org/
MarkUp/Guide/</a></li>
<li><a href="http://www.w3schools.com/html/">http://www.w3schools
.com/html/</a></li>
<li><a href="http://www.webmonkey.com/tutorial/tag/web_
basics">http://www.webmonkey.com/tutorial/tag/web_basics</a></li>
</ul>
</td>
</tr>
</tbody>
</table>
<br>
<br>
</body>
</html>
```

Now launch a Web browser and open the page by selecting **File**, then **Open File**. (You can view your new Web page only on your computer. It's not on the Web until you upload it to a Web server. Until then, it's only on your local machine.)

Notice how the HTML tags control the way a Web browser displays the content on the page. You can see how the HTML code created

- a headline (see the <h1> tag)

- a paragraph (see the <p> tag)

- boxes (see the <table> tag)

- bullets (see the <li> tag)

▶ Images and HTML

Web sites without images are boring; even the most basic Web design should include photos, logos or other graphics.

→A preview of how the HTML will display in the browser. ←

Building a Web page is different from using a print design program like InDesign or word-processing software like Microsoft Word. You can't put an image on a Web page. Instead, you call it into a Web page. Here's how:

1. Use the <img src> tag to tell the Web browser where to look for the image on the Web server by declaring the source (src) of the image (img).

2. The Web browser then visits that location and makes a copy of the image to display for a user with the Web page.

A full image tag looks like this:

<img src="http://www.website.com/images/picture.jpg">

An image tag can carry many attributes, affecting the way the image is displayed on the Web page. For example, we can add the following attributes:

- alternate text (alt): displays when you mouse over an image

- border: draws a border around the image

- width: shows width in pixels

- height: shows height in pixels

- align: determines the alignment of the image—left, middle, right—and forces the text to wrap around the image

- hspace: shows horizontal space in pixels around the image

- vspace: shows vertical space in pixels around the image

How would it look if we added an image to the page called "sample.html" from the exercise we started earlier? Here is the full code, with the new code that will call in the image shown in boldface type:

```
<html>
<head>
<meta content="text/html;charset=ISO-8859-1" http-equiv="Content-Type">
<title>HTML Tutorials</title>
</head>
<body>
<table style="text-align: left; width: 300px;" border="1"
cellpadding="2" cellspacing="2">
<tbody>
<tr>
<td style="vertical-align: top;">
<h1>About HTML</h1>
```

```
<p><img alt="PBS" src="Images/picture.jpg"
style="border: 1px solid; width: 73px; height: 73px;" align="right"
hspace="5" vspace="5">There is a lot more you can learn about HTML.
And the best place to turn for complete information on any topic related to
Web design is, of course, the Web. The following sites offer helpful tutori-
als so you can learn more about HTML.</p>
</td>
</tr>
<tr>
<td style="vertical-align: top;"><br>
<span style="font-weight: bold;">HTML Tutorials</span><br>
<ul>
<li><a href="http://www.w3.Org/MarkUp/Guide/">http://www.w3.Org/
MarkUp/Guide/</a></li>
<li><a href="http://www.w3schools.com/html/">http://www.w3schools
.com/html/</a></li>
<li><a href="http://www.webmonkey.com/tutorial/tag/web_
basics">http://www.webmonkey.com/tutorial/tag/web_basics</a></li>
</ul>
</td>
</tr>
</tbody>
</table>
<br>
<br>
</body>
</html>
```

Here is how it displays in a Web browser:

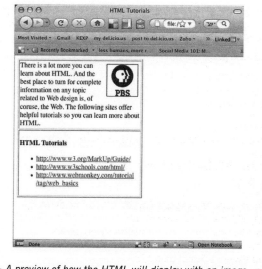

→ *A preview of how the HTML will display with an image.* ←

DRILLING DOWN

Paths If you design a Web page but the image you want displayed doesn't appear, then the **path** is wrong. If both the HTML page and the image are stored on the same server, you can use a **relative path**, which is a shortcut of a URL, to call the image into the page. So, instead of using a full URL for the location of the image, you would use <img src="/images/picture.jpg">. Alternatively, you can link directly to an image that has already been published on the Internet by using the full URL (known as an **absolute path**).

Note: This will work on your computer only if you have the PBS logo stored on your local machine. You can download a copy from the Web for this exercise. Just be sure to create a folder called Images in the same location as your HTML page and put the logo in there. You can see how the code will make a Web browser look there for the image, since the code reads <img alt="PBS" src="Images/ picture.jpg">.

▶ **HTML editors**

As you might have guessed by now, Web sites are no longer created by someone writing code line by line, as I did in 1995. Web designers use HTML editing software such as Adobe Dreamweaver, also known as WYSIWYG editors (What You See Is What You Get, pronounced wizzy-wig). These tools enable you to see how the page will look in a browser as you create and edit it.

But you don't need to spend hundreds of dollars on a new software program to get a taste of working with a WYSIWYG editor. There are several free online HTML editors that handle basic design tasks quite well, including those available at www.online-html-editor.org and www .ckeditor.com.

▶ **HTML tutorials**

You can learn a lot more about HTML. And the best place to turn for complete information on any topic related to Web design is, of course, the Web. The following sites offer helpful tutorials:

- www.j-learning.org

- http://webdesign.about.com

- www.webmonkey.com/tutorial/tag/web_basics

⑦ CSS (CASCADING STYLE SHEETS)

HTML was created by computer scientists—for computer scientists. It has been driving designers crazy ever since.

HTML is extremely efficient at transferring information across the Internet, but it is limited in its ability to make Web pages look nice. Enter CSS, or cascading style sheets, which gives Web designers the power to realize their creative visions in Web browsers.

In short, CSS makes Web sites look cool.

A basic understanding of how CSS works is important for anyone who plans to do any work online. CSS enables you to edit, modify and troubleshoot existing Web pages and designs. For example, if you set up a blog on WordPress and use one of the hundreds of freely available themes (prebuilt templates) created by real Web designers, knowing a little CSS will enable you to go into the code and make small changes to your design.

So, even if you don't plan to design a Web site from scratch, at times you'll want to use CSS to make changes to the sites you work with.

The key to CSS is the ability to set a style for a group of elements on your Web site or blog—for example, how the headlines or body text should be displayed. CSS is really just a collection of rules. Here's how the logic flows:

1. Declare a font, color, size and other attributes for a specific type of content.

2. Set it in the style sheet.

3. Then, when a page is loaded, the Web browser checks the style sheet and displays the information according to the declarations you have selected.

⬇ ADD CSS TO HTML

Using the sample page we created with HTML, let's add some CSS:

1. Create a separate document in TextEdit or Wordpad and give it the extension .css (for example, stylesheet.css).

2. Enter the code below to set the styles we want to apply to our HTML document (named "simple.html").

```
body {
    font-family: verdana,arial,sans-serif;
    font-size: 14px;
    line-spacing: 2em;
}

h1 {
    font-size: 200%;
    color: #0000FF;
    font-weight: bold;
    text-align: center;
}

ul {
    text-indent: 1em;
    list-style-type: square;
}
```

3. Save the document in the same location as the HTML file.

4. Add a line of code to the head of the HTML document—in between the opening <head> and closing </head> tags. This will tell a Web browser where to look for the style sheet.

Here's the code: <link rel="stylesheet" href="stylesheet.css">

So, what's going on here? By creating a universal style sheet for our Web page, we were able to modify the appearance of the headline, body text and bulleted list without editing any of the HTML. The best part is that all the pages on a Web site refer to one style sheet, so you can control and modify all the styles with one document instead of editing every single page.

Here's a quick translation of the rules we set with our CSS code, so you know how it works. We declared a new style for all the text in between the <body> tags with the following statement:

```
body {
    font-family: verdana,arial,sans-serif;
    font-size: 14px;
    line-spacing: 2em;
}
```

The following is inside the browser window image:

About HTML

There is a lot more you can learn about HTML. And the best place to turn for complete information on any topic related to Web design is, of course, the Web. The following sites offer helpful tutorials so you can learn more about HTML.

HTML Tutorials

- http://www.w3.org/MarkUp/Guide/
- http://www.w3schools.com/html/
- http://www.webmonkey.com/tutorial/tag/web_basics

⟶ *A preview of how the HTML will display using CSS.* ⟵

Explanations:

- font-family: verdana,arial,sans-serif means that the Verdana font should be used, and if the user doesn't have Verdana, then try Arial, and if not Arial, then whatever sans-serif font is available.

- font-size: 14px means that 14-point type is specified.

- line-spacing: 2em means that the lines should be spaced apart at a distance twice the height of a regular line of text.

Next, we made a declaration about the headline style, which will affect any text between the <h1> tags, with the following code:

```
h1 {
    font-size: 200%;
    color: #0000FF;
    font-weight: bold;
    text-align: center;
}
```

Explanations:

- font-size: 200% means the font should be 200 percent larger than normal.

- color: #0000FF means the color of the type should be blue; "0000FF" is a hex code for a particular shade of blue (search for HTML hex codes if you want to see the entire palette).

- font-weight: bold means that the font should be in boldface.

- text-align: center means that the text should be centered on the page.

Finally, we made two declarations for our bulleted list, which appears on the page between the <ul> tags (ul = unordered list):

```
ul {
    text-indent: 1em;
    list-style-type: square;
}
```

Explanations:

- text-indent: 1em means that the text indent should be one more than normal. (Em is a proportional sizing element that works for all sizes of type.)

- list-style-type: square means that the bullets will be styled to be square.

▶ CSS essentials

Now that you've learned the rules, let's examine how they work.

Each rule consists of a selector and a declaration. The selector is the HTML tag or attribute outside the curly braces. The declaration is everything inside the curly braces. Each declaration contains a property (for example, font-weight) and a value (for example, bold).

There are two types of selectors: element selectors (H1 and P) and class selectors (which begin with a period and are added to HTML through the class attribute).

Each rule should be written with the selector first, followed by an opening curly brace and then the first declaration. If a particular selector has more than one declaration, each declaration should end with a semicolon.

Finally, end the rule with a closing curly brace.

▶ CSS tutorials

Obviously, you can learn a lot more about CSS. The following sites offer helpful information, examples and tutorials:

- www.w3schools.com/css

- http://webdesign.about
  .com

- www.csszengarden.com
  (contains a very cool
  demonstration—a user
  can quickly change the site's design by selecting different CSS designs)

Scratching the surface: If you have mastered this much basic HTML and CSS, you are ready to begin exploring more advanced concepts on your own. This is just the tip of the iceberg when it comes to Web design and development, but once you understand how the basic concepts work, you should be comfortable enough to start getting your hands dirty with actual Web development.

What is it? | What's Next? | Summary

XML (EXTENSIBLE MARKUP LANGUAGE)

As we discussed earlier, RSS is a powerful tool for delivering content from a Web site. It lets your audience subscribe to a feed and receive updates automatically. RSS feeds are based on XML, and although you don't have to learn how to write XML, you should understand how it works.

XML is not a replacement for HTML; it is a complement. It uses tags to describe what data are, not how they should look (as HTML does). And it's customizable, so a user can create a personal set of tags.

XML is most commonly used in RSS feeds. Because most content-management systems and blog engines create their own RSS feeds, you probably won't have to worry about creating your own XML to enable people to sign up for your feeds. Here's an example of XML in an RSS feed from an events calendar:

```
<item>
   <title>Event: Northwest Singles Club—Monthly Meeting at Cascade
   Pizza, Wed, Jan 14 6:00p</title>
   <description>Dinner and Monthly Meeting</description>
   <summary>Come meet some new people and have a good time.</
   summary>
   <phone>398-1852</phone>
   <pubDate>Thu, 20 Nov 2008 16:26:23 +0000</pubDate>
</item>
```

Pretty simple, huh? Each item in this feed would have a title, a description, a summary, the phone number and the date the item was published.

XML is an important piece of the emerging semantic Web, also called Web 3.0. Classifying information by its content instead of its structure enables people to search for information more intuitively. To learn more about XML, start with these Web sites:

- http://xmlfiles.com

- http://webdesign.about.com

- www.w3schools.com/Xml/

What is it? | What's *Next?* | Summary

⁂ CONTENT-MANAGEMENT SYSTEMS

The modern Internet is not driven by hand-coding pages, but rather by content-management systems, also known as CMS. These Web-based systems make it easy to publish text, audio and video to Web sites and also manage that content and the sites' look and feel.

There is an entire industry of companies that build, sell and maintain different content-management systems. Clickability, Newsbase and Saxotech are just a few that are popular with news companies. Gannett, The Washington Post, Vox Media, BuzzFeed and The Texas Tribune are among the many news publishers that built their own CMS.

WordPress, which started as primarily a blogging platform, is the world's most popular CMS. The company boasts that more than a quarter of all the Web sites on the Internet are powered by its CMS. WordPress is behind global news destinations like CNN.com and is also the backbone for neighborhood blogs.

Over the past few years, an alignment of stars has led many news sites of all sizes to switch from traditional content-management systems to blog platforms like WordPress. The two forces at work: rapid development from the WordPress community, which has grown the back-end framework from a simple blog system to a powerful CMS, and online news publishers' collective need to have more flexible, social news sites that are more than just static, digital representations of the old print model.

Learning to use WordPress for Web publishing is an important skill for today's journalists. Even if you don't end up working at a news company that uses WordPress, the basic principles of using a CMS that you will learn from WordPress will be applicable to whatever CMS you end up using in your job.

WordPress is also the best way to self-publish on the Internet. When I graduated from journalism school at Gonzaga University in 1991, I had to find a job in order to be published, because it wasn't feasible for an individual to own a printing press or broadcast station. The Internet, of course, changed all that. And with WordPress, you have the opportunity to do whatever job you dream about. Want to be a music critic? A food or fashion blogger? A political writer? You don't have to wait for someone to hire you—simply launch a WordPress blog and get going.

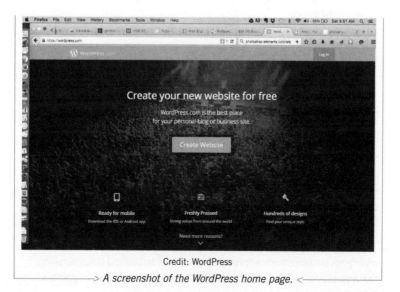

Credit: WordPress

A screenshot of the WordPress home page.

WordPress is an open-source platform where developers from all over the world continuously improve the system by building plug-ins, themes and widgets that make the basic CMS increasingly powerful. It's free to set up and install, as are many of the extras built by the developer community, but don't let the lack of a commercial price structure fool you. This is a world-class publishing platform.

What is it? **What's *Next?*** Summary

⬇ LAUNCH A WORDPRESS SITE

The first question to answer when choosing WordPress is which flavor do you prefer? If you have no budget for hosting, then head over to WordPress .com and sign up for a free WordPress blog that will have "WordPress.com" in the domain name (e.g., mysite.WordPress.com).

You can upgrade to a premium WordPress.com account and have WP host your blog and get your own domain name if you don't mind spending a few dollars. It's important to note that, in order to customize your design, you'll need to add the custom CSS feature. See the WordPress.com Store at http://en.WordPress.com/products.

If you want the flexibility of hosting your own version (and a better domain name), then go to WordPress.org. Most Web-hosting companies offer an option where they will install and set up popular Web services like WordPress for you much as your computer would install software. If you choose to host your own, your first act will be to decide where to host your site. There are too many options to list here, but you can start your search with these hosting companies, all of which feature one-click installation of WordPress and are recommended by the WordPress.org site:

DreamHost

JustHost

Laughing Squid

Media Temple

BlueHost

▶ Publishing with WordPress

A big advantage to WordPress is that the act of publishing content is very simple, even if you're not technically inclined. If you're new to WordPress,

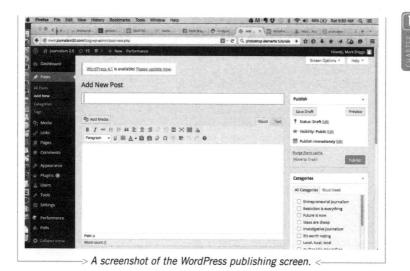

--> *A screenshot of the WordPress publishing screen.* <--

check out the video tutorials available at WordPress.tv for a complete menu of step-by-step instructions. To get you started quickly, though, here's a brief overview of the basic function of publishing content on WordPress.

New articles are called "posts" in WordPress, so the first step is to find one of the many links on the WordPress dashboard to **Add New Post**. Once there, you'll see a fairly standard publishing window (standard now, mostly because of WordPress), with a headline box, a content toolbar and an open box for text. Simply add a title or headline and then enter the text for your post into the open box.

The content toolbar in WordPress is easy to use and features the functions that are universally recognized by anyone who's done any word processing. Text style, alignment, formatting and all the usual suspects are here, so use the features to make your text look the way you want.

One of the best features in WordPress, and one that has become fairly standard in all CMS platforms, can be found in the top right corner of the open text box. There are two tabs—one labeled **Visual** and the other **Text**—that you can use to toggle between the WYSIWYG view of how the text should appear when published and the HTML view of the code behind the scenes that determines the look and layout.

Use the **Text** tab to learn how the basic HTML tags work. As you add formatting (e.g., bold, italic), use the **Text** tab to see what specific tags were added by the system. This simple technique has helped countless Web

Strip Out Bad Code If you're copying and pasting from another program like Word into a CMS like WordPress, it's a good idea to paste it into a plain text program like TextEdit (Mac) or Notepad (Windows) first to strip out the formatting. In TextEdit, select the **Make Plain Text** option under the **Format menu**. If you don't take this step, the proprietary formatting code from programs like Word will conflict with your CMS (e.g., WordPress) and mess up the display and layout of the text.

workers learn the ropes of HTML and computer coding. (Think of it as riding a bike with training wheels.)

Once you have written the post and added the photo(s) or video(s) you want, you're ready to publish. Be sure to use the **Preview** button on the far right to see what your post will look like before you share it with the world. If you want the post to be published at a later time, click **Edit** next to **Publish Immediately** and set a date and time. This is called "future publishing" and is a handy way to manage your time, since you can write more than one post during a writing session but schedule the posts to publish on a predetermined schedule.

WordPress offers many more useful features. Become familiar with them by experimenting directly in the CMS or by searching terms on the WordPress.tv site or the Web to find more in-depth tutorials.

▶ Customize the theme

By now you're probably wondering why we bothered with those primitive HTML and CSS exercises. Think of it as something like learning your multiplication tables before you got your first calculator. The exercises provide a foundation of understanding that will help you realize the possibilities and achieve your goals—in this case, designing a great-looking WordPress site.

A "theme" in WordPress controls how the site will look for everyone who visits it. A basic installation of WordPress gives you choices among a number of attractive themes for your site; you can find them by selecting the **Themes** link from the left menu.

You can try different themes and use the **Live Preview** function to see what each would look like on your site before making the switch. If you want even more options, simply search "free WordPress themes" online

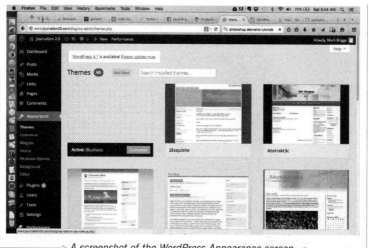

> A screenshot of the WordPress Appearance screen. <

and try to find one that fits your needs. Even more themes are available if you have some money to spend. For $50 you can buy a professional-looking theme—a tremendous value when you compare that to how much a custom-built Web site would cost (hundreds of dollars, or maybe thousands).

One big advantage of using WordPress for your Web site or blog is the ability to customize the theme. Even after you find a great theme, you will probably want to make some small changes to make it truly fit your objectives for your site. This is easy to do with WordPress.

Click the **Appearance** link on the left menu to reveal the available options for that particular theme. These features are simple to use and understand; they offer radio buttons and drop-down menus for making various selections, with some text boxes for customizing headers and titles.

Also, you can go deeper in your customization and actually get into the code by clicking the **Editor** link under **Appearance**. This will reveal the CSS style sheets that are controlling your theme and give you the opportunity to modify the code. This is the best way to learn the basics of coding. Working with existing code, making small changes and then seeing the outcomes of those changes is how countless computer programmers have learned their trade. You should experiment with the CSS style sheet on the WordPress site, if only to get some code-level experience in CSS and Web site design.

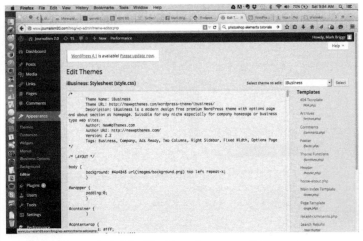

> A screenshot of the WordPress Appearance Editor screen. <

Don't Break Your Site If you're modifying the code in the WordPress theme editor, be careful. You could break your site if you make the wrong change and lose the original code that was working fine. It's a good idea to open a blank text document and copy the code you want to modify there first to protect it. That way, no matter what crazy modification you add to your live site, you will always have the ability to revert to the previous version of the code that was working fine. Think of it as a safety net for your experimentation.

WordPress is an extremely flexible and powerful publishing platform. This brief overview barely scratches the surface of what you can do with your WordPress site. The key to getting the most out of WordPress is to make time to investigate how best to use the system and do some experimentation with your site, if only to learn what features and capabilities are available to you. There are meetups in larger cities, plus conferences (called WordCamp) and other opportunities to meet with and learn from the WordPress community. And, of course, countless online resources are available—search for sites where skilled developers and designers share their tricks and tips.

CHAPTER 1

⚡ MOBILE APPS VERSUS MOBILE WEB

With so much of the digital audience consuming news and information on mobile devices these days, it's critical to consider how your Web site will be presented on smartphones and tablets. There are two basic ways that people get news and information with mobile devices: native apps and mobile versions of standard Web browsers.

Here's an easy way to think about the difference: If you visit CNN.com in Safari on your iPhone or Chrome on your Android device, that is considered the mobile Web. If, however, you download the CNN app from iTunes or the Google Play Store and launch it on your phone or tablet, then you are using the native app. (It's called "native" because the app was built specifically to run on iOS or Android, so it's native to that operating system.)

In most cases, the native app offers a better user experience, because the content and formatting have been optimized for that platform. Many users, however, consume news and information through the mobile Web, largely through following links from e-mails or social media posts. If you click a standard Web link on your phone, the browser on your phone will launch to display the article, photo or video.

> **DRILLING DOWN** ▲▼
>
> **Make Your Site "Responsive" for Mobile** If your site looks good on any size screen, on any device and on any operating system, then it is considered "responsive" because it responds to those variables. Just a few years ago, responsiveness was considered an advanced feature on Web sites, but today it's a standard that should be followed by anyone leading a Web publishing project, even if it's as simple as starting a blog.

⬇ MAKE A WORDPRESS SITE FOR MOBILE

Fortunately, WordPress makes it easy to build a site that displays appropriately on mobile devices. There are many options for WordPress themes and widgets that do an excellent job of formatting your site to fit any size screen on any operating system. Such "responsive" Web design is the standard nowadays.

BURT HERMAN

▶ **CO-FOUNDER** | Storify
(@burtherman)

Credit: Photo courtesy
of Burt Herman

We're now in the age of the new printing press, living through a revolution spawned by digital publishing. And the wonderful thing about this revolution is that the "press" costs virtually nothing. For the first time in world history, anyone can easily communicate to a mass audience across the world. If you can get someone to notice you, and leverage social networks, you can go global in a way that only the richest media networks or broadcast conglomerates could do in the past.

None of this happens without computer code. Just as printing presses were fueled by ink, the Web is fueled by code like HTML, CSS, Javascript and other languages that bring media to life online.

That's not to say that every journalist needs to give up writing and become a rock-star engineer. Learning code, just like learning any other language, requires years of practice.

But there are steps journalists can take to get some basic digital literacy that can help them in this new digital age that will serve them well as we increasingly move to an all-digital world. It's only a matter of time before paper as a medium disappears entirely, with the declining costs of screen technology and better touch interfaces.

Here are a few tips for journalists to make sure you remain relevant in this new world:

- **Learn HTML and CSS:** It's quite simple to get a basic grasp of how Web pages are presented, which means you'll be able to go in and change simple things as needed on a site.

- **Learn how to read API documentation:** APIs (application programming interfaces) are the way that sites and applications interact with one another. It's how you can take data from a social network like Twitter or Facebook and integrate it with Google Maps or a timeline application. Being able to read the API documentation means you can see the possibilities for building applications and new ways to tell stories.

- **Learn how to customize blog sites like WordPress:** Doing some basic work to customize a blog will make you comfortable with tinkering with a site and publishing online. Much can be done with out-of-the-box open-source technology, and getting some initial confidence will encourage you to try more and see how far you can bend the available tools to what you need.

- **Embrace new tools:** Try out new tools as they come out and use them for journalism, or see how they could inspire journalism-related work. Always be open, as technology moves quickly and it's good to stay aware of trends online to see how new technologies could have media-related uses.

[*Source:* Written by Burt Herman at the request of the author.]

When searching for a new theme to try on your site, be sure to check to see that "responsive" is one of the features. The same applies to widgets and plug-ins. Once you find a new theme that you like, make sure you actually test it on as many devices as you can, since the results will vary from theme to theme. There was a time not so long ago that Web designers needed to test their sites on a handful of different browsers—and versions of browsers. There is less need for that these days, but the need to test on various mobile devices has never been greater.

Pay attention to how different Web sites display on your phone or tablet, especially if you click on a link in an e-mail or on Facebook or Twitter. This is the standard user experience for millions of people every day "reading the news." So it's important to understand how people access the news. (We will be taking a deeper dive into the mobile audience and the distribution of news on social media later in the book.)

What is it?   What's Next?   **Summary**

☒ START TO SEE DIGITAL OPPORTUNITIES

The more you understand about how digital content works, the better prepared you will be to work for a digital-content operation. Basic knowledge of HTML, CSS and XML will enable you to see more clearly the opportunities for your journalism in the digital world.

Use the simple lessons here to begin exploring these concepts. When you come across a piece of jargon or an acronym you don't understand, toss it into Google, do a couple of minutes of research and then keep going. It's all there; you just have to want to learn it. The only limits on your understanding of how the Web and digital content work are your curiosity and willingness to try something new.

GET GOING Checklist ✔

☐ **Check your browser:** Check to see whether your Web browser is the most up-to-date version (in Chrome or Firefox, select **About** in the top menu to find this information). Today, most browsers update to new versions automatically, so this is not as important as it used to be.

☐ **Download a new browser:** Download a new Web browser, especially if you are not currently using Chrome or Firefox. Other options include Safari, Internet Explorer and Opera. All browsers are going through constant improvement, meaning they all get better all the time.

☐ **Subscribe to news alerts:** Create a news alert at Google and download a news reader app to your smartphone or tablet to get started with RSS.

☐ **Create a Web page:** Complete the HTML and CSS exercises described earlier; add your own content and styles to the sample Web page using additional HTML tags and CSS styles.

☐ **Start a blog on WordPress:** Follow the instructions earlier in this chapter and begin publishing online. Treat your blog as a sandbox for experimentation until you know what area you want to focus on with your content.

☐ **Make sure your WordPress site is mobile-friendly:** Test your WordPress site on as many devices as possible. Ask your friends and family—anyone whose smartphone or tablet is different from yours—to help.

CHAPTER 2

Blogging and Microblogging: Publish, Distribute and Connect

Every college journalist should have a blog. And a Twitter account. Period.

Working reporters with beats maintain blogs in addition to filing traditional stories. They also use Twitter to distribute their journalism and cultivate sources. So if you're hoping to get a job in journalism, you might as well start now.

Maintaining a blog used to be the most effective way for a journalist to connect with an audience. Social media platforms, especially Twitter, changed that and brought many new options and opportunities to a journalist's toolbox.

"In Internet time, 'blogging' seems to have become an antiquated term," wrote Matt Thompson in the second edition of "Journalism Next." "Some would say it's also an antiquated idea—a retirement home for early adopters stuck in the era of the Internet Superhighway."

"I'd argue quite the reverse," continued Thompson, who has been an innovative force at NPR since 2010. "Blogging's become such a basic pattern for information on the Internet that it feels almost weird that it still has a name."

Twitter is also known as a form of microblogging, since the content is published in small doses compared to a traditional blog. The concepts are similar, as are the benefits, so we will tackle blogging and microblogging together in this chapter.

"Gone are the days of journalists passively publishing information that is simply read, viewed or listened to," says Ellyn Angelotti, digital trends and social media faculty member at The Poynter Institute. "The news cycle is now interactive. Journalists use microblogging to publish, share and find information, links, photos, videos and polls with large audiences from anywhere."

Today things are changing fast, and one of the biggest changes is microblogging. As you are about to learn, microblogging is much more than a publishing technology. It is a relatively new form of social networking that allows journalists to connect more closely with other journalists and with readers. It's a means of participating in the "live Web," which means information being published and consumed in real time and constantly updating. This gives a journalist the best sense of what's happening right now online. And it's the fastest way for a journalist or news organization to report breaking news and promote other work.

Similarly, blogging helps journalists to develop community with readers or viewers so they can test ideas, receive early and direct feedback and publish or broadcast in the timeliest manner possible. For college journalists, blogging means learning a new content-management system, building an audience for their writing and reporting and cultivating a collaborative community once they have that audience.

By blogging and microblogging, professional reporters can publish information beyond the traditional news cycle and in something other than the traditional story format, both of which help enhance their authority on a beat. Blogs also help news organizations establish deeper relationships with readers and leverage the wisdom of the crowd to broaden coverage.

"It's always been important to me to be as close to my readers as possible, and blogging is about as close as it gets," says Dwight Silverman, who has written TechBlog for the Houston Chronicle since 2008 and has more than 20,000 followers on Twitter (@dsilverman). "I consider the community in TechBlog to be collaborators. My blog is not just about me—it's about us."

A good blog is a continuing conversation. You facilitate it, but if it works, your audience may dominate it. If that happens, you win, the news organization wins and, most important, the readers win.

"Readers are our friends," says Ben Mutzabaugh, who has blogged about business travel for USA Today for more than 10 years and has more than 180,000 followers on Twitter (@TodayInTheSky). "In print, it's easy to feel you are at odds with readers because people will find one little thing wrong. So, as a journalist you get defensive. The readers on a blog chime in and help you. They want you to get the story right. Readers help make the blog stronger than any single author could make it alone."

The rules are different with blogs. Blogging reporters play off other information they find online, even linking to stories and blogs that might have been thought of as competition just a few years ago. Online, all relevant information is an essential part of the virtual-community conversation on a given topic.

Thankfully, most news organizations have realized the importance of effective blogging. Blogs are no longer an extra feature on news Web sites. They have become the cornerstone of coverage for news organizations of all sizes. Blogs are also powering a growing wave of independent journalism start-ups. So understanding how to blog is essential to anyone learning about journalism.

Blogs are not magic. Be warned: Writing a successful blog takes dedication and determination.

"I was working hard before as a print journalist, but nothing like what I do now," said John Cook, a former business reporter for the Seattle Post-Intelligencer who leveraged the success of his newspaper blog into a venture called GeekWire. As co-founder and one member of a small team of writers for GeekWire, Cook is considered one of the leaders in the coverage of the start-up-technology industry, but this recognition didn't come easy.

"I am constantly on guard for the next story, blogging on Thanksgiving Day, checking e-mails on Christmas Eve and waking up in the middle of the night with a good lead on a story," Cook said. "Guess you could say I am a bit obsessed. There's never a break. It is hard work, but I love it. The great thing about a blog for an old-fashioned beat reporter like me is that it is journalism at its core—pounding the pavement looking for the next scoop and making sure that you stay two steps ahead of the competition. That drive was always in me as a beat reporter, but a blog elevates that to a much higher level."

A blog is a simple form of communication that is now an essential part of the news organizations that once considered it controversial. Blogging can help you cover a beat and build a loyal community of readers whose interactions contribute to your coverage.

In this chapter you will learn the following:

- How microblogging works

- How some journalists and news organizations have used blogs

- How to get started with a common blog platform and use RSS feeds to beat the competition

- How to build and manage a community of followers and drive traffic to a blog

- How individual journalists can make microblogging and social media work for them in their professional lives

⚠ BLOG BASICS

Blogs have forever changed the way that information is shared in our society. They're fast. They're interactive. They're freewheeling. They can be influential or incredibly boring—it all depends on the writer(s) powering the blog. A blog is simply a different way to publish content. It's a technical term that refers to a content-management system, not necessarily a writing style.

Three characteristics define a blog:

- It's a frequently updated Web site with entries displayed in reverse chronological order (that is, the most recent stuff is on top).

- Each entry, called a post, has a headline and a body. Most entries include links to other news and information on the Web, and many contain photos or other graphics.

- It contains a link for comments that lets readers post their thoughts on what the blogger is writing about. Not all blogs allow comments, but most do.

▶ Why blogs are important

The first information revolution, in the 1990s—when everyone started creating Web sites just to have them—gave way to a more authentic information revolution between 2001 and 2005, with the advent of blogs.

The Internet of the 1990s purportedly enabled anyone to become a publisher. But it turned out that "anyone" needed to know a little bit about computers and, specifically, how to build a Web page. As a result, most individual publishers were computer-code jockeys or graphic artists and designers, many of them more interested in pushing the cosmetic limits of this new medium than in polishing the content. In essence, individuals' Web sites at that time were style over substance. Lots of flashy Web sites were built, but once you visited them and saw the pretty graphics, there was little reason to return.

Blogs flipped this model on its head. They're not always pretty to look at, but they can be published by anyone who can click a mouse and type. The software makes this kind of publishing so easy that you can update a blog several times a day with about the same effort required to send e-mail.

▶▶ *Blogs changed Web publishing*

After the terrorist attacks of September 11, 2001, blogs became an effective way for people to share their responses to events and discuss what they thought was happening to the country. The personal connections those early bloggers created with readers, at a time when nerves were still raw and people were reeling, ushered in a new era of interactivity between writer and reader. And the energy created by those post-9/11 blogs morphed into passionate discussion and debate during the run-up to U.S. military action in Iraq, and evolved further in 2004 as election season shifted into high gear. Presidential candidates and the Republican and Democratic national committees hosted blogs, altering the perception of a blog as a grassroots communication tool and further mainstreaming the medium.

Since then, blogs have continued to gain momentum, readers and participants. Many blogs have become media companies and developed into essential information sources, which has only made the term "blog" that much more murky. TechCrunch, paidContent and TreeHugger all started as one-person blogs but evolved into companies with dozens of employees. And all three were acquired for millions of dollars by other media companies. Meanwhile, mainstream news companies such as The New York Times feature dozens of blogs to complement their other digital coverage.

▶▶ *Blogs changed journalism*

Dan Gillmor is credited with launching the first blog for a mainstream news organization, the San Jose Mercury News, in 1999. Since then, thousands of blogs have been launched on the Web sites of newspapers, magazines and TV and radio stations and as independent journalism start-ups.

The blog-publishing platform fits journalism. Its simplicity, immediacy and interactivity improved journalism throughout the first decade of the new century, bringing journalists and their audiences closer and removing the constraints of time and space that once limited a journalist's ability to report a story and engage an audience.

Many journalists are still trying to figure out how to make blogs work for them. News organizations remain in experimental mode, launching new blogs aimed at ever more targeted niche audiences. The Los Angeles Times, for example, launched 21 blogs in 2008, maintained 15 in 2012 and then grew to 32 in 2014. In 2012 The New York Times had 67 active blogs but by the end of 2014 had pared that down to 35. CNN had 46 in 2012 and 51 in

2014. The topics covered span a wide range, including food, motherhood, old age, applying to college, chess and what's on TV.

The more experimentation, the greater the likelihood of success. In Seattle, nearly three dozen hyperlocal news blogs unaffiliated with traditional news organizations cover specific neighborhoods. Meanwhile, local newspapers and TV news stations each have dozens of blogs. This level of blog saturation for one location can be seen in many other cities in the United States, too.

Scott Karp, an entrepreneurial journalist who once ran digital strategy at Atlantic Media Co., wrote on his blog, Publishing 2.0, that one lesson any journalist learns through blogging is what it's like to feel the power and responsibility of being a publisher. You decide how often to publish to your blog. You decide what form the content will take. You decide the layout of your blog. You decide how to interact with the audience. And you decide how to edit the content and what the headlines say.[1]

And if no one reads your blog, guess who's responsible?

This applies even if you work for a mainstream news organization. Especially if you work for a mainstream news organization. In some newsrooms, the competition to be tops in the Web site traffic rankings has replaced the competition to get a story on page one. When I was editor of the Web site for The News Tribune in Tacoma, Wash., reporters were increasingly anxious to see the monthly report I compiled that ranked our 30-some blogs according to pageviews. (Eventually I gave most of them access to the online reporting tool so they could pull the numbers themselves.)

Consider the experience of Curt Cavin, a motor-sports reporter for The Indianapolis Star. He had been answering questions in a weekly Q&A on the newspaper's Web site for five years when he decided to take on a daily Q&A to try to improve the newspaper's Web site traffic rankings (competition is a great motivator).

"From my perspective, more questions meant more opportunities to communicate what I knew about the sport and my experiences in it," Cavin wrote at the Online Journalism Review. "I made [it] conversational and friendly, showing my vulnerabilities and enjoyment of life and the sport. It was blog-like, one might say."

It worked. At the peak of the IndyCar racing season, he receives about 150 questions a day and answers about 10, almost all before 9 a.m. And he eventually ranked first in Web features at IndyStar.com.

---

[1] Scott Karp, "Every Newspaper Journalist Should Start a Blog," Publishing 2.0, May 22, 2007. http://publishing2.com/2007/05/22/every-newspaper-journalist-should-start-a-blog.

Ask the Expert: 2014 IndyCar teams shaping up

(Photo: Philip Abbott Philip Abbott for Chevy Racing)

f 3   CONNECT   TWEET   in 1 LINKEDIN   COMMENT   EMAIL   MORE

TAGS

Indianapolis 500   Indianapolis   Milwaukee   NASCAR Sprint Cup Series   Juan Pablo   Juanjo

Question: My family and I are interested in going to the IndyCar race at Barber in April. This would be our first road/street race we have attended because our preference is ovals. Is there a certain area of the track you would recommend we sit? Also, we were planning on attending the Milwaukee Mile again until they moved the date from June to August. Why was the race moved? Was it to spread out the ovals more on the schedule? (Steve, Winston, Ga.)

Answer: The beauty of road courses, in particular, is the ability to move around the facility to watch from different places, and Barber Motorsports Park is as good in that regard as anywhere. The viewing mound in Turns 2-3 is terrific. Bring a blanket, lawn chairs and munchies. There's a video board there, and it's terrific. There are several other good places, too, which won't disappoint. Plus, there are more classes of cars on the track, so there's always something to watch, and the scenery is great. It just occurred to me that we'll be there a bit later in April, which means it should be even prettier. As for Milwaukee, one of the advantages to holding the event later in the summer was to benefit from the publicity of the fair. I don't know if that was the only reason, but it was a big one.

Question: Now that the Iowa Speedway has been sold, do you see the eventual demise of its IndyCar race as usually happens when ISC or SMI buys a track? (Dave, Indianapolis)

Answer: No, I don't so long as track officials make the effort, and I think they will because there won't be a Sprint Cup race to carry the load. As it stands, the IndyCar

Credit: Indianapolis Star

The AskTheExpert blog on IndyStar.com makes it easy for readers to participate by featuring an email address for questions at the top of the page, and then posting answers to several reader questions below.

In 2007, his readers suggested a get-together over cheeseburgers to talk IndyCar racing. Overwhelming interest led to a community event during the weekend of the Indianapolis 500 that became known as the Carb Night Burger Bash. About 700 people attended, and more than $8,000 was raised for local charities.[2]

For John Cook, the former Seattle Post-Intelligencer reporter, his Venture blog was a place to pour out his passion for innovation in journalism. Over the years he wrote memos to top management, pleading with them to dedicate more resources to the online part of the operation. He and a colleague, Todd Bishop, even drafted a business plan for launching a technology news Web site at the P-I. But when management turned a deaf ear to their proposal, they started considering other options and eventually quit their jobs at the P-I to launch TechFlash with the Puget Sound Business

---

[2]Curt Cavin, "Daily Posts, Perseverance Make the Difference in Building Newspaper Blogs," Online Journalism Review, October 15, 2008. www.ojr.org/ojr/people/curtcavin/200810/1547.

This tech CEO doubts Seattle will dominate cloud computing — and he's completely wrong

Latest News   Most Popular

Credit: GeekWire

> GeekWire, a site launched by former Seattle P-I business reporters John Cook and Todd Bishop, allows users to catch up on news about some of the largest tech companies, such as Microsoft, Amazon, Apple and Google, which are featured prominently in the dropdown menu. <

Journal (the predecessor to GeekWire). Several months later, more than 100 P-I journalists lost their jobs when the newspaper ceased print publication and began publishing online only.

"I could see what was happening to the industry and just wanted to keep moving forward and find new ways to cover my beat," Cook said. "The blog allowed me to do that without having to worry about the rest of the operation."

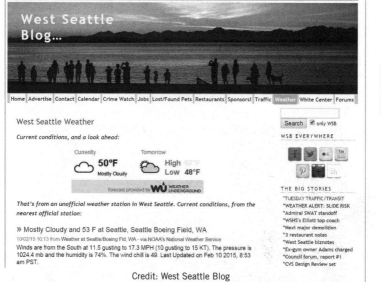

West Seattle Weather

Current conditions, and a look ahead:

Currently	Tomorrow
☁ **50°F** Mostly Cloudy	⛅ High 57°F Low **48°F**

forecast provided by **WU** WEATHER UNDERGROUND

That's from an unofficial weather station in West Seattle. Current conditions, from the nearest official station:

» Mostly Cloudy and 53 F at Seattle, Seattle Boeing Field, WA

10/02/15 10:13 from Weather at Seattle/Boeing Fld, WA - via NOAA's National Weather Service

Winds are from the South at 11.5 gusting to 17.3 MPH (10 gusting to 15 KT). The pressure is 1024.4 mb and the humidity is 74%. The wind chill is 49. Last Updated on Feb 10 2015, 8:53 am PST.

Home | Advertise | Contact | Calendar | Crime Watch | Jobs | Lost/Found Pets | Restaurants | Sponsors! | Traffic | Weather | White Center | Forums

Search ☑ only WSB

WSB EVERYWHERE

THE BIG STORIES

*TUESDAY TRAFFIC/TRANSIT
*WEATHER ALERT: SLIDE RISK
*Admiral SWAT standoff
*WSHS's Elliott top coach
*Next major demolition
*3 restaurant notes
*West Seattle biznotes
*Ex-gym owner Adams charged
*Council forum, report #1
*CVS Design Review set

Credit: West Seattle Blog

The West Seattle Blog is a comprehensive hyperlocal news site, providing its readers with such specific information about their communities as the weather.

Many other journalists have launched blogs without big ambitions only to be surprised by the audience and opportunity. Tracy Record started a blog in 2005 to share random thoughts about her neighborhood. A lifelong journalist who was working for the local Fox affiliate at the time, she named it West Seattle Blog and started out writing just a few items a week.

Then, in 2006, a storm knocked out power and brought down trees throughout the region. Traditional news Web sites supplied readers with an overview of the damage, but residents had nowhere to turn for

DRILLING DOWN ⬍

Organize Feeds With Hootsuite and TweetDeck To consume massive amounts of real-time information efficiently, use Hootsuite or TweetDeck to organize social media feeds into columns that make it easy for you to track updates as they happen. All news organizations rely on these tools to keep tabs on what is happening on social media. On many assignment desks, these tools are as critical as a police scanner. RSS is also a great way to read dozens of blogs regularly. Refer to the RSS section in chapter 1 (pages 12–17) and use the lesson on setting up feeds in an RSS reader to help you consume your new blog diet efficiently.

truly local updates. Record started posting frequently on her blog, providing firsthand reports from the neighborhood, and word of her blog spread.

Suddenly she had an audience, one that continued to grow, thanks to Google searches for "West Seattle." In 2008, she quit her job at the TV station and, with her husband, turned West Seattle Blog into a full-time operation that pays their salaries through local advertising.

"I don't have an entrepreneurial bone in my body," Record says. "But I do like to work long hours and always want to know what's going on." Because people had nowhere else to turn for truly local news in West Seattle, her self-created job of running a local news blog has turned out to be a good fit.

As these examples show, innovation and experimentation are easier with a blog. Its flexible format enables an author-publisher to forge a personal identity with a unique voice, maintain a pace that matches the audience's needs and write with a style and focus that can adapt to new interests or pursuits.

What is it? | What's *Next?* Summary

⚠ MICROBLOGGING BASICS

If blogging started as an online journal, think of microblogging as an instant messaging journal. A microblogging service allows users to publish brief text messages, usually no more than 140 characters, with links to other Web sites, photos or videos. Messages can be submitted in a variety of ways, including text messaging, with a smartphone app or simply through posting to the Web.

The messages can also be consumed in many ways, including on mobile devices, via e-mail and on Web sites such as Twitter.com. The services make it simple for you to subscribe to, or follow, an individual and receive that person's updates in various forms and to secure your own messages and restrict access only to those individuals you want reading your updates.

▶ Why is microblogging so popular?

The ease of publishing, combined with the ease of consuming, has contributed to microblogging's rapid growth. Blogging can intimidate writers who don't feel they can consistently write anything of interest, but anybody can contribute something with a 140-character limit. And when you find someone worth reading, you can easily follow that person, meaning you'll automatically receive updates from that person on a Web site or on your mobile device.

Twitter is the most popular microblogging service. In fact, the platform is so popular that the term "microblogging" is no longer parlance for the activity. The Twitter service was launched in July 2006, and by the end of 2014 it had nearly 300 million users and was seeing more than 500 million tweets per day. But Twitter isn't the only way to become a microblogger. You're also doing it when you post status updates on a social network such as Tumblr, Facebook or LinkedIn.

Services like Twitter invite users to post quick updates on what they might be doing, thinking or planning at any given moment. The more updates that people post for one another, the more connected friends and colleagues become, 140 characters at a time.

Social scientists call this "ambient awareness" or "ambient intimacy." It's the ability to maintain a constant connection with others without a direct communication tool such as phone or e-mail, which is one-on-one. Ambient awareness allows for one-to-many communication, making it persistent but passive. If a friend or colleague doesn't have time to stay tuned to your every thought or move, that person simply doesn't check your updates—much more polite than ignoring an e-mail or a phone call. But the updates remain there, so whenever the person has time and interest, he or she is easily able to find out what you've been up to.

"Each little update—each individual bit of social information—is insignificant on its own, even supremely mundane," Clive Thompson wrote in The New York Times Magazine. "But taken together, over time, the little snippets coalesce into a surprisingly sophisticated portrait of your friends' and family members' lives, like thousands of dots making a pointillist painting. This was never before possible, because in the real world, no friend would bother to call you up and detail the sandwiches she was eating. The ambient information becomes like 'a type of E.S.P.,' as [Ben] Haley described it to me, an invisible dimension floating over everyday life."[3]

---

[3]Clive Thompson, "Brave New World of Digital Intimacy," The New York Times Magazine, September 5, 2008.

▶ Why is microblogging important?

To understand why microblogging is important, you need to understand how it started. Microblogging is the product of three previous forms of short, text-based communication: Internet Relay Chat (IRC), Short Message Service (SMS, or text messaging) and instant messaging (IM). Twitter's founders sought a way to blend these different forms of communication to keep tabs on friends. But the service has exploded beyond any of the projected uses its inventors envisioned.

Two keys to Twitter's rapid growth are its simplicity and its flexibility. Open application programming interface (API) technology allows new tools and technology to be built on top of Twitter, thus not only providing more functionality for users but also creating deeper investment by a community of developers.

Around the same time that Twitter launched in 2006, Facebook unveiled its own microblogging feature. News Feed pushed any update to a person's profile out to all the person's friends without any additional action by the individual. This feature brought ambient awareness to average users of the Web and in some ways probably paved the way for the microblogging movement and entered us all into the era of status updates.

Twitter's first spotlight moment came at South by Southwest (SXSW), a festival of music, media and technology that regularly draws many thousands of people to Austin, Texas. Attendees at the March 2007 SXSW found Twitter a useful tool for tracking the conference happenings and organizing meetups with friends. The company spurred the spontaneous usage by displaying the stream of messages relating to the conference on large flat-screen television monitors.

At the end of the conference, Twitter won the award for best mobile application. The next week, the number of Twitter users grew 55 percent, according to an article in the Financial Times.

"The success is sort of shocking," Dan Fost wrote in the San Francisco Chronicle a week after the 2007 SXSW conference, "considering that most information-overloaded people believe they have no desire to invite hundreds of new messages onto their cell phones. Yet once started, many people find Twitter strangely addictive, to say nothing of useful."

It's incredible to think that as early as 2007 a technology writer would observe that we were already overwhelmed with information on our phones. After Twitter rose to prominence, it was quickly followed by Instagram, Tumblr, Snapchat and many others.

Twitter's simplicity led to its first-mover advantage. But as users grow accustomed to the practice of microblogging, they may desire more features. Tumblr produces a full-featured microblog and allows users to post any form of media from any type of device.

The reason some new-media experts think so highly of Twitter, Facebook and Tumblr is that these applications signal the emergence of the "real-time Web." By unlocking so much information that previously would not have been published, platforms such as Twitter and Facebook have unseated Google for some users who want to know what's happening online right now. Google is not sitting still, however. It unveiled Google+ in 2011 in an attempt to compete with the aforementioned platforms and by 2014 claimed to have more than 300 million active monthly users. Google+ has not been seen to have an impact on journalism at the same level as Twitter or Facebook, however.

In the past, a user had to wait for a news organization to publish a story on a breaking news event such as a plane crash. With Twitter, users on the scene start spreading the word immediately. And marketers don't have to wait for a survey or brand study to see how their products are being received. They simply run a search on Twitter for their product name and, because the vast majority of Twitter users don't protect their posts, read what people are saying about them right now.

Even Google search can't do this.

As Clay Shirky noted in "Here Comes Everybody," the new concept is publish first, filter later.[4] We'd already moved, years ago, from an information ecosystem that featured a scarcity of information to one that offers abundance. This fundamental shift created the opening for microblogging to emerge as a community navigation tool, producing information that people want right now and helping people find what they are looking for.

---

[4]Clay Shirky, "Here Comes Everybody: The Power of Organizing Without Organizations" (New York: Penguin Press, 2008).

SHORTY AWARDS

The Shorty Awards, highlighting the best microblogging on Twitter as chosen by Twitter users, were first held in January 2009. The winners have to limit their acceptance speeches to 140 characters. See www.shortyawards.com.

Some journalists have a hard time thinking about writing a news story 140 characters at a time. But it can actually be an excellent frame to work within, as Paul Bradshaw discussed on his Online Journalism Blog.

"One great thing about Twitter—and this is why it is so useful for student journalists—is that after a while it trains you to look for interesting things around you (and think how you can communicate that in 140 characters)," wrote Bradshaw, a journalism lecturer in Birmingham, England. "Those who write off the minutiae of Twitter need to realize: it's the writer who makes it interesting."[5]

News organizations, with stables of writers paid to make things interesting, have flocked to the new medium. In addition to making it easy for people to participate in the live Web, a microblogging platform such as Twitter is an important social media tool that is critical for every journalist in the digital age.

"When I started running social media for The Cincinnati Enquirer in early 2008, there weren't many social media editors out there," says Mandy Jenkins, who went on to run social media at The Huffington Post and now works at Storyful, the self-described "first news agency of the social media age."

"Most of us were former reporters, producers or editors who'd caught the Twitter bug and wanted to share it," Jenkins said. "We were part of the newsroom power structure from our former jobs, which helped move our practices into the rest of the operation."

Jenkins and Liz Heron, a social media expert who has worked for The Washington Post, The New York Times and The Wall Street Journal and now works for Facebook, both believe that if news organizations were proficient in social media, the jobs of social media managers at news

---

[5]Paul Bradshaw, "10 Things You Can Tweet About on Twitter," Online Journalism Blog, February 16, 2009. http://onlinejournalismblog.com/2009/02/16/10-things-you-can-tweet-about-on-twitter.

organizations would be obsolete. If all newsroom staffers knew how to use social media as well as they know how to use e-mail and other communication platforms, social media would be considered a core competence, not a specialty.

These tools are especially powerful for helping journalists tap the power of the crowd, as discussed in chapter 3.

"Social media platforms such as Twitter enable budding reporters to be part of a more open journalistic culture," wrote Alfred Hermida, an assistant professor at the Graduate School of Journalism, University of British Columbia, and founding news editor of the BBC News Web site. "Traditionally, the work of journalism has been hidden behind the walls of the newsroom. Through social media, journalists can be more open about their work, offering insights into the process of news, and connect with audiences in a way that simply wasn't possible a generation ago."[6]

In 2011, the "Arab Spring" emerged as one of the most powerful examples of social media mixing with journalism. Twitter was the best place to find out what was happening—as it was happening. Instead of waiting for reporters to gather information, write stories and submit them to editors for posting online, the people-formerly-known-as-sources were posting their observations, experiences, thoughts and fears immediately to Twitter for the millions of people using the service to read. NPR's Andy Carvin used these sources to cultivate and curate an informed stream of real-time updates as citizens of Egypt, Tunisia and other Arab countries fought (often violently) for their freedom.

The Washington Post called Carvin "a one-man Twitter news bureau" in describing how he chronicled fast-moving developments throughout the Middle East. "By grabbing bits and pieces from Facebook, YouTube and the wider Internet and mixing them with a stunning array of eyewitness sources, Carvin has constructed a vivid and constantly evolving mosaic of the region's convulsions."[7]

---

[6]Alfred Hermida, "Budding Journalists Use Twitter, Blogs to Open Doors," PBS MediaShift, February 10, 2009. www.pbs.org/mediashift/2009/02/budding-journalists-use-twitter-blogs-to-open-doors041.html.

[7]Paul Farhi, "NPR's Andy Carvin, Tweeting the Middle East," The Washington Post, April 6, 2011. www.washingtonpost.com/lifestyle/style/npr-andy-carvin-tweeting-the-middle-east/2011/04/06/AFcSdhSD_story.html.

"I see it as another flavor of journalism," says Carvin, who left NPR in 2014 to join Pierre Omidyar's new journalism venture, First Look Media. "So I guess I'm another flavor of journalist."

Carvin's skill on Twitter goes beyond republishing tips and links. He questions, crowdsources and verifies information and answers questions. Most of it is done out in the open on Twitter for all to see.

"In a lot of ways, this is traditional journalism," says Mark Stencel, NPR's former managing editor for digital news. "He has just turned the news-gathering process inside out and made it public. He's reporting in real time and you can see him do it. You can watch him work his sources and tell people what he's following up on."

▶▶ *Effective medium for breaking news*

The first assumption most journalists make when they see a microblogging platform such as Twitter for the first time is that its primary use would be for publishing breaking news alerts. True, it's an effective platform for that. But when it comes to breaking news, it's equally as important to be on Twitter to receive information as it is to use Twitter to send it.

The last few years have brought countless examples of news stories breaking first on Twitter. In many cases, these stories kept developing on Twitter before established news organizations could assemble even their quickest coverage. For example, on April 1, 2011, Shawna Redden used Twitter and the photo-sharing site Twitpic to share eyewitness accounts from an emergency landing of a Southwest Airlines flight after a six-foot hole opened in the roof of the aircraft just five rows behind where Redden was sitting.

Redden (@BluestMuse on Twitter) communicated with news organizations in Sacramento on Twitter, relaying information from 35,000 feet after the cabin lost pressure and air masks dropped from the ceiling. "Happy to be alive," Redden tweeted to the CBS 13 news account, responding to a question. "Still feel sick. 6 foot hole in the skin of the plane five rows behind me. Unbelievable."

She also posted a handful of photos to Twitpic, including one of the hole that caused the emergency. News organizations around the world republished the photo, just as they did the iconic image that Janis Krums captured in 2009 of passengers loading into life rafts after the emergency landing of a commercial jet in the Hudson River. In the days afterward, Redden was interviewed by "Good Morning America," Fox News, MSNBC and The Associated Press, among others.

The primary goal of using social networks, however, is not publishing. It's connecting. Learning about breaking news is one benefit of listening to

BluestMuse Shawna MalviniRedden
@CBS13rightnow Happy to be alive. Still feel sick.6 foot hole in the skin of the plane five rows behind me. Unbelievable.
1 Apr

BluestMuse Shawna MalviniRedden
Sky! twitpic.com/4fv02d
1 Apr

BluestMuse Shawna MalviniRedden
@countupir mechanical. Hole ripped in the skin of the plane!
1 Apr

BluestMuse Shawna MalviniRedden
@KTXL_Kathy was calm. Pilot landed safely. Excellent crew!
1 Apr

BluestMuse Shawna MalviniRedden
@KTXL_Kathy terrifying but happy to be alive. Explosion sound, then a rush of air... masks dropped and a woman screamed. Everyone else was
1 Apr

BluestMuse Shawna MalviniRedden
Yikes! twitpic.com/4fuozb
1 Apr

BluestMuse Shawna MalviniRedden
Loss of cabin pressure, hands down the Scariest experience of my life.
1 Apr

BluestMuse Shawna MalviniRedden
@SouthwestAir Emergency landing in Yuma. SW pilots are amazing!

Credit: https://twitter.com/BluestMuse

those in your network, but learning about what they're thinking, talking about, reading and doing is even more important. At no other time in the history of journalism have writers had this kind of access to their audience.

Even with ordinary citizens tweeting away about breaking news, journalists still play an important role by verifying facts and publishing updates as more information becomes available. People were already turning to news organizations' Web sites for the latest developments in the news, and now they turn to those organizations' Twitter feeds for even more immediate information.

Twitter has made an impact in courtrooms, too, where the quick publishing format fits nicely into trial coverage. A federal judge in Kansas ruled in March

2009 that Ron Sylvester, a reporter for The Wichita Eagle, could use Twitter to provide constant updates from a racketeering gang trial.

U.S. District Judge J. Thomas Marten said jurors are always told to avoid newspaper, broadcast and online reports. And Twitter, he decided, was not an exception.

"The more we can do to open the process to the public, the greater the public understanding—the more legitimacy the public system will have in the eyes of the public," Marten said in an interview with The Associated Press.[8]

When journalists and news organizations first discovered Twitter, many perceived it as nothing more than a new channel for publishing breaking news. They set up a service called Twitterfeed that allowed them to publish headlines automatically from their Web sites onto their Twitter accounts. But that's like putting Twitter on autopilot—and gradually journalists began to realize that doing that was preventing them from engaging in the community conversation that is essential to getting the most out of the live Web.

"Be a human presence on Facebook and Twitter; don't just attach your RSS feed to them and walk away," says Tracy Record, founder of the West Seattle Blog. "We have two main Twitter feeds. One is just RSS for those who only want links. The other one is all human, all the time, and if I send out a link there, it's because I did it myself. Answer questions, post fragments, let people post to your wall/page. Be present."

▶ Becoming a blogger

Before you wrote your first news story, you read news stories. Knowing the best practices of the medium is essential to understanding the fundamental components, like the lede, the nut graph and the walk-off. It's the same with blogs.

You have to read blogs in order to write an effective blog. Finding the ones that are right for you will take a little searching, but it's worth the time. Here's where to start:

Visit other news Web sites whose journalism you respect, and check out their blogs.

---

[8]Roxana Hegeman, "Twitter Boosts Public Access to Federal Courtrooms," Associated Press, March 6, 2009.

Credit: Janis Krums, http://twitpic.com/135xa

Janis Krums brought down the Twitpic servers when he posted a photo on Twitter of the famous 2009 plane crash in the Hudson River.

Find blogs that cover a subject that you hope to cover someday. Whether your interest is the environment, politics, sports, food or fashion, you should be reading blogs every day to immerse yourself in your topic of interest.

As you read other blogs, take time to analyze what is or isn't working on each one. Notice which posts you like the most, and then distill that information:

What makes them interesting? Is the writing crisp? Is it compelling? Are the topics relevant? Are there enough links to related material?

Note ways you could incorporate the best elements that you see elsewhere into your own blog.

Track the frequency of posts. Is the blog updated as often as you would like? Or too often, creating too much material to keep up with?

The concept of a blog has evolved greatly. What started as a single person's online journal has morphed into a flexible and powerful publishing phenomenon. The most popular blogs—Mashable and TechCrunch, for example—are really professional news Web sites that have chosen the blog as their publishing format. That decision has enabled these sites to build community around the news they report through the comments to their posts, which also helps increase their audience.

▶ Learn the language

Bloggers use specific terms to describe the mechanics of the medium, and it's important for you to know what they mean. Some of these terms are rarely used these days, but knowing them will give you a good foundation to build on.

Post: An entry on a blog or, as a verb, to make an entry on a blog.

Permalink: A link available on each post that provides direct access to that post, usually with comments visible. This is helpful for other bloggers to link directly to a given post or for readers to e-mail a link to a specific post to friends.

Trackback: A mechanism for communication between blogs, enabling one blogger to let another know that he or she is linking to their material. Trackback helps readers easily follow a conversation and helps bloggers know who is linking to each post. A **pingback** performs essentially the same function but uses slightly different technology.

Blogroll: A collection of links usually found on the sidebar of a blog. It is designed to inform blog readers of the sites that the blogger visits frequently. The thinking goes: If you like my blog, then you'll probably like other blogs I read. The links in a blogroll are most commonly to other blogs, but they can be to general or news Web sites, too.

▶ Crowdsourcing and building community

Tapping into your network of followers on Twitter is similar to engaging readers of a blog. While the audience may be different, the responses and

Credit: TechCrunch

> *TechCrunch, one of the most popular blogs in the world, provides its users with the most relevant information by showing them which topics are currently trending.* ←

reactions are usually more immediate, more diverse and more substantive. Even at 140 characters, those responses and reactions are the whole point of microblogging.

Sites such as CNN.com and nytimes.com have hundreds of thousands of followers of their breaking news accounts. So there is obviously a demand for such services. But getting the most out of building a community on Twitter takes a personal touch. A microblogging platform such as Twitter is, after all, really a social network disguised as a short-message publishing platform. There is power in finding new people to follow, and thereby extending your network. There is **social capital** to be earned through actively participating in that network, where you give information and ask questions and expect your followers to do the same.

For journalists, the biggest benefit of microblogging is learning about the audience. By following the people who follow you, you get a glimpse into what your readers are doing, thinking and reading. **That's information that's never been available to journalists before.**

Twitter Best Practices   Follow first, tweet later. The best way to get going on Twitter is to start following a few people who interest you and then see who they follow and retweet (RT) and follow them. Try to build up to about 20 people to follow each week. Then really listen to what is being said and shared by those you follow.

Going forward, it's a good idea to follow most of the people who follow you (as long as they're real people and not spambots).

Once you are ready to post on Twitter, follow these guidelines:

- **Be relevant and timely:** Don't clutter your followers' streams with severely off-topic or old content.

- **Be informative:** Provide value to the stream with good or simply interesting information. Share links to other sources often.

- **Be instructive:** Tips and advice are always welcome.

- **Include links:** When 140 characters isn't enough, use a link shortener such as bitly.

- **Reflect your personality:** Be personable, but don't get carried away.

- **Build relationships:** Ask questions judiciously. Answer questions, especially those directed to you, as often as possible.

Once a journalist starts microblogging, new doors open. Professionals who blog have discovered that Twitter can be particularly useful in providing real-time guidance and feedback on their journalism. By posting an item announcing an upcoming interview and then asking for suggestions on questions to ask, journalists invite audiences to work with them.

Posting also works when a journalist doesn't have someone to interview but is instead looking for leads, background or other information on a particular subject. It's like interviewing the public, but in an efficient and timely manner.

Twitter can be useful for performing public interviews. Putting out single or multiple questions into your Twitter networks in a call-and-response fashion will allow you to compile valuable research quickly and efficiently.

Sure, the collection of followers any journalist has on Twitter or another microblogging service is just a slice of a potential audience. But the tips, reactions and feedback found in a journalist's feed can be a gold mine of leads to follow. It's up to the journalist to use them responsibly.

"Twitter is very effective at finding news leads," says Lauren Spuhler, a former Web producer at the Knoxville News Sentinel. "People Twitter about fires or other news they see as they're driving by. Then we follow up."

As more news organizations establish online identities through Twitter, Facebook and other forms of social media, tips on breaking news come faster and more often from people who are starting to think of themselves as more than just readers.

Because everyone has the power to choose whom they follow, your community grows only if you post messages that offer some benefit to your followers. The best postings on Twitter get "retweeted" with a simple "RT." This is a recognition that you have posted something of value that someone else wanted to share.

Later in this chapter we'll look more closely at how you can build your network of followers.

▶ Marketing and building your brand

The old business models for journalism have been crumbling; innovation in journalism today must include an awareness of new business models and marketability. Can marketing save journalism? It sounds like a heretical question because journalists have long valued their profession as more "pure" than marketing and public relations. Yet, as these seemingly disparate forms of communication start to meld, journalism can benefit from integrating new marketing strategies and tactics.

"More than ever, the hard work of growing our audience falls squarely on the newsroom," states the first line of the recommendations in a 97-page report released by The New York Times in 2014. That line is under a subhead that reads, "Make developing our audience a core and urgent part of our mission."[9]

"Strategies" doesn't mean advertising or slogans or logos. As marketing has evolved in the digital age, it has become more transparent, authentic and collaborative—which I will argue in chapter 9 are all traits that describe good journalism today as well.

---

[9]The New York Times, "Innovation," March 2014. www.scribd.com/doc/224608514/The-Full-New-York-Times-Innovation-Report#scribd.

Follow the 80–20 Rule On a personal microblogging account, use 80 percent of your posts to add something of value to the community—a link to an interesting news article, a tip on a new Web site or anything else that your followers might find interesting. The other 20 percent of the posts can be self-promoting, such as links to your latest articles or blog posts or asking for help.

If you take too much from your community without giving, you will limit the growth of your followers.

News organizations and independent journalists create social capital by becoming the "trusted center" within a structure of relationships through digital communication. French sociologist Pierre Bourdieu suggested that social capital can be developed through purposeful actions and then transformed into economic gains. This concept is similar to the traditional business model for news of generating revenue based largely on a public service (for more, see chapter 9).

The opportunity of social media is especially important to younger journalists just starting out. News companies expect that interns and fresh-out-of-college new hires will possess a proficiency in social media. In fact, proficiency with new technology can help you land your first job.

"In social media, a budding journalist has an incredible platform to demonstrate their talents and engage with others in a way that just wasn't possible when I was in journalism school," says Hermida of the University of British Columbia. "At the very least, students should have a Web site that contains everything they produce. Better still if they have a blog which invites comments and discussions."

What is it? | **What's *Next?*** | Summary

⬇ MAKE A PLAN, CREATE A BLOG

Enter "start a blog" into Google and one of the first links that appears is www.wikihow.com/Start-a-Blog. This site provides an intuitive, step-by-step description that you can follow to create your own blog. An Internet search will yield many other sites as well, but most blog systems are so easy to use, you won't need any help.

Before you create your blog, take some time to think about what you will blog about. This will help you as you set up the software and will guide your early activity with the blog. But realize that you can always change course.

First, determine the goal of your blog. If you are just starting out and want to use your blog as an example of your journalistic work, pick a topic you can write about with authority. It can be cooking or jazz or knitting, but it should be something you are passionate about, so that you'll be motivated to keep to a regular posting schedule.

If you are working for a news site and want to add a blog to your coverage, then set a goal for your blog that is different from the coverage you are already doing with news articles or broadcasts. It should complement, not repurpose, the coverage you are already providing.

To create a basic plan for your blog, answer these three questions:

> What will you name your blog? (1–3 words)
>
> What is a good short description of of or catchphrase for your blog?
>
> What will you write about in your blog? What is its mission? (2–3 sentences)

Feature this information on your blog so readers will know immediately what you are all about. Stumbling onto a new blog and being unable to figure out quickly its reason for being is frustrating.

For example, Silverman's blog is named TechBlog and its catchphrase is "Upgrade your geek with Dwight Silverman." John Cook's GeekWire blog promotes "Dispatches from the digital frontier" as its catchphrase.

DRILLING DOWN

Hosting Fees Because WordPress is used by so many news companies, you should consider paying the small monthly fee for a hosted WordPress blog. This offers several advantages, including getting experience with this powerful content-management system. Also, you will gain the ability to choose from a larger number of themes and edit the CSS on your theme, as well as install dozens of plug-ins (which are similar to the gadgets in Blogger). In addition, the fee buys you a personalized domain name without "wordpress" in it (for example, mycoolblog.com). See chapter 1 for more information on getting going with WordPress.

For more information on hosting your own WordPress blog, go to http://wordpress.org/hosting. The hosting plans on this page provide one-click installation of WordPress and cost less than $10 a month.

▶ Choose a blog system

Although you can find lots of easy-to-use blog platforms—many of which are free—I recommend that you create a blog at WordPress.com. Because it is the leading platform, using it can help you in the future. You may find yourself interviewing for a job at an organization that uses WordPress, and your knowledge of how the system works will give you an advantage.

As we discussed in chapter 1, creating a blog at WordPress.com is quick and painless; there are demos and video tutorials to help you get started. It's also free.

Another option is Blogger.com, which is easy to use and also free, but is not widely used in professional settings.

Once you know what you'll name your blog and where you'll be blogging, you're ready to start.

Name: The name you choose for your blog will display at the top of the page and also in the URL. For example, a blog called "My Cool Blog" would have the URL http://mycoolblog.wordpress.com on WordPress.

Theme: You can choose how your blog looks by picking from several different themes. You select fonts and colors just as you would in a word-processing program.

▶ Customize your blog's appearance

You can use basic CSS to customize the look and feel of your blog. But don't let that scare you away. In fact, it's a great environment in which to get your hands dirty with some rudimentary CSS.

Page elements: Simply click **Edit** next to any of the sections on the page you wish to modify. Upload your own header image and add a short description in the **Header** field.

Fonts and colors: Choose from various colors and fonts.

Edit HTML: This is inaccurate; it's really Edit CSS, because the code you will access from this link is mostly the CSS style sheet.

Pick new template: Choose from several stock templates and change your blog's look and feel with two clicks.

Select **Appearance** from the left navigation menu of the dashboard after you have logged in. From there, you can select a new theme for your blog

The user interface for WordPress.

with two clicks. Or modify the following sections (links appear at the top of the page, next to the **Options** label).

Widgets: Quickly add some extra functionality to your blog; examples include a search box and a calendar that shows your recent posts.

Extras: Not much to see here; move along.

Custom image header: Upload your own header image.

Edit CSS: You can experiment with CSS styles, but you can't save the changes and make them public unless you upgrade to the WordPress Custom CSS Editor (that costs about $15 a year). Or you can host your own WordPress blog and have complete access to the style sheets.

Extras, gadgets and widgets: It's easy to add some very cool features to your blog using WordPress. Everything from a display of recent comments to a list of blogs you follow is just one click away.

In Blogger, these features are called gadgets, and you add them from the **Layout** page. Click on the **Edit** link next to **Gadgets** and select from the dozens available. Click the plus sign next to the gadget you wish to add and follow the steps to configure the gadget for your blog.

On a basic WordPress blog, these features are called widgets and can be accessed from the **Widgets** link under the **Appearance** header in the left navigation menu. Find a widget and click **Add,** then click **Edit** to

It's easy to add extras and add-ons to a blog with WordPress.

configure the widget. Setting up the widgets in WordPress can be a little more confusing. For example, when using certain widgets (such as **Links** or **Categories**), you can configure them only if you access them from separate links in the left navigation menu. So if you add a widget but can't figure out how to customize it, scan the links in the left navigation menu for a matching item and use it to build out the widget the way you want it.

What is it? **What's Next?** Summary

⬇ HOW TO BUILD AN AUDIENCE FOR YOUR BLOG

All writing is more fun when you know someone is reading it. With a blog, you can publish a steady stream of words and ideas, but there is no guarantee that anyone will ever see them.

The formula for driving traffic to your blog is simple. Executing it is not.

Regularly publish high-quality posts.

Write effective headlines.

Participate in the community.

Although veteran news reporters, with years of research behind them, are at an advantage when it comes to reporting and distilling facts and information, they are at a disadvantage when it comes to crafting blog posts. All those years spent writing inverted pyramids and anecdotal leads bog down many professional journalists when they blog.

Put the reader first: A successful blogger knows what readers want and can clearly and effectively communicate an idea, news or analysis quickly. If you write to impress the readers, you will distract them from the content.

Organize your ideas: Use a traditional outline to arrange your thoughts. Each post should be limited to as few items as possible; everything you include should complement your primary idea. Anything else just distracts the reader.

Get to the point quickly, too. Introduce the topic, provide a little background, and then fill in the details.

Be direct: It's important to use short sentences, short paragraphs and even short words. Simple, declarative sentences are the most effective for blogs. Posts should vary in length but should always be direct and to the point.

Be the authority, with a personality: The narrower the topic, the better. Your audience will clearly understand the subject matter covered, and you will have a better chance to present yourself as the best source of timely information on that particular topic. Add a distinctive voice and a conversational writing style, and you've got the formula for a successful blog.

"I've had a column at every newspaper I've worked at, and my blogging voice is very similar to my column voice," TechBlog's Silverman said. "It's not really anything I found; I just fell naturally into it. That said, not everyone is in that position. I tell newbie bloggers to write as though you're telling news to a friend via e-mail. In fact, sometimes I'll suggest they write their first blog posts in Outlook, just so they feel like they're in the right zone."

The right voice is key. It has to be comfortable for you, the author, and engage readers at the same time. Pretending to be someone you're not is a recipe for failure. You can model your voice after those you like in other blogs, but eventually you'll need to develop a style that works for you and your audience. You won't find your blogging voice immediately, so trial and error and experimentation are essential.

"My blogging voice varies depending on what I am writing," Cook said. "Sometimes, in complex legal stories I play it straight in typically journalistic fashion. Other times, I write in the first person. Other times, I attempt humor. The blog allows you to experiment—one of the other reasons I love it. I like to try to surprise readers. One way to do that is by changing your voice and trying new things to see what works. Fail early and move on. Overall I would say that my writing style has become much more conversational and chatty over the years. I don't think that it's a bad thing."

How's this, Mom? Om Malik, the journalist-turned-blogger behind the successful GigaOM network, offered a good piece of advice in a Slate article on how to blog: Write, then wait 15 minutes before publishing to provide enough distance for you to edit yourself dispassionately. Malik also suggested that you write your posts as if your mother were reading your work. This will help you maintain civility and keep your writing clear.[10]

Make your posts scannable: Use different typographical techniques to make your posts easy for busy readers to scan (because those are the only readers you've got). Bulleted or numbered lists, bold text, subheads and quotes set apart from the rest of the text are simple ways to boost scannability.

Link, summarize and analyze: Attribution is important, and in a blog attribution takes the form of links. A great post is sprinkled with links to other sites, news articles and even other blogs. Some blogs publish entire posts that are nothing but links to other articles and material that is related. (Silverman simply headlines these "Linkpost.")

Be specific with headlines: A good blog headline is effective for both readers and robots (see chapter 9 for more information). It should be specific to the point of the post and include keywords that a user who is searching for this type of information would enter into a search engine.

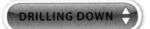

DRILLING DOWN

Ads If you want to try to make a few dollars from your blog, sign up for Google Adsense or Amazon Affiliate Ads. You won't get rich overnight, but you might make enough each month to buy some new iTunes. Remember, though, if you are publishing a blog with ads, you have a commercial Web site, even if you are making only $2 a month. This may limit your use of some third-party content

Have a good attitude: Mike Masnick from Techdirt.com suggested in a Slate article that attitude is an important blogging tool. "When in doubt, write. When really in doubt, ask your readers for their opinions. Don't beg for traffic. Don't worry about traffic. Just write what you're interested in, communicate with others, and enjoy yourself."

---

[10]Farhad Manjoo, "Advice From Arianna Huffington, Om Malik, and More of the Web's Best Pundits," Slate, December 18, 2008. www.slate.com/id/2207061.

▶ Use photos and screenshots

Blogs without images are lame. Would you read a newspaper or magazine if it had no pictures, graphics or art of any kind? Of course not. Don't expect readers to flock to a boring blog without visuals.

If you work for a newspaper or magazine, you have access to a treasure trove of images. And as a reporter-blogger, you will probably write about subjects that have been covered previously, so reusing file photos should be easy.

If you are on your own, you need a basic understanding of copyright and a healthy respect for other people's material. Yes, adding an image or graphic from the Internet to your blog is technologically simple. But that doesn't make it right.

You need to ask permission to use anyone else's photo or graphic you find on the Web, unless the creator is making it available through a Creative Commons declaration. If you are publishing a blog without ads (a noncommercial Web site), you probably have a good chance of receiving permission to use someone else's image, provided that you include a credit and a link.

To search for photos and images that are freely shared by their owners, try these Web sites:

> http://search.creativecommons.org

> http://flickr.com/search/advanced (check the box at the bottom of the page to "Only search within Creative Commons–licensed content")

You can brush up on what's acceptable and what's not by visiting this handy page from the Electronic Freedom Forum: http://w2.eff.org/bloggers/lg/faq-ip.php.

Most blogging software makes adding a photo to a post as simple as adding an attachment to an e-mail.

Some systems will even resize the photo so you don't have to. If yours doesn't, and if you pull a high-resolution image from archives and need to reduce it to save your page load time (big pictures make Web pages load very slowly), use an online service such as PicMonkey or FotoFlexer to resize it quickly without having to download and learn new software. (For more information on handling digital photos, see chapter 5.)

▶ Post early, post often

One of the first questions a new blogger is likely to ask is, "How often should I post to my blog?" There is no hard-and-fast rule. When it comes to reporting news on a blog, many veteran journalists have struggled to free themselves from the once-a-day news cycle of the newspaper.

A blog's mission will determine how often it should be updated. Technology and gadget blogs, for example, produce a steady stream of new content, 24 hours a day, 365 days a year. But posting daily updates is not a reasonable goal for a one-person blog, so here's a more practical guide, especially when you're starting out:

Post approximately once a day: If you can keep your posts short, you can easily add at least five or six a week. Hitting that minimum is important if you plan to build an audience, and maintaining it forces you beyond your comfort zone; it requires you to consider writing about some new and different angles that will help you broaden your area of expertise.

It's important to find the point in your day when you are most inclined to blog. Maybe in the morning with a cup of coffee, or the afternoon when you're fully awake. Whenever the words flow most easily, schedule yourself some time to blog. Then stick to that schedule for 30 days. It's the best way to make blogging a habit.

If you work for a news organization as a reporter or columnist, you will post even more frequently. After all, if your beat is worth covering, there will be plenty of action to write about.

I'm too busy! Sure—we all are. But successful bloggers have found ways to make their blogs work for them, saving them time, instead of simply becoming an added burden. Here's how:

> Use the blog as a notebook, compiling your notes and story ideas as drafts in a blog system, and then making them public one at a time.

> Seek public feedback and use it to focus your future writing.

DRILLING DOWN

The Screenshot To add some visual interest, insert a screenshot of a blog or Web site you are writing about. There are many different ways to make a screenshot; it depends on which computer and operating system (OS) you are using. Do a Web search for the word "screenshot" and your OS (Windows or Mac), and you'll find several good how-to explanations.

You will discover that you often don't know enough about a particular topic to feel comfortable writing about it. Don't let this stop you. Instead, use it as an opportunity to learn enough to write about something new.

▶ Participate in the community

Take advantage of your blog's interactive and community-building potential to increase your exposure and your audience. You should not start a blog unless you're willing to allow—and manage—comments. Some mainstream news blogs don't allow comments, severely undermining the community-building function of the medium. Others take a hands-off approach and allow open discourse to develop and, sometimes, dominate the blogs. Neither extreme is desirable.

"Comments are, in my mind, essential to a blog," said GeekWire's Cook. "I love comments even though sometimes they can get out of hand. They are, in many ways, a reporting tool that helps guide me on a story. I can't tell you how many times I've been tipped off to a great story through comments. Other times I have received an insight/question that I may not have recognized before."

Embrace comments as a valuable reporting tool; don't view them as a burden or necessary evil, as many traditional journalists do.

"We moderate comments at chron.com, and I think that's important," Silverman said. "Moderated comments raise the quality of the discussion, and doing so is not a burden or necessary evil at all. It's part of the process of building a healthy and respectful online community."

You can cultivate comments by adding your own to any discussion that needs clarification, redirection or simply a vote of confidence. For example: "Great comments, everyone. Keep them coming!"

You can highlight astute observations or pertinent questions by turning them into full blog posts. This will give you easy blog fodder and let your readers know that they matter to you. That's important, because one of the reasons blogs are popular is that they embrace interactivity and give readers a sense of participating.

Comments can enrich your blog; they can also spoil it. Don't let a few bad apples ruin the conversation for everyone else. Shepherd the comments so people stay on topic and are respectful. A good comments section is akin to the animated conversation in a pub on a Friday night. But sometimes people get out of hand and deserve to be thrown out.

Whatever the focus of your blog, you can be sure that some other blogs cover the same, or similar, topics. In the old-media world, these other blogs would be seen as competition, to be kept at arm's length or ignored altogether. In the new-media world, however, it's better to jump in and join the community. Here's how:

Read other blogs: They'll help you stay on top of current news and developments related to your blog's focus and also help you find new blogs to follow.

Comment on other blogs: When you submit comments, sign your name and include your blog's URL so that blog readers know where to find you.

Link to other blogs in your posts: When you link to blogs because they have interesting posts, write to the authors. Compliment them and notify them that you are linking to them. You're paying them a sincere compliment, and most likely those bloggers will check out your blog and possibly return the favor, earning you some new readers.

▶ Use RSS feeds to beat the competition

Once you have a blog, you need something to blog about. Once you have something to blog about, you need a community to participate in.

Remember RSS (Really Simple Syndication)? It's an essential tool for any blogger because it provides the most efficient way to follow a dozen, or several dozen, blogs and news sites, giving you endless material to comment on—and link to. It's also the best tool for finding new blogs and news sites to follow.

DRILLING DOWN

Create a Blogroll Use your favorite 10 to 15 RSS feeds for your blogroll, the list of links on the side of your blog that notifies your readers about the blogs you regularly follow. You can also use the blogrolls on other blogs to find more feeds to add to your RSS reader.

In chapter 1, you learned how to set up an RSS reader and subscribe to news feeds. Build a comprehensive list of RSS feeds from blogs that you want to follow, and as you find new blogs and Web sites of interest, add them. You should also use RSS for news searches so you can efficiently track anything new on the topics you are interested in blogging about.

Start by compiling a list of 10 topics you want to blog about. They could be company names, names of people or a small geographic area like a town or a neighborhood in a city. Then set up RSS feeds for those searches and let the robots do the work for you.

Adding a Web search to an RSS reader is easy (review from chapter 1):

> Perform the news search (in Google News or Yahoo News).
>
> Click on the RSS icon or link on the first results page.
>
> Copy the URL.
>
> Open your RSS reader and select **Add a Feed**.
>
> Paste the URL into the address box.
>
> Hit **Subscribe**.

⬇ START USING TWITTER

The great thing about microblogging, especially on Twitter, is how easy it is to get going. It takes just a few minutes to register for a new account, upload a profile picture and post your first tweet.

Before you get "on" Twitter, though, you need a sense of what you're going to do with it. Not everyone has the same goal, of course. And while you don't have to stick rigidly to one approach with your microblogging, it's helpful to know what you are hoping to accomplish:

- Are you a reporter hoping to build community with readers?

- Are you an editor aiming to build a network of readers around a specific topic?

- Are you a journalist hoping to network with other journalists?

- Are you an aspiring [insert dream job here] looking to build your personal brand?

Identifying what you want to accomplish will help determine your Twitter ID (or username). If you are part of a news organization, your username should be consistent with the organization's brand. If you are hoping to build a personal brand, then use your full name. If you want to network with others around a shared interest, you can have a little fun with your Twitter ID (and your profile picture), but you should still add your real name to your profile.

So what are you waiting for? Go to Twitter.com and sign up, already.

▶ Learn the Twitter basics

To participate in any community, you first need to know the language. And we can all be thankful that there are only a handful of "insider" terms you need to know in order to be a functioning member of the Twitter community.

DM: Direct message, which is a tweet that goes directly to one Twitter account and is visible only to that account.

@: It precedes a Twitter ID in a reply (for example, @markbriggs).

Tweet: As a verb it means sending a message on Twitter; as a noun, it means the message sent or received.

RT: Retweet, meaning copying someone else's tweet and posting it so your followers can see it, too.

Hashtag: A common label for any tweet that should be tied together with others' tweets, preceded by a # symbol; especially effective for a news event or a conference (for example, #sxsw for the South by Southwest conference).

There are four main things you can do on Twitter: post a message, read other people's messages, read reply messages that other people intend for you, and send and receive direct messages, which are private. (We'll cover searching on Twitter separately.) Here's a look at each activity:

Post: It's easy, but there's a 140-character limit.

Read: It's easy, too, since the messages of the people you follow automatically display on your Twitter home page (after you sign in).

Reply: Reading reply messages is easy, too: Just click "@Replies." If you want to reply to someone, simply add the "@" sign before the person's Twitter username (or click the arrow on the person's tweet you wish to reply to).

Send and receive direct messages: Sending a direct message is easy, too. You can simply begin your tweet with the letter "d" followed by the username of the person you are messaging, or you can use the "Direct Message" feature on Twitter's Web site or TweetDeck or Hootsuite. That person will receive an e-mail notification regarding the receipt of a direct message (or DM), and the message will not be public.

▶ **Build your network**

When you start on Twitter or Tumblr or Google+, you don't have a network or a community. But you can build one with a little time and effort.

The first step is to find people to follow. Go to search.twitter.com and search for terms you are

DRILLING DOWN

B Brf   Don't use up your entire 140 characters with a lengthy URL. Posting links to interesting news articles is a great way to add value to your network, but remember to keep URLs short with a URL shortener. Twitter offers this service from its Web site or you can use an outside service such as bitly (http://bitly.com) to convert a long URL into a short one that, when clicked, directs the reader to the full URL. You can also accomplish this by using a third-party client such as TweetDeck or Hootsuite, which, like bitly, offers analytics and reporting. This can help you gauge which links get the most clicks by your followers.

interested in, such as "journalism" or "newspapers" or "iPhone." When you find a post that looks interesting, click on the profile of the person who posted it. If other posts from that person appear interesting, you should add him or her to your feed. Then click to see whom that person is following, and when you find someone whose interests seem aligned with yours and whose posts look interesting, follow that person, too.

Now posts from those people will appear on your Twitter, Tumblr or Google+ home page. When someone reposts another post, follow it and you'll probably find someone else new to follow. Following just a few new people every day will quickly increase the depth and breadth of the posts flowing into your home page.

This also helps in the next step, which is to get people to follow you. On Twitter, each time you click the "Follow" button on someone's profile, that person receives an e-mail notification about your decision to follow his or her tweets. Usually, that person will then click the link to your profile, and, if your tweets seem interesting enough, will click the "Follow" button on your profile.

The best way to build a network is by posting good content and promoting those you follow. As Sarah Evans noted on Mashable: "Twitter is all about karma. The more good you put out there, the more you receive."

Evans continued: "When you find others with great information, don't be shy in sharing with your community. It's a great feeling when you promote one of your followers (instead of yourself) and it results in dialogue among your community. It ultimately reflects support for you and credibility for your followers. Win-win!"

Also, it's a good idea to add your Twitter, Google+ or Tumblr URL to your e-mail and other electronic signatures. Then, in addition to your e-mail, Web site and blog, people you are communicating with will know your microblogging ID, too.

▶ Search on microblogs: The live Web

The idea of the live Web is easiest to understand during a breaking news event.

But a breaking news event isn't the only time you should turn to the live Web on Twitter. At any given moment, you can see the most popular topics that are being discussed on Twitter by visiting any number of Twitter applications or going directly to http://search.twitter.com. Normally you will see a combination of hashtags and actual brands or people. Click on **Advanced Search** to filter and focus your search.

Here you can also enter search keywords to find information on a specific topic. Sure, Google and Wikipedia have become great reporting tools, but neither is fast enough to match Twitter.

If Apple has released a software update for the iPhone and you're a business reporter who wants to know whether people like it, you could post an invitation to your blog and ask people to comment or e-mail. But that is limited and slow compared with searching Twitter. Here you'll find people who may never visit your blog, and you'll find out very quickly whether the masses love or hate the upgrade. If you want to contact one of them, use @reply or send a direct message. You can also ask questions publicly by following whatever hashtag people are using (in this example, probably #iphone).

▶▶ Start following

Before you post even a few tweets, spend some time finding a few people to follow. Social media is often compared to a cocktail party or professional networking event, and one of the first things you (should) do when arriving at a party is listen to the conversation that is already in progress. Apply that same line of thinking to Twitter and spend a little time "listening" by reading what people are writing, specifically those people who interest you.

"I have one simple rule—follow people back," Linda Thomas wrote in the second edition of "Journalism Next.""Imagine you're at a party and for some reason you've captivated three people who are listening to you, when a fourth person walks up. It would be rude to turn your back and ignore him or her. But that's what you do when you don't follow people back on Twitter. That person might have had a great story to share, or a useful idea. You'll never know."

Credit: https://twitter.com/search?q=iphone&src=typd

Twitter is easy on a mobile device because the messages are short.

Refer to the suggestions covered in the earlier section on building a network and the methods listed below to find 20 people to follow each week. It takes only a few minutes to find and follow someone, so this assignment shouldn't take more than half an hour per week. (It takes only a couple of minutes to follow three people a day.)

Here's how to find people to follow:

Search: Use http://search.twitter.com and search for names or topics. Also try Twellow.com and Tweepz.com to search for people.

Use your followers: Scroll through the people your followers are following.

Use the followed: Scroll through the people you are following.

Follow the influentials: Services such as Tweepz rank people by their numbers of followers so you know which are the most popular. These people probably aren't "in your network," but it's fun to follow a few celebrities and the A-list people on Twitter. Following them might give you ideas about how to use the service most effectively.

▶ Start tweeting

People getting started with microblogging often worry they have nothing to say. Twitter's 140-character limit seems constricting at first, but it can be liberating because it lowers the bar on what's worth contributing.

Here's your tweeting assignment—five different types of tweets to post to your new Twitter account:

What are you reading? Use your RSS reader to find interesting links to post. This is the easiest way to add value and build followers.

What are you thinking? Start listening to the internal conversation you have going on in your head. At least once a day there's got to be something worth sharing.

What are you doing later? Not right now, since what you're probably doing right now is sitting in front of a computer trying to think of something to say on Twitter. But later on, are you attending an event or meeting that's interesting or hitting a deadline on a project that's worth noting?

What are you liking on Twitter? Find a message posted by someone you follow that's interesting or helpful and retweet it. This gives the original poster a public pat on the back and gives your followers access to something interesting they might otherwise have missed.

Credit: https://twitter.com/nytimes

The Twitter stream from The New York Times provides news updates.

What can you ask or answer? Asking questions on Twitter is effective for many types of information. But you should also answer people's questions if you want them to answer yours.

▶▶ Go mobile

Download the Twitter app on your iPhone, Android or Windows phone and use Twitter to post and read updates from anywhere. You can also go to the Twitter home page with your phone's Web browser, but downloading and using the native app will get you a better mobile Twitter experience.

Reporters are using mobile phones to post Twitter updates from breaking news events, press conferences, high school sports events and more. The 140-character limit makes it an especially comfortable medium, and it also offers an easy and effective way to capture and share photographs from the scene (see chapter 5 for more on photography).

The interconnections of information—be it news, marketing or conversation—are critical to journalism in the digital age. Understanding microblogging and tapping into the power of community are the best—and easiest—ways to get going.

Credit: Photo courtesy of
Matt Thompson

MATT THOMPSON

▶ **EDITORIAL PRODUCT
MANAGER** | NPR
(@mthomps)

In Internet time, "blogging" seems to have become an antiquated term. Some would say it's also an antiquated idea—a retirement home for early adopters stuck in the era of the Internet Superhighway.

I'd argue quite the reverse. Blogging's become such a basic pattern for information on the Internet that it feels almost weird that it still has a name.

A little history's in order. When the term "blogging" emerged, a lengthy, scrolling list of content was mostly anathema to news organizations. Users don't scroll, the conventional wisdom contended, well after usability scholars started knocking it down in 1997. It took almost a decade for news organizations to warm up to the simple idea of a stream of material largely ordered by recency.

If you reread coverage from the traditional press of The Huffington Post's 2005 launch, you might have thought the Pulitzers had created a "Derisive Sniffing" category. (On the site's fifth anniversary, the Columbia Journalism Review rounded up the top five old-media jeers given at the launch of "Arianna's blog.") But by 2007, blogs like HuffPo and Perez Hilton had skyrocketed past their blog-averse old-media counterparts, upstarts like Talking Points Memo were winning prestigious journalism awards, and old media was hustling, as usual, to catch up.

Meanwhile, many of the same digital natives who'd brought us the simple idea of blogging were innovating on the format. In 2005, Jason Kottke (who'd been blogging at that point for seven years) noted the emergence of the "tumblelog," a subset of blogging he described as just "a quick and dirty stream of consciousness," super-brief, minimalist posts, devoid of the chatty rambling many folks associated with blogging at the time. Soon, this type of posting composed most of the material on Kottke's site, with only the occasional longer post. People had started to call it "microblogging," and it was catching on. The next year, a few guys at a podcasting start-up launched a prototype of a thing they'd call Twitter. The year after that saw the launch of a start-up called Tumblr.

I recount this history because the blog was one of the first information structures unique to the internet, and it's useful for us to remember how foreign it once seemed when we consider how far it's now spread. Your Twitter timeline, your Facebook news feed, your Pinterest page—all of these would once have been described as subgenres of the blog. But the pattern's now so baked into our understanding of how digital information flows that we still somehow think of "blogging" as a separate practice, inextricably bound to the tone and aesthetic of its snarky pioneers.

I think one of the most essential, revolutionary ideas that blogging taught us will hold true for the foreseeable future: the stream is ultimately more important than the story. Whether you're blogging in the classical fashion, tweeting, tumblring, or pinning, you build the most significant value not with a single post, but with a stream of material that turns passersby into followers, hooking them back again and again. The growing crowd you convene around the work you do is your journalism's most powerful asset. Master the art of cultivating such a stream, and you assure yourself enduring relevance, as many of blogging's pioneers still claim today.

[*Source:* Written by Matt Thompson at the request of the author.]

☑ LOVE IT OR LEAVE IT

Most journalists got into the field because they liked it, and then found they had a talent for it. The same is true in the blogosphere. You need to be passionate about your blog, just as you are passionate about your craft or your beat. If you're not, you'll be wasting your time.

"Today's journalism demands social media skills, like it or not," said Thomas, who spent four years as morning news host on KIRO Radio in Seattle and is now managing editor for online news and content strategy at Starbucks. "I love it. You will too if you use microblogging to create your own community of news consumers, to develop unique stories and to break news."

When I ran thenewstribune.com, I used to tell reporters, "You have to love your blog." They would laugh and wait for me to say that I was joking, but I was serious. Many of those journalists stopped by my desk a few months later and, grinning broadly, whispered, "Mark, I love my blog."

Although blog love can't be measured, it becomes obvious after six months who loves and who loathes their blogs. Mostly we found that reporters, editors and even photographers—once they got started—wished they had more time to spend on their blogs and Twitter accounts. For some, blogging became the cornerstone for all their work. Those reporter-bloggers can't imagine working in a world without a blog, just as others can't imagine doing journalism today without e-mail or the Internet.

If you can find the fire to blog and participate in the world of Twitter, you will reap the rewards.

"I think one of the most essential, revolutionary ideas that blogging taught us will hold true for the foreseeable future: the stream is ultimately more important than the story," says Matt Thompson. "Whether you're blogging in the classical fashion, tweeting, tumblring, or pinning, you build the most significant value not with a single post, but with a stream of material that turns passersby into followers, hooking them back again and again. The growing crowd you convene around the work you do is your journalism's most powerful asset. Master the art of cultivating such a stream, and you assure yourself enduring relevance, as many of blogging's pioneers still claim today."

BLOGS ON BLOGGING

Some of the tips in this chapter are courtesy of a blog on blogging called Copyblogger. It's among a handful of online resources that can provide a constant stream of suggestions and inspiration as you continue blogging. Here are some sites to get you started:

Copyblogger.com

Problogger.net

Weblogs.about.com

GET GOING Checklist ✓

Blogging

☐ **Evaluate other blogs:** Find three blogs that cover topics you find interesting and determine the following:

   ☐ Each blog's biggest strength (immediacy, analysis, depth, style?)

   ☐ How each blog plays to that strength

   ☐ How each blog builds community through interaction with readers and links to other blogs or sources

☐ **Complete the quick plan:** Think about what your blog will cover:

   ☐ What will you name your blog? (1–3 words)

   ☐ What is a good, short description of or catchphrase for your blog?

   ☐ What will you write about in your blog? What is your blog's mission? (2–3 sentences)

☐ **Create a blog:** Set up your blog on WordPress.com or Blogger.com. Don't use the default theme; find one you like.

☐ **Post to your blog:** Start with some basic posts, on topics such as which RSS reader you are using and which feeds you have subscribed to. Make a post with an image; don't steal one, though.

☐ **Add a blogroll:** Include at least six blogs you are following with your RSS reader.

☐ **Join a community:** Make three comments on any of the blogs that you are now following.

Microblogging on Twitter

☐ If you don't have a Twitter account already, create one.

☐ Use the search functions on the service to find new sources of information.

☐ Follow the steps listed in this chapter to start following others and then start tweeting to build your Twitter network.

☐ Visit http://multimedia.journalism.berkeley.edu/tutorials/ twitter to explore further using Twitter as a journalist.

CHAPTER 3

Crowd-Powered Collaboration

Way back in 1970, Phil Meyer wrote one of the most important books on news reporting. He began his book, "Precision Journalism," with an observation that seems even more prescient today:

"If you are a journalist, or thinking of becoming one, you may have already noticed this: They are raising the ante on what it takes to be a journalist."

More than four decades later, it's more accurate than ever.

As the tasks of journalism get tougher, most news organizations have made staff cutbacks, asking journalists to "do more with less." Meanwhile, independent journalism start-ups are changing the rules about who is a journalist and what's needed to report the news. They're operating without the infrastructure that's traditionally been seen as necessary for doing serious journalism.

Whether in traditional newsrooms or new-style organizations, trained journalists are looking for ways to leverage their assets—their news judgment and their reporting and editing skills—in order to work more efficiently without sacrificing their values. The best journalists are embracing technology and a more open approach to gathering and presenting information. They're discovering that the power of the people can help them jump-start the process of finding sources, experts and new angles, and it also provides instant—and constant—feedback.

"I am a big believer that my readers are much smarter than me and have a better grasp of what's going on, so why not leverage that wisdom to do a better job of reporting?" asks John Cook, co-founder of GeekWire and a former newspaper reporter.

This chapter is not about how to use a particular technology. It's about how to harness a wide array of digital tools to knock down barriers, to bring journalists closer to readers and readers closer to journalism. News organizations venturing into this territory find it pays off in all sorts of ways.

At The Dallas Morning News, for example, a project called Neighborsgo offers readers a place to publish their own stories; the best ones then turn up in print. "Neighborsgo has helped The Dallas Morning News strengthen community connections and reinforce the concept of journalism as a conversation," said Oscar Martinez, who helped lead the project from 2007 to 2012. "Collaborations with readers are a permanent part of the media landscape, and what we've learned with Neighborsgo will be informing community coverage efforts at The News for years to come."

New reporting methods such as crowdsourcing, open-source reporting and pro-am journalism are becoming the focus for more and more news operations in the United States. Although these terms and their definitions are still fluid and sometimes overlap, this chapter will approach each separately.

Crowdsourcing: The Internet allows enthusiastic communities to come together and provide the value for a given Web site. Crowdsourcing focuses that community power on a specific project and demonstrates how a group of committed individuals can outperform a small group of experienced (and paid) professionals.

Open-source reporting: The term "open source" refers to design, development and distribution "offering practical accessibility to a product's source (goods and knowledge)." Applying this concept to journalism means using transparency in reporting in order to provide a benefit to your audience and possibly acquire benefits from your audience.

Pro-am journalism: The most unfiltered form of collaborative journalism allows the audience to publish directly to the same platform, or Web site, that professional journalists use to publish their news. This is commonly referred to as user-generated content, or UGC. Because journalists can no longer be gatekeepers, creating opportunities for an audience to self-publish and then adding a layer of journalism on top produces broader and deeper coverage than the journalists could produce by themselves.

⚡ CROWDSOURCING

"Crowdsourcing" is a term coined by Jeff Howe in a 2006 article for Wired News. Think of crowdsourcing as a form of outsourcing, the term it spun off from. Crowdsourcing harnesses the sustained power of community to improve a service or information base.

Or, as my mother likes to say, "Many hands make light work."

The online version of the Encyclopedia Britannica, for example, cannot keep up with Wikipedia in terms of updating articles and information. And Microsoft, with all its resources, struggled to keep pace with the development of the Firefox browser, a project powered by volunteers collaborating under the nonprofit Mozilla Foundation.

In journalism, crowdsourcing—also known as distributed reporting—usually relates to reporting a specific project or answering a specific question. News organizations have used crowdsourcing to find instances of voting problems, to follow local distribution of disaster payments from the federal government and to map potholes on city streets.

In these cases, and many others, logistical hurdles would have made it impossible to tap into so many sources even 10 years ago. But in a world where one person can ask hundreds, or even thousands, of people to lend a hand with an investigation or data collection, crowdsourcing becomes a powerful new tool for reporting news.

While the concept of crowdsourcing might seem to lend itself especially well to grassroots organizations and projects, some of the most notable projects have been done by some very big companies. Here are some examples from outside journalism.

Way back in 2001, a Web site called InnoCentive began offering some generous cash rewards to freelance scientists if they could solve problems that scientists had thus far not been able to solve. More than 350,000 people from more than 200 countries have registered to participate. Lilly now works with other companies as a sort of crowdsourcing broker, allowing them to use the site to solve problems of their own. See www.innocentive.com for more information.

Amazon.com describes its Mechanical Turk project as "artificial artificial intelligence." It pays people to complete tasks—"human intelligence tasks"—that people do better than computers, such as identifying subjects in photographs and translating text. This is the opposite of the InnoCentive project: The pay is low and the tasks can be done by anyone. People need to perform a high volume of tasks to make any real money, but the tasks are so simple that thousands of people have registered to "turk." See www.mturk.com.

Box 3.1   **READER CONTRIBUTION AT THE NEWS TRIBUNE**

During a snowstorm in 2012, The News Tribune built an online map plotting all the different snow accumulations around Tacoma, Wash., and asked the public to submit their own measurements. Readers were also invited to comment on the locations and add photos, enhancing the original service. John Henrikson, assistant managing editor for interactive news at the newspaper at the time and now news director at MSN News, used a Google Fusion service to build the map "as a quick fix to a deadline problem":

"How to tap our users to report on a widespread weather event. Our developer wasn't available that day, and even if he was, it would hardly seem worth it to develop a programmed solution for a one-time use."

Here's how Henrikson described the production of the collaborative snow map:

1) Created a Google form with fields for each item of information we sought. (Important: Take some time to think through the type and format of data you want to end up with and design it into the form. This will make for cleaner data and save you time in the long run.)

2) When you build the form it automatically creates a Google Doc spreadsheet to capture the information.

3) We placed a bug in our print edition asking readers to contribute their conditions on the form. We also primed the pump by asking all News Tribune and Olympian employees to fill out the form at their homes when they got up.

4) Once we got a critical mass of reports in the spreadsheet, I cleaned it up a bit and imported it into Google Fusion tables, a free tool to create maps and other visualizations from datatables. I had worked with fusion tables for a dozen or so other projects, so it was easy and fast. (Although it's relatively easy to use, I would not recommend trying to learn it on deadline.)

We got more than 300 datapoints from contributors and 12,000+ pageviews from readers. We included optional contact info fields in the form and were able to use that info for reporting leads.

▶ Why crowdsourcing is important

Crowdsourcing in journalism remains an experiment; most news organizations are constantly looking for ways to leverage the power of the crowd to help them improve their reporting and publishing.

"Right now, there are three aspects to crowdsourcing that I use for everyday news gathering and news reporting efforts," says Misty Montano, digital content manager at KUSA-TV in Denver, whose 9news.com site is an industry leader. "Listening to comments on articles, in tweets, on posts from our Facebook community helps direct editorial decisions. Stories or story angles are chosen from what we're hearing and seeing from those posting on our digital and social platforms. Listening will also tell us when our audience is getting tired of a story."

Montano says that "eavesdropping" outside of one's own digital and social networks leads to stories and story angles. "Yes, I spend time each day looking at what's being said on competing websites and social networks," she admits.

"Asking and being responsive is the final aspect. We'll outright ask what people want us to ask during a story. We ask people to share story ideas. We ask people to share their photos and videos. Also, we set up branded hashtags that are consistently used on all of our platforms. Our audience knows them and uses them. Instead of tweeting us, they'll use our hashtag to get our attention and be a part of our ongoing conversation."

Montano adds that, since the news organization asks for audience participation, it also tries to follow up in some way, from saying thanks to asking for more information. "We get involved in conversations happening on Facebook posts. We don't just let the comments flow. We answer questions and talk with everyone else in the thread of comments."

The Public Insight Network (PIN) is a more formal version of this new brand of collaboration. It started in 2003 at Minnesota Public Radio and is now operated by American Public Media and widely used by other public radio and TV stations, including NPR. It is also used by commercial news organizations such as The Washington Post, The Miami Herald and The Charlotte Observer, and by universities such as Arizona State, Missouri and Montana. (See www.publicinsightnetwork.org.)

The "network" is really just a powerful online database and system of tools for finding sources, making it easier for reporters to find people with specific expertise or personal experiences relevant to particular story assignments. Anyone can register to be a PIN source by filling out a form online and providing personal information, including information on any subjects they might know more about than most people. These might include career expertise, hobby interests or local insight.

"It's common for journalists—whether professionals or students—to be limited in their thinking about finding sources for a story," says Steve Outing, a longtime digital media analyst and consultant. "The 'typical suspects' are public officials, business owners, community leaders, athletes and coaches or the random 'man or woman on the street.' But by using PIN, journalists can find not only experts in all sorts of fields but also 'regular people' who have personal expertise or skills, say in rock climbing or mountain rescue, or who have had personal experiences that might fit with a story, such as students who have recovered from drug addiction, or people who have family members in prison."

In March 2012, for example, PBS "NewsHour" was reporting from Texas on crucial issues related to the region's water supply system. These included record high temperatures, depleted groundwater, vanishing lakes and how people were tapping into alternative approaches to adapt.

To get a better understanding of the size of the problem, "NewsHour" used the Public Insight Network to learn more about the limitations of water supplies across the nation, asking readers to share their thoughts and concerns about their own access to water. Here is one excerpt from the responses received:

"Living in the desert, we are hyper-aware of water use," Sarah Mattson of Tucson, Ariz., wrote. "We joke that Tucsonans can smell clouds. Still, I think we could all do more to conserve water. The good news is that by conserving and by supplementing the water supply with Colorado River water, groundwater levels are rising in some areas of the valley. However, to truly maintain a sustainable water supply for a city population, I feel more creative and innovative means need to be devised. For instance, why are we flushing drinking water down our toilets? What would it take to recycle household water through toilets? How can we make safer use of our 'gray' water for landscape and garden watering? How can we better deal with the greater strain on the water supply from the mining and agriculture industries without sacrificing those necessary industries?"[1]

▶ ▶ *Thousands of contributions*
In 2000, Joshua Micah Marshall was a doctoral candidate in early American history at Brown University and the Washington editor of a liberal magazine, The

---

[1] Saskia de Melker, "Do You Worry About Access to Water?" PBS "NewsHour" Web site, March 23, 2012. http://www.pbs.org/newshour/rundown/2012/03/do-you-think-about-where-your-water-comes-from.html.

American Prospect, when he started a blog called Talking Points Memo (TPM) as an outlet for his ideas and to track the presidential election recount in Florida.

The blog has grown into a full-blown professional news organization, with 2 million visitors to a family of Web sites each month, a staff of seven and offices in Manhattan and Washington, D.C. In 2008, TPM received the George Polk Award for legal reporting in recognition of its groundbreaking coverage of the scandal that led to the firing of eight U.S. attorneys and the resignation of Attorney General Alberto Gonzales. In 2009, Time magazine named TPM one of the 25 Best Blogs on the Web.

The award-winning coverage would not have been possible without crowdsourcing. In addition to following news tips from readers, the site regularly doles out assignments to its readers. In the case of the U.S. attorneys scandal, the assignment was combing through thousands of e-mails and internal documents released by the Department of Justice and forwarding salient leads and tips back to the reporters, and Marshall, at TPM.

"There are thousands who have contributed some information over the last year," Marshall said of TPM's coverage of the U.S. attorneys story in an article published in The New York Times.

Writing on a blog for his journalism students, Dan Kennedy, a media critic who teaches at Northeastern University, called the announcement of the Polk Award "a landmark day for a certain kind of journalism."

TPM readers, Kennedy continued, "relentlessly kept a spotlight on what other news organizations were uncovering and watched patterns emerge that weren't necessarily visible to those covering just a small piece of the story. This is crowdsourcing—reporting based on the work of many people, including your readers."

Another online-only news site, The Huffington Post, used the same crowdsourcing approach in 2009 to enlist readers' assistance in covering the federal economic stimulus bill. With millions of dollars distributed to thousands of sources, harnessing the power of the crowd was the only feasible way for a news organization to cover the story and catch fraud, misuse of funds, conflicts of interest and other malfeasance typically found when so much money is involved.

The NBC affiliate in Denver where Montano works used Facebook in 2013 to build community and collaborate with its audience during that year's flooding in Colorado. Crowdsourcing went beyond news gathering, Montano says.

"Of course photos, videos and stories were crowdsourced, but the 9NEWS Facebook page became a place for people to share information and

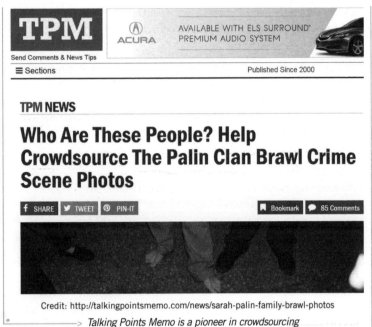

TPM NEWS

Who Are These People? Help Crowdsource The Palin Clan Brawl Crime Scene Photos

f SHARE **y** TWEET **ⓟ** PIN-IT   **🔖** Bookmark **💬** 85 Comments

Credit: http://talkingpointsmemo.com/news/sarah-palin-family-brawl-photos

Talking Points Memo is a pioneer in crowdsourcing journalism, evidenced by this story where readers were asked to identify the people in the photo by sending an email to TPM.

resources. People found help because our community was doing its own crowdsourcing on our Facebook page. We encouraged it. We used our other platforms of TV and digital to let people know these conversations were happening on our Facebook page."

Projects and stories like these, and many others, were not possible before the Internet made the distribution of information and communication so cheap and so easy. It has become standard operating procedure for journalists to leverage the audience when fact-finding, reporting and assessing the importance of particular news stories.

What is it? | What's Next?   Summary

⸮ OPEN-SOURCE REPORTING

Today a news organization's journalism must be transparent, authentic and collaborative. That's why blogs and Twitter are helpful for news organizations.

Neither will replace traditional journalism, and that's not the objective. These new digital tools bring journalists closer to readers and readers closer to journalism by removing barriers to conversation.

This spirit of openness and collaboration is behind a burgeoning crop of independent and hyperlocal journalism start-ups. Many of these new sites are powered by professional journalists who have left traditional news organizations and now write without the constraints of an institutional voice or hierarchical editorial control.

The concept of open-source or distributed reporting is a form of transparency. Traditionally, readers learn about stories a news organization is working on only when the stories are finished and published. While it's still common to keep big story ideas secret to prevent the competition from stealing them, the open-source reporting model means a news organization will go public with most story ideas early in the reporting process. Disclosure invites readers to help report the story.

▶ Why open-source reporting is important

Unlike in crowdsourcing, where a reporter is asking for a specific kind of direct assistance, open-source reporting means pulling the curtain back on the reporting process and welcoming the audience's feedback. Whether or not people respond, opening the process helps journalists increase their credibility and social capital. When people see how the process works, they are less likely to hang on to any perception that reporters are biased or operating with nefarious motives.

How it started: Although the terms used to describe the practice are new, open-source reporting has been around for many years. The Spokesman-Review in Spokane, Wash., began using distributed reporting in 2001 with a database of e-mail addresses—something it called a "reader network"—that it used to correspond with readers while reporting stories. This model has been copied by newspapers everywhere and is used effectively in many situations, especially when journalists are looking for sources to interview on a specific topic or collect reactions from regarding a current issue in the news.

Most reader networks were started with e-mail addresses from readers who had contacted the newspaper, either by sending a letter to the editor or by asking a reporter about a news story. Through its Web site, a news organization can also build the database by advertising the network and inviting readers to join. By collecting as much information as possible, the news organization can slice the network several different ways and target

Sources The concept remains the same while the technology keeps changing. E-mail first made possible the efficient management of a database of contacts who could easily be sent queries for news coverage. Message boards and online forums serve a similar need but are much more passive (the audience needs to come to them). Comments on blogs work well if the bloggers have built a vibrant community with sufficient interaction. Today's social media networks, especially services such as Twitter and Facebook, are the next iteration.

specific subsets for certain queries—people who live in a particular ZIP code, for example, or fans of a particular sports team.

Some newspapers now have more than one reader network. It can make sense to create and manage separate contact databases for education stories (if you need direct contact with teachers) or business stories (if you need to get feedback from local business leaders only).

As Clay Shirky wrote in his book "Here Comes Everybody," news companies correctly understand that work produced by the "mass amateurization" of publishing may not meet the same standards as the journalism in established media outlets. Publishing or posting is now so easy that journalists have no choice but to get comfortable with some new definitions and practices.

"The change isn't a shift from one kind of news institution to another," Shirky wrote, "but rather in the definition of news: from news as an institutional prerogative to news as part of a communications ecosystem, occupied by a mix of formal organizations, informal collectives, and individuals."[2]

Thus, the bottom line becomes: How can we harness this new movement of mass publishing and networked information to do better journalism?

▶ Link curation taps the power of the Web

Links power the Web. They're what makes it such a deep, rich, interactive information medium. Some journalists quickly recognized the power of linking and used it to provide easy access to source documents or previous coverage. But for years, linking to "the competition"—other news sites—was either explicitly or tacitly prohibited. "If we send readers somewhere else, they might not come back," the thinking went.

---

[2]Clay Shirky, "Here Comes Everybody: The Power of Organizing Without Organizations" (New York: Penguin Press, 2008).

Fortunately, that kind of backward thinking has mostly moved to its rightful place in the graveyard of ideas. The link has proved to be more than just an add-on feature in journalism. It is a powerful form of content that builds readership and brings readers back. Look no further than Google, the world's dominant search engine, for proof. All Google does is send people away from itself. And all people do is come back.

In journalism, the recognition that no one can corner the market on any specific form of news or information has led to the opening of minds. This, in turn, has led to the development of new and innovative ways to use links to do better journalism.

Jeff Jarvis, director of the TOW Knight Center for Entrepreneurial Journalism at the City University of New York, is famous for telling news organizations to "do what you do best and link to the rest."

Enter a relatively new journalism concept called curation: using editorial judgment to provide links to other sources of news and information, based on the needs and interests of a particular audience. Anyone can collect links, and algorithms can aggregate. But only trained editors have the skills to select and collect the best information and build a loyal audience.

Cultivating an audience on social media requires effective link curation. Posting links to interesting news, photos and videos is a surefire recipe for success when building an audience on Facebook and Twitter. Many of those links, of course, will be to outside news sources, since the demand of posting new, fresh content to those streams easily outpaces most news organizations' or journalists' ability to publish their own content. High-quality, frequent link posts drive audience growth. And the larger the audience, the more potential visitors to the journalists' or news organizations' own links when posted in the mix.

DRILLING DOWN

Use Storify to Curate

Links The social media stream is often more like a fire hose. For journalists hoping to filter out the noise and produce more signal for their audience, a tool called Storify should be added to the toolbox.

Storify makes it easy to click and drag links from Twitter, Facebook and Web sites into a consolidated stream of the best news, information, photos and reaction around a single topic. Check it out at www.storify.com.

⚠ PRO-AM JOURNALISM

The do-it-yourself (DIY) movement first gained popularity with home improvement tasks and projects. It helped launch entire TV networks and dozens of Web sites. But DIY journalism? Yes, people sometimes want to play reporter, too.

Although news organizations were slow to warm to the concept, most have realized that their audiences are going to be reporting everything from breaking news to church club events somewhere online. It might as well be happening on organization news sites, alongside their own reporting, thus providing a fuller selection of news and information for the audience.

Starting a digital publishing platform, where the costs of publishing are practically zero once you have an operating Web site, allows readers the chance to publish their own news or other forms of content.

Arguing about whether the text, photos or videos uploaded to a news site constitute journalism misses the point: We are operating in an entirely new information ecosystem. As Clay Shirky observed, "Everyone is a media outlet."[3]

The essence of pro-am journalism is simple once you understand that no news organization can be everywhere all the time. Readers can help provide the "what"; journalists can then provide the "why."

CNN's iReport is probably the best-known example of pro-am—or participatory—journalism. The site invites anyone to contribute photos and video, and some of the content produced by regular citizens ends up airing on CNN programs.

CNN launched iReport in 2006. There are now more than 1 million contributors to iReport from nearly every country on the planet. Just as important, the audience for iReport is also sizable, with 350,000 Facebook "likes" and 200,000 Twitter followers by the end of 2014.

Lila King, a member of the founding team, said that iReport started as a news-gathering engine. "We wanted to take advantage of cellphone photography and people's ability to capture a news event with a photo or video," King said. "We now have a more nuanced understanding of what it has become; it is more of a community."

---

[3]Shirky, "Here Comes Everybody."

Curation and crowdsourcing are both forms of community management, which is one of the hottest job segments in digital media. Community management is a skill and a practice that some journalists find natural and easy, while others struggle to adapt. You could file many tasks under the category of community management—everything from managing comments on a news story or blog post to dealing with reactions to your news story on social media to full-fledged crowdsourcing efforts like iReport.

"It has taught journalists at CNN a great deal about community management," said King, who left CNN in 2014. "We have learned to nurture, to build and keep alive a community of similar interests. It's not what we were really thinking when we started it."

King said that her favorite iReport project was one that won a Webby Award in 2011.[4] On the first day of spring her team members wanted to see if they could construct a walk around the planet. "We asked the iReport community to take a 60-second walk and shoot video of what they saw. Then we took the most interesting and stitched them together. The video edit looks very lovely," King said.

"It kind of stretches the definition of what counts as news on CNN. It takes on a new meaning. It sort of lets us be more creative and whimsical as news producers—and all of us exploring how to create new things out of the cameras in our pockets."

Credit: http://ireport.cnn.com/community/assignment

CNN's iReport provides community members with topic suggestions at the Assignment Desk and equips them with tools such as writing, photography and videography tips.

[4]"We Won a Webby!" CNN, May 3, 2011. http://ireport.cnn.com/blogs/ireport-blog/2011/05/03/we-won-a-webby.

CNN started making assignments to the iReport community early on and, according to King, "about half of the content that ends up on-air is driven by assignments." Much of it is cultural or personal-interest stories. "Since you can't predict when breaking news will happen, it became more important to develop [iReport] as a community," King said.

One of the great misunderstandings around crowdsourcing and pro-am journalism is that they are "free." It's true, there is no monthly charge for the content that users send to newsrooms, whether through a platform like iReport, via e-mail or as postings on Facebook. The challenge is that generating content of a certain quality—and quantity—from your audience requires real effort. Manual effort.

"Doing work with user-generated content is just as much work, if not more, as producing through traditional journalism means," King said. "There's been a common misconception that it's free stuff, free work. That couldn't be further from the truth.

"With collaborative journalism you get a different kind of reporting and storytelling. You get richer angles than you would normally get. But creating a piece of work with your audience is a very different version of journalism."

King described how, "with every new iteration, iReport has gotten closer to CNN proper. In the beginning it even had a blue and orange logo, while now it is a part of CNN.com. Another example is a feature we rolled out last year called Open Story. It's built on a big scale involving lots of places and topics, from natural disasters" to the Ferguson protests in 2014. "We built it so that CNN and iReport contributions would have equal weighting and play in the same space," King said.

"It's the job of the editor to find the best, most relevant of all the pieces we have to produce the best packages. It's the most important thing we can and should do," King said. "Keeping citizen journalism or crowdsourcing in the corner really limits its power to contribute and limits our abilities to tell the entirety of the story."

▶ Know where you stand on legal grounds

It is also the job of news organizations to make sure they operate within legal boundaries when republishing or rebroadcasting content created by the audience. The laws in this area, as with most digital-content issues, are still emerging and evolving. If you work for a news organization, be sure to check with a company-employed legal resource. You should also check—and actually read—the terms of service on your news organization's Web site. Here are some general guidelines that can be helpful when you are determining what user-created content to publish:

- If someone posts a photo on your branded Facebook wall or sends one to you via a Twitter direct message, you must vet the photo to ensure its authenticity and determine who owns the photo.

- If you find a photo on a social media platform and want to republish it, you must make a screenshot of the photo on the platform to be covered by fair use under copyright law.

- If you or your news organization asks people to post photos to social media with a specific hashtag that you have created, that should qualify as tacit approval by the user for his or her photo to be republished. For example, at KING 5 we frequently ask users to post photos of the season and use the hashtag #k5summer or #k5fall. When someone posts such a photo to Twitter or Instagram with that hashtag, we are clear to republish those images on our Web site or social media networks.

- While tacit permission is good, explicit permission is the best, so whenever feasible reach out and ask the user submitting the content to give you permission, in writing, to reuse the content.

▶ Newspapers tap the power of the crowd

The Bakersfield Californian newspaper jumped in early with regard to crowdsourcing. In 2004, it launched Northwest Voice, the first "citizen journalism" project at a U.S. newspaper. At the time, the best example of citizen journalism could be found in South Korea: the prolific OhmyNews, with tens of thousands of correspondents and a creative compensation system that spawned a number of would-be copycats in the United States. Many U.S. newspapers launched similar projects, but very few were as successful as Neighborsgo in Dallas and MyCommunityNOW in Milwaukee.

The Dallas Morning News launched a print-only community newspaper called Neighbors in 2005; two years later the newspaper turned it into Neighborsgo and launched a corresponding Web site. The idea behind the project: Offer readers a place to publish their news on a separate area of the Web site of The Dallas Morning News, with the lure of print publication for the best stuff. In addition to the Web site, 18 different weekly print editions were launched, each targeting a separate geographic area. (As of 2012, the company was producing 11 editions.)

Credit: The Dallas Morning News

Neighborsgo is a source for members of specific communities near the Dallas area to both contribute and consume news stories that affect them.

▶ Print can still be a powerful tool

The readers responded. Editors were inundated with submissions and e-mails. Oscar Martinez concluded that the motivation for most of them was the prospect of seeing their words on paper.

"The innovation of neighborsgo isn't the social-media aspect of neighborsgo .com or the amount of content generated by users," said Martinez. "It's the resulting print product, which is a mash-up of user- and staff-generated content. Print still has an incredible power to validate shared experiences and strengthen community connections."

Another great story for newspapers is how the editors at neighborsgo have gone about getting to know their audience. As Martinez said: "Before you can mobilize an audience, you need to know who they are. More important, they need to know who you are."

Martinez described how "Neighborsgo editors display their personalities online and interact daily with readers across multiple platforms—including prompt e-mail and phone replies, and outreach via external social media sites such as Facebook and Twitter. Occasionally, editors meet with readers face-to-face, informally, over coffee or participate in community events. For example:

- Veterans Day Luncheon—Veterans and military families profiled in Veterans Day editions were invited to lunch. More than 100 people attended.

- Media Catalyst Summit—Neighborsgo editors conducted a seminar for PR professionals who submit stories and photos on behalf of others to explain the community connection we seek in all stories that get published in print. (Similar sessions were held for aspiring photographers—how to shoot better photos that will be published in print—and for pet-adoption organizations.)

- Lonestar Volleyball Facility in Frisco, Texas—One sign promoting neighborsgo and neighborsgo.com. Thousands of girls' volleyball teams and their families every weekend."

MyCommunityNOW is a similar project launched by the Milwaukee Journal Sentinel in 25 neighborhoods. The basic premise is the same: Leverage an inexpensive and efficient digital platform to allow an audience to self-publish; then use the best submissions for localized print editions. The Journal Sentinel recognizes that its reporters and editors can't be everywhere; neither can they cover every event readers might want to know about. With the lure of print as an added draw for the audience, MyCommunityNOW provides expanded coverage in each community.

"Let's face it, if there is a ribbon-cutting ceremony at a new grocery store in town, the odds are slim that the newspaper will send out a staff photographer or reporter to cover it," said Mark Maley, former NOW online editor. "But if the chamber of commerce president has a digital camera, we strongly encourage him to take a few shots and post on the local NOW site. It's providing a facet of coverage that newspapers—especially in this era of downsizing and staff cuts—often can't provide.

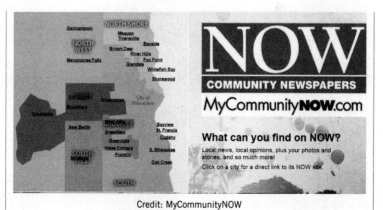

Credit: MyCommunityNOW

The Milwaukee Journal Sentinel covers dozens of local communities with MyCommunityNOW, providing photos and stories on separate websites organized by location.

"But beyond that, we are giving people a chance to actively participate in how their community is being covered and to interact with others in their community through our sites. Just as people like posting videos to YouTube and photos to Flickr, they like to use similar tools to interact with other residents in their hometown."

ℒ₂ MANAGING NEWS AS A CONVERSATION

"The speed of communications is wonderful to behold. It is also true that speed can multiply the distribution of information that we know to be untrue."

—Edward R. Murrow[5]

Murrow's distinguished journalism career ended some 35 years before the Internet made digital news and communication a part of daily life. Today his observation is truer than ever.

Now that news is a conversation, one of the greatest challenges facing journalists is how to manage, and leverage, that conversation.

The socialization of news is clearly the right direction for journalism. It is often said that "information wants to be free," but it is truer in the digital age that information wants to be analyzed, shared, synthesized, curated, aggregated, commented on and distributed. Even journalists feeling overwhelmed by new technology can see that more interaction with the audience carries big benefits. But every opportunity creates questions and challenges:

- How do journalists participate in the conversation without sacrificing their objectivity or credibility?

- What about legal and ethical issues now that everyone can publish anything they want on professional news sites?

- And what happens when you really want the audience to participate, but they don't?

This section aims to address these questions and more. Interactive discussion is an integral part of the news process today. But the quality of that discussion can vary greatly. Learn how to use technological and human resources to cultivate constructive conversation around news coverage.

---

[5]Edward R. Murrow, speech to the Radio-Television News Directors Association, 1958.

"As news organizations increasingly incorporate social media and other reader-feedback tools into their reporting, knowing how to manage conversations is becoming essential to digital strategy," says Meghan Peters, a former digital producer at The Seattle Times and community manager at Mashable who now works at Facebook. "The Web allows anyone to create his or her own content and exchange ideas. It has democratized the news and information market, meaning newsrooms are no longer the gatekeepers of publication. For news organizations, this change means new resources—quality feedback and reader-created content—that can enhance their reporting."

Let's get this out in the open: Many journalists (maybe most journalists) have long preferred news as a lecture. Only begrudgingly have they come around to the idea that a future in journalism means managing online communities and participating in various social networks.

That's OK. We're just getting started here.

The idea of news as a conversation is frequently trumped by reality. Participants are rarely as constructive or respectful as journalists (and other readers) would like. And there are either too many for news organizations to manage or too few to generate an actual conversation around the news. Part of the blame for comment areas that are cesspools of inanity rests with the publishers of the Web sites.

Three areas of evolution suggest a brighter future for comments on news stories: The technology is getting better, newsrooms are accepting more responsibility and the commenters are expecting more from each other. Even though many comment areas on news sites have dark pasts, it is worthwhile to keep investing time and energy in making them better than the ghettos of personal attacks and flame wars that they have all too frequently been.

As new formats and concepts emerge, new issues involving ethics and standards develop, too. Learn to apply your journalism values and ethical know-how to vexing new issues as well as familiar ones.

▶ Making conversation

What began as comments on news stories and blog posts has mushroomed into full social networking tools on news sites and full participation by journalists in dominant social networks such as Facebook, Twitter, Google+, Tumblr and Pinterest (to name just a few). While the primary motivation for offering social tools on news sites is to stay technologically relevant, the reward goes beyond giving the audience a chance to play, too. These are effective tools for building better relationships with readers and viewers and helping to build loyalty to your news brand (and your personal brand as a journalist).

How do you do it? Mandy Jenkins, who has held community management and social media positions at several news organizations, including The Huffington Post, offers these "rules of engagement":[6]

- Answer all questions.
- Address criticism (without spats).
- Publicly or privately respond.
- Share good responses.
- Publicly correct yourself.
- Always acknowledge news tips.

Credit: Flickr.com/Jack Lail

In May 2009, the Knoxville (Tenn.) News Sentinel held a community forum to discuss comments on the KnoxNews.com Web site.

---

[6]Mandy Jenkins, "Making Community Engagement an Everyday Process," Zombie Journalism, April 2, 2011. http://zombiejournalism.com/2011/04/making-community-engagement-an-everyday-process.

▶ ▶ *Conversing through comments*

Most online news stories are accompanied by comments links. At a glance, the concept is simple: For centuries, people have discussed current events and today's news with each other, so why not add some simple technology to allow online readers to take that discussion public with people they may or may not know? Unfortunately, the results haven't always been so simple.

Often, those simple comments are downright ugly and mean.

In February 2009, for example, defense attorneys for four suspects charged in a carjacking and gruesome slaying asked a judge in Knox County, Tenn., to require local media, including the Knoxville News Sentinel, to either shut down those portions of their respective Web sites that allow readers to post comments about the case or make it mandatory that commenters reveal their true identities rather than use screen names.

Rarely do these controversial conversations end up in court (see the section headed "Know your legal responsibilities" later in this chapter). Criminal court judge Richard Baumgartner said such an order would be a prior restraint on the media. Prior restraint repeatedly has been ruled unconstitutional.

"So long as people are not committing any wrongdoing they should be free to anonymously participate in the online forums," Baumgartner wrote.[7]

Journalism and news editing today bear little resemblance to the days of Murrow, or even the occupation I encountered at my first newspaper job in the early 1990s.

And although audio, video and microblogging are disruptive, transformative technologies, the most tectonic shift for journalism in the past decade has less to do with technology and more to do with people. Changes, even good ones, often make people nervous.

You see, sometime shortly after Web sites made it easy to interact with news, the audience decided to. First through message boards and forums, then through blogs, and then through comments directly on news stories and now on social media platforms, people quickly transformed news from a lecture or one-way communication to a conversation with fluid changes in the content from one consumer to another.

---

[7]Jamie Satterfield, "Judge Won't Seek to Limit Online Comments on Carjack Case," Knoxville News Sentinel, April 14, 2009. www.knoxnews.com/news/2009/apr/14/judge-wont-seek-limit-online-comments-carjack-case.

Daily newspapers publish a few hundred letters to the editor each month. But online, readers post tens of thousands of comments a month on newspaper Web sites, Facebook and other digital platforms. "Some of the comments are intelligent. Many are inane," says Jack McElroy, editor of the Knoxville News Sentinel. "A few are downright cruel."

While many journalists and news organizations fought this development because of the problems McElroy cites, the audience always chooses what kind of journalism it wants—and it always will. So, it has become standard operating procedure for news sites to offer readers opportunities to comment on news stories, to publish their own news or photos and even to participate in social networking so that they may connect with one another.

▶▶ *Conversing through social networking*

Social media represents a new way to connect with people and communicate information. Reporters and journalists always need to do that. Like the telephone and e-mail before it, social media is the latest change in how people are connecting and communicating. But the change is purely tactical; the standards and values of journalism do not change.

Social media offers many benefits to news as a conversation:

- It creates transparency in the reporting process.

- It enables an immediate feedback loop.

- It spreads awareness of news coverage through word-of-mouth marketing.

That last benefit is the most important, especially in today's challenging economic climate for news. The marketing potential to be gained from authentic participation in social networks and conversations is huge. It is commonplace for people to discover news on Facebook and Twitter, among many other social media sites. In fact, an oft-cited assumption about news in a networked, digital world is "If the news is important, it will find me."

That means your news, your journalism, must be part of this ecosystem to survive. If you want a larger audience, you have to go where the audience is and participate in the way the audience participates.

This is easier said than done, of course.

Cultivating an interactive community around news online has real value. Despite the potential headaches of offensive anonymous posts and the additional burden of juggling reader feedback with more traditional tasks of journalism, the benefit earned through a constructive and collaborative relationship between journalists and their audience is well worth the effort.

"Once journalists can stop teasing their stories and start talking about their stories, they'll find their social communities can help them tell a story," says Montano of 9news.com. "Journalists need to listen, eavesdrop, ask and respond, just as the news organization does."

Story tips are often discovered and links are shared in the comments after an article or blog entry is posted online. As Dan Gillmor famously said when he became the first newspaper reporter to have a blog in the late 1990s, "My audience knows more than I do." It's important to remember that your communities know more than you do. If you do, then it's easy to understand why engaging those in the know in conversation will lead to better journalism.

Mike Davidson, who co-founded the collaborative news site Newsvine in 2005, says the back-and-forth exchange of information makes the news better. His Newsvine site was acquired by MSNBC.com in 2009, and Davidson continued to work on both Newsvine and other technology needs for its parent company before becoming vice president of design at Twitter.

"Increasingly editors and writers are realizing that they only know part of the story," says Davidson. "And instead of pretending that they know all of the story, they can create a conversation by beginning that discourse, either online or on-air, and by having their audience, ideally, add to it."

"Community manager" has become a new job description, and even a job title, at many news organizations. Others refer to these duties as weaving, cultivating or mobilizing.

"In traditional news gathering, reporters typically do not look to their audience to find subject-matter experts. Rather, they call go-to sources or representatives of credible organizations," Peters says. "The Web brings to light people who would ordinarily be outside of these groups, yet may have a deep knowledge or unique perspective. By connecting with the communities they cover and harnessing their digital contributions, reporters can not only make their storytelling richer but also establish loyalty."

What is it? | **What's *Next?*** | Summary

⬇ BUILD AND MANAGE A COMMUNITY ONLINE

Now you know ***why*** you should build community online, but you may still be wondering ***how.*** It's definitely more art than science—as is so much of journalism—but we can draw from some of the more successful journalists and news organizations and learn the basic rules of the road.

▶ Make news collaborative

The power of the Web comes from its interactivity. The link, which connects one piece of information to another, is the primary building block of the digital age.

The secondary building block is the comment, or contribution, that an audience can easily make to any page of news or information. Contributions come in all shapes and sizes. In addition to comments on news stories and blog posts, audiences routinely contribute the following content on news and information sites:

Photos

Video

Event listings (on calendar sites)

Edits (on wiki sites)

Message board posts

Blog posts

Votes and recommendations

Promotion on other social media sites (for example, Digg, reddit and StumbleUpon)

Even though anyone can contribute content to a Web site, most people will not. But those who will can make a dramatic improvement in the distribution and even the quality of the content. That's the basic concept behind something called the 1-10-100 rule for participatory audiences.[8]

The 1-10-100 rule for participatory online communities states:

> 1 percent of the user community—including the journalists on news sites—actually create primary content.

> 10 percent of the user community will "synthesize" the content by posting a comment, e-mailing a link to a friend, authoring a blog post on a separate site and linking back to it, voting it up or down, etc.

> 100 percent of the user community will benefit from the actions of the first two groups.

This is the phenomenon many experts have noted with the most active user-generated communities on the Web. Wikipedia, Flickr and even YouTube receive the vast majority of their content from a vast minority of their users. Wikipedia's founder, Jimmy Wales, performed a study in 2007 that found that more than 50 percent of all the edits on Wikipedia are done by just 0.7 percent of the users.[9]

Despite the millions of pageviews each of these sites receives, the content is actually created by a relatively small group of users. This illustrates the power of enabling the crowd with the tools and access to contribute content or synthesize the content that is published by journalists.

After a relatively slow start, mainstream news sites have made significant progress in this area in recent years. Independent journalism sites mostly launch with this technology "baked in." Notice how different the user experience is when you visit Mashable, The Huffington Post or BuzzFeed, for example, compared with a local newspaper or TV news site? When you are fighting for audience, making news participatory is an important strategy, creating brand loyalty among members of a user group that is all too promiscuous, constantly jumping from one news source to another.

---

[8]Bradley Horowitz, "Creators, Synthesizers, and Consumers," Elatable, February 16, 2006. http://blog.elatable.com/2006/02/creators-synthesizers-and-consumers.html.

[9]Wikipedia. http://en.wikipedia.org/wiki/Wikipedia.

▶ Journalists must get involved

Unfortunately, user collaboration and user-generated content do not come easily. As Len Brody and many others who have direct experience have pointed out, they take a lot of work.

User-generated content and community are not free. They don't cost money, as the Associated Press wire does, but maintaining them takes a commitment of time, energy and resources that in some cases could be comparable. But there is no alternative. You can't buy community or license it. You have to build it.

There are opportunities for journalists to build community in many different ways, not just hyperlocal "community news" projects. Breaking news, especially, brings excellent opportunities to tap the power of the crowd and build social capital for the news organization, the journalist or both.

If you get a tip about a breaking news event, for example, acknowledge to your audience who sent the tip and how. This is especially effective if the tip came through social media (such as Twitter or Facebook), and you can use that social media platform to give your tipster the proper thanks.

If the breaking news event is significant, establish a post on your Web site or Facebook page so your audience can ask and answer questions with each other. This also works for long-running stories, such as a teachers' strike or a high-profile court trial. But you can't just "set it and forget it." Any news topic that will draw significant audience probably is controversial, and a forum for comments will spin out of control if left alone.

It's a brave new world—and time to recognize that traditional roles for journalists are no longer relevant. New roles and new job titles have become the new normal.

▶ Develop sources, find scoops through LinkedIn

Journalists can use social networks to develop deeper sources around specific reporting beats. They can accomplish this in different ways, such as by finding sources through the dominant social networks: Facebook, Twitter, Google+ and LinkedIn.

LinkedIn launched in 2003 and now has more than 300 million members. It was the first social networking company to turn a profit and went public in 2011. Because it is a professional social network, it is especially powerful for anyone covering business topics. Anyone working in journalism today—or planning to tomorrow—should have a LinkedIn profile and should constantly be cultivating contacts.

In extolling the virtues of LinkedIn to college students when I visit campuses, I describe the social network as a digital Rolodex. If you grew up in the age of phone books and newspapers, you remember the Rolodex, a small filing system for organizing business cards and keeping track of contact information for different people. It's ink (or pencil) on paper, though, which means when someone gets a new job or a new phone number, your record of that person is immediately out of date—and therefore useless.

LinkedIn, on the other hand, is constantly updated with new job and contact information (so long as the person getting the new gig remembers to update it). This is especially important for college students who have yet to even start their careers; LinkedIn allows them to maintain connections to classmates who will go on to land jobs at all manner of different companies.

One of the most basic functions on LinkedIn is search. A reporter can search for people in a specific company, industry or location. But the way the social network is designed limits the ability to contact people. Direct connections, those who have agreed to be among your LinkedIn connections (like friends on Facebook), are dubbed 1st Degree, and you can send them messages or view their contact information (if they have provided it in their profiles). The ability to contact people who are either 2nd or 3rd Degree connections is more limited, though, so the larger your personal network, the more power and flexibility you will have when trying to reach potential sources.

The Center for Public Integrity received the George Polk Award in 2014 for its "After the Meltdown" series, which revealed that many of the executives responsible for the 2008 financial crisis faced few consequences.[10] Daniel Wagner's piece was driven by LinkedIn profile searches, according to May Chow, manager of corporate communications at LinkedIn.

The social network has also evolved into a powerful jobs marketplace and publishing platform, both of which can be effective tools for journalists. Companies rely on LinkedIn when looking for candidates to fill open positions, and job seekers use it to learn about prospective employers and the people who work there. Many smart journalists have also discovered gold in those job postings.

Scott Martin was one of those journalists when, in 2013, he broke the story of Twitter's pending IPO for USA Today. He surfaced a job opening that Twitter

---

[10]Daniel Wagner, "After the Meltdown," Center for Public Integrity, September 11, 2013. http://www.publicintegrity.org/2013/09/11/13327/subprime-lending-execs-back-business-five-years-after-crash.

DRILLING DOWN

Power Tips for Journalists on LinkedIn Investing time and effort into LinkedIn will pay dividends for any journalist. Here are some fundamental suggestions:

- **Treat it like a social network:** LinkedIn has become a powerful publishing platform, so if you are regularly publishing news stories or blog posts, add links on LinkedIn and regularly scan the stream for interesting content. Add "likes" and comments to the posts of others and build social capital.

- **Change settings to be anonymous:** As you view other LinkedIn members' profiles, the platform keeps track. You can prevent others from knowing you were "LinkedIn stalking" them by setting your preferences to anonymous.

- **Use advanced search to find sources:** Use one of the many filters available to fine-tune your searches by industry, company, geography and more.

- **Save searches:** If there are commons searches you anticipate running repeatedly, save those searches to make your work more efficient.

- **Take advantage of free upgrades for journalists:** A little-known benefit available to journalists (as of early 2015, anyway) is an upgrade to LinkedIn Premium at no charge.

- **Make use of different apps:** LinkedIn offers a variety of mobile apps to help users best leverage the platform. For example, the Connected app makes it easier to keep tabs on people, and the Pulse app turns LinkedIn into a river of news and links posted by people in your network.

- **Join the crowd:** The LinkedIn for Journalists group had more than 50,000 members at the start of 2015. Join and receive updates and tips on how to leverage the platform for your journalism.

had posted for someone to come on board to help write an S-1 document, which a company must file with the Securities and Exchange Commission to start the process of going public.

"After my story published, Twitter actually pulled its LinkedIn job posting for somebody to write its S-1," said Martin, who is now director of content and media strategy at the Bateman Group. "The LinkedIn research in the story was the basis for a later print piece in USA Today saying Twitter's IPO is near."

Credit: https://www.linkedin.com/vsearch/f?adv=true&trk=federated_advs

> *Advanced search on LinkedIn offers many filters and powerful features.* <

Analyzing the types of jobs that a particular company is hiring for is a good way to learn what is happening at that company and can also inform larger trend stories. The New York Times, for example, broke a story that JPMorgan Chase's corporate site had been hacked when DealBook reporters found out through LinkedIn that JPMorgan was hiring digital security experts.[11]

▶ Collaborate with your community

It has been said that, in the digital era, when everyone can publish anything from anywhere, the audience will increasingly provide the "what" while journalists provide the "why" and the "how."

We've seen this play out in global stories (the Arab Spring, the Ferguson protests, and so on): Regular citizens are using mobile phones to report breaking news. While critical to the overall reports, those text messages,

---

[11]Matthew Goldstein, Nicole Perlroth and Jessica Silver-Greenberg, "Cyberattack at JPMorgan Chase Also Hit Website of Bank's Corporate Race," New York Times DealBook, October 15, 2014. http://dealbook.nytimes.com/2014/10/15/cyberattack-at-jpmorgan-chase-also-hit-website-of-banks-corporate-race.

videos and photos cannot tell the whole story without someone to connect them and provide needed context. A journalist can do this by producing a traditional news story with a narrative or by using a new medium, as Andy Carvin demonstrated with his use of Twitter to cover the Middle East while he was at NPR.

This is a form of pro-am journalism, and it is happening on a local level, too. Rather than competing with citizens who can supply firsthand accounts and footage of news events, journalists are learning how to collaborate with them. It also works in non–breaking news situations as bloggers and other independent publishers contribute meaningful content to public awareness. And it is a significant advancement in the evolution of journalism.

It is no longer a surprise to see the home page of a mainstream news site link to a competitor or even to a local blog. It is commonplace for network news programs to broadcast messages and video published by citizens.

A layer of journalism on top of whatever the public publishes can help filter the information and add value to it. And when you can add value, you have the makings of a business model.

One of the more ambitious examples of adding a layer of journalism over the contributions of community is Global Voices Online. With more than 500 bloggers, translators and editors all over the world, the site is a kind of new-age foreign wire service.

"These days, when people read or experience something important they will usually blog it, or tweet it, or put a link on Facebook for their friends. This happens millions of times every day, all over the world in hundreds of languages," says managing editor Solana Larsen. "At Global Voices, we pick up on local reactions to world events and translate illuminating opinions for a global audience. It could be Iraqi bloggers describing the scene of a suicide bombing, or Chinese bloggers discussing the pros and cons of the Olympics in Beijing. Or people on Twitter in Madagascar describing street riots as they happen. The world is always talking, and journalists can get a lot out of listening."

The authors at Global Voices "are usually bloggers from the countries they are writing about," according to Larsen. "They are able to identify credible blogs and online sources, and write stories that offer both context and links to different citizen media text or images. Increasingly, reporters and producers will e-mail Global Voices to figure out how to get in touch with a blogger from a country that's in the news. We help make it easier for journalists (and other bloggers) to diversify their sources and look at things from a different perspective. This kind of curiosity is important considering how many countries in the world don't

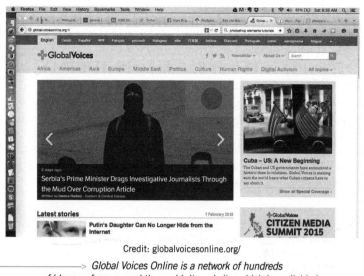

Credit: globalvoicesonline.org/

Global Voices Online is a network of hundreds of bloggers from around the world. Its website, which is available in over a dozen languages, features stories about specific regions such as Africa, the Americas, Asia, Europe and the Middle East, as well as topics that affect all regions such as politics, culture, human rights and digital activism

have a free press. Ordinary citizens are putting out news every day that their own media or government wish to silence," says Larsen.

Collaboration among journalists is also flourishing in the digital age. Technology makes it easy for reporters, editors and photographers to share tips, resources and even news coverage, which is possible now that most news organizations understand they are not competing with one another.

Twitter, Facebook groups and LinkedIn have proven to be important resources for journalists of all stripes for discussing current projects or recent developments in the industry and even finding jobs.

What is it? | **What's *Next?*** | Summary

⬇ KEEP CONVERSATIONS ACCURATE AND ETHICAL

Human nature being what it is, each new communication technology that becomes part of journalism brings with it some potential pitfalls. Social media is no different, and news organizations have been leery from the start about reporters having sources as friends on Facebook or starting personal blogs to voice opinions that would never make the news pages.

The technical hurdles are low. Unlike editing video or designing a Web site in CSS, the primary skills involved here are communication and judgment, two characteristics most journalists take pride in having.

▶ Set guidelines for participants

The biggest news organizations have continually made news (in industry circles, at least) by releasing and updating policies regarding social media. The New York Times, for example, includes the following passages in its policy:

- Be careful to not to write anything on a blog or a personal Web page that you could not write in the Times—don't editorialize, for instance, if you work for the news department.

- Should we avoid consenting to be Facebook "friends" of people in the news we cover? Mostly no, but the answer can depend on the situation. A useful way to think about this is to imagine whether public disclosure of a "friend" could somehow turn out to be an embarrassment that casts doubt on our impartiality.

The Wall Street Journal, meanwhile, released its own set of rules in 2009. They include these proscriptions:

- Don't recruit friends or family to promote or defend your work.

- Consult your editor before "connecting" to or "friending" any reporting contacts who may need to be treated as confidential sources. Openly "friending" sources is akin to publicly publishing your Rolodex.

Shortly after the Journal released its policy, a writer for the social media Web site Mashable asked me whether ethics policies at newspapers and TV stations should include rules on social media. I don't see how social media is any different, as far as ethics are concerned. If a newspaper or TV station already has an ethics policy, it should apply to social media, too. Was a new ethics policy needed when reporters started using the telephone or e-mail? I hope not.

A news organization should look to its terms and conditions on its Web site and see what it is expecting or requiring from the audience that is now contributing content. Be real. Be nice. Don't lie. Don't take credit for something that is not yours. Basic rules like that. You know, the stuff my kids learned in kindergarten.

Much of this seems like common sense to digital natives who grew up interconnected with one another's thoughts and opinions. Plus, writing policies and rules is trying to bring black-and-white thinking to an area that is still very gray. For example, The Wall Street Journal's policy prohibits "arguments online with critics." How do you define that? An intelligent debate and exchange of ideas is healthy, but a name-calling flame war is not. How do you decide where to draw that line?

Some journalists wonder whether they represent themselves with their personal accounts, or are they always on the job representing their news organizations? In general, journalists should use social media the same way they use offline social interactions. How do you conduct yourself when talking to people in public—at a coffee shop or restaurant, for example— who may or may not know you are a journalist? That's a pretty good guide for how you should behave online, too.

Most ethical dilemmas can be solved through transparency. If everyone knows what you're doing and why you're doing it, there is a very low risk of impropriety. For example, promoting your stories or coverage from your news organization through social bookmarking sites such as reddit and Fark, or social networking sites such as Facebook and Twitter, is OK as long as it's obvious you have a bias and a reason for promoting such content.

▶ Monitor postings for offensive content

The kind of situation that occurred in Knoxville, Tenn., where a vicious crime made news and subsequently drew offensive attacks to the comments section of the news publisher's site, is unfortunately quite common. Online audiences, especially those with anonymous screen names to hide behind, push agendas and grind axes in a very public way in the comments sections on news sites.

At their best, story comments add layers to a news story that a newsroom simply cannot. Local expertise, interaction, discussion and a healthy exchange of ideas supplement the news in the report.

At their worst, story comments are nothing more than senseless drivel. They can descend to mean-spirited personal attacks between people who know each other's screen names intimately but know very little about their adversaries in real life.

Hot-button topics are obvious triggers, but locally sensitive issues tend to spill over into all areas as well. For example, in 2008 editors at The San Diego

Union-Tribune found that the commentary on any news story they published quickly turned into a debate over illegal immigration, because that was the issue of the day at the time. This happens every day on all manner of news Web sites, so be aware of the stories and sections on your site that have the potential to become regionally, racially, politically or even religiously charged.

Technology, community management and commenter behavior continue to improve, but not fast enough. Most editors have better technology to handle comments than they did five years ago, as well as more awareness of potentially explosive situations. If a news story turns controversial, some editors will turn off the comments to avoid the predictable ugliness that could appear. Others will simply keep a closer eye on the trend of the commentary.

Comments posted to news stories generally create the most controversy. Comments to blogs on news sites or those posted in message boards and forums are generally cleaner and more focused to the topic, according to a survey conducted by Ryan Sholin, a new-media professional who writes the Invisible Inkling blog.

"I expected commenters on news stories, where more people could see their words, to be more civil than commenters on blog posts on a news site, which theoretically have a smaller audience, and I expected the worst of the lot to show up on message boards, buried deep in the bowels of the sites that haven't flushed them from their systems yet," Sholin wrote. "I was wrong."

Blogs tend to be more watched, managed communities than mainstream news sites, where there is less direct responsibility for managing comments. This dictates behavior and, as one respondent to Sholin's survey said, "getting out of line there would be like yelling in someone's house."

Anonymity continues to be a huge issue at most newspaper Web sites because those organizations have traditionally used a rigorous system of checking and confirming identities before publishing the original user-generated content: letters to the editor. It has taken years for many traditional journalists to come around to the idea that comments are a different animal and therefore deserve different rules. Anonymity is often blamed for the proliferation of destructive comments and the presence of trolls in comment areas. But many editors now believe that requiring commenters to provide their actual identities would stifle valuable input, as some people would not feel free to comment at all.

"Verification became a central tenet of journalism in the 20th century, and in recent decades, newspapers imposed strict rules on the use of anonymous sources," Jack McElroy wrote in "The Case for Anonymous Comments" in the Knoxville News Sentinel. "But anonymity is not, in and of itself, anathema to healthy public discourse."

McElroy acknowledged that local news organizations must do more than provide news. If they are to remain relevant—and survive—they must facilitate community dialogue and position themselves at the center of that conversation.[12]

As online culture evolves, the discourse in the comments on news stories will too. User-generated content is not free. News sites that seek thoughtful, constructive commentary now know it won't happen without their involvement. As one respondent to Sholin's survey observed, "We do little to 'cultivate' our commenters and so the inmates have taken over the asylum."

The commenters are getting better, or at least less anonymous, too. The proliferation of Facebook and other social networking sites has created value in the establishment of an online identity. New technology such as Facebook Connect, which allows users to use their Facebook accounts to sign in to other Web sites instead of registering new accounts, helps, too. When you use Facebook Connect, you are who you are on Facebook, so if you comment on a news story, everyone will know who you are, too.

Another option for news sites is to enlist the community's help. It is now routine for sites to include a link near each comment to allow other users to flag it as inappropriate. Some news sites have "deputized" small groups of regular contributors and asked them to police the comment streams. The obvious question this raises is, Why would we trust the foxes to guard the henhouse? But if you can find a group of noble, trustworthy citizens, this approach can be incredibly powerful. Otherwise, consider what would motivate community members to do a good job. Some news organizations have offered free T-shirts (which also serve a marketing purpose), and some have hosted somewhat frequent get-togethers over pizza and soda.

Most online editors welcome the idea of allowing readers to hold the journalists accountable, just as the journalists try to hold those in power accountable to the community. They hope for an exchange of ideas between locally or topically interested citizens on the subjects of the news stories. But they now also know that moderation and management are

---

[12] Jack McElroy, "The Case for Anonymous Comments," The Upfront Page, Knoxville News Sentinel, March 13, 2009. http://blogs.knoxnews.com/knx/editor/2009/03/the_case_for_anonymous_comment.shtml.

critical; a completely open forum is likely to devolve into a cesspool of personal attacks and bitter name-calling (human nature being what it is).

"Yes, everybody has an opinion but not everybody's opinion matters," Davidson said while he was still running Newsvine. "Part of the key is to foster a culture of moderation, self-moderation. We're not really concerned with users who come by one time and leave a comment. What we care about, and what we measure, is how many people come back to the story 5 times, 10 times, 50 times because they care about what people have said in relation to their own comment."

Treat your comment areas like a garden: A little care and nurturing every day will go a long way toward making a healthy community. And remove any weeds as soon as they appear.

▶ Know your legal responsibilities

For years, news organizations operated social and interactive sections of their Web sites under a false assumption: If you edit any of the user content, you'll be responsible for publishing it and therefore liable for its veracity and potentially libelous statements.

Fortunately, that's not what the law states.

When David Ardia was the director of the Citizen Media Law Project at Harvard University's Berkman Center for Internet & Society, he tried to help news organizations and journalists understand the law. He would point to Section 230 of the Communications Decency Act, passed by Congress in 1996, as the basis for how news organizations and other Internet publishers should handle comments, message boards and other controversial content submitted by users.

The law states: "No provider or user of an interactive computer service shall be treated as the publisher or speaker of any information provided by another information content provider."[13]

"So, basically what that said is: We're going to hold you to distributor standards, not to publisher standards, for things that you publish online. And courts have taken that provision and essentially run with it," Ardia said.

This allows Web publishers to open their sites to all manner of interactivity without having to worry about verifying every statement published by users.

---

[13]"Protection for Private Blocking and Screening of Offensive Material," U.S. Code Collection, Cornell University Law School. www.law.cornell.edu/uscode/47/230.html.

The Online Media Legal Network (OMLN) is a network of law firms, law school clinics, in-house counsel, and individual lawyers throughout the United States willing to provide *pro bono* (free) and reduced fee legal assistance to qualifying online journalism ventures and other digital media creators.

«« about us »»

THE CLIENTS »

Online publishers and creators of digital media who innovate, create, and inform.

THE LAWYERS »

Lawyers offering their expertise in media law, intellectual property, and business advising.

WHAT PEOPLE ARE SAYING ABOUT OMLN

The web, it is often said, has lowered the barriers to entry in the publishing and journalism worlds. And that's true, but for one exception: legal services. There, start-ups, bloggers and stand alone journalists are at a disadvantage compared to Big Media. This network is trying to level the playing field for independent online producers. That's why it matters. That's why I support it.

- Jay Rosen, professor of journalism at NYU

Credit: http://www.omln.org/

The Online Media Legal Network website connects its two audiences, journalists, or "The Clients," and lawyers, to provide a free legal referral service and resource center for journalists.

Many misconceptions have prevailed around this topic for years, but the fact is that the law gives more power to the publishers than most people have realized.

"The one thing that's clear from this act is that it does not immunize the original creator of content itself," Ardia said. "So, the author of the defamatory statement, if they're a user and they post a comment on one of your articles, they can still be held liable. It's just the Web site operator that has immunity under this provision."

Ardia cautioned publishers not to consider themselves untouchable because of this law, however. A publisher could still be subpoenaed to appear in court if there is litigation around a defamatory comment or one that invades someone's privacy. "So, there are other things to be concerned about, even if you don't have liability for the comments," he said.

The next issue that usually presents a dilemma for publishers is how to respond to commenter complaints about comments posted by other users. If someone flags a comment as defamatory, libelous or an invasion of privacy, does the publisher bear responsibility for removing that content as soon as possible?

"The answer to that is no," Ardia said. "The cases have been very clear in saying that you have no obligation to remove material from your site if you've been notified that it's defamatory or otherwise problematic. If you think about that, it might strike you as: 'Geez, that doesn't sound right.' But courts don't want to put you in the position of having to determine if something is defamatory or not."

This is good news for news organizations, and it's even better news for independent journalism start-ups that don't have the luxury of corporate counsel. Hyperlocal and topical bloggers, for example, should take heart in the protection of Section 230 and use it to their advantage. It may be more important for these smaller operations that rely on audience participation to a greater extent than newspapers or TV news stations do. (For more information, go to www.citmedialaw.org/legal-guide/online-activities-covered-section-230 or visit the Online Media Legal Network at www.omln.org.)

Of course, the law simply establishes the ground floor below which you're not allowed to sink, so you should still bring professional and ethical responsibility to bear on these issues. Just because you can leave defamatory material published by someone else on your site doesn't mean you should.

▶ Correct errors

Accuracy, of course, is a hallmark of the best journalism. But perfection has always been elusive. Nobody's perfect, after all, so mistakes will be made.

In the digital age, accuracy is an even rockier road. Transparency and interactivity mean errors will be highlighted in very public ways. Immediacy means the time spent verifying information has diminished, so the chances for error have increased. Meanwhile, the acceptance by journalists of a world where more mistakes are made and mistakes are more public hasn't been easy.

"Corrections are journalism's equivalent of Puritan-era stocks, clamping a wrongdoer's feet, hands or head inside heavy wood frames, on humiliating display in the town square," Chip Scanlan wrote on The Poynter Institute's Web site.[14]

Craig Silverman launched RegretTheError.com in 2004 to provide a Web site focused on highlighting the typos, grammatical errors and factual mistakes made in the mainstream press. (He has since moved his writing to the Web site of The Poynter Institute.) His goal was to bring accountability to the press

---

[14]Chip Scanlan, "We Stand Corrected: When Good Journalists Make Stupid Mistakes," Poynter Online, December 12, 2007. http://poynter.org/column.asp?id=52&aid=134345.

by exposing its transgressions. He found fertile ground to cover and, in 2007, published a book containing the most entertaining mistakes.

Unfortunately, errors are no laughing matter for news companies.

"Newspapers, and other media as well, are losing more than their stock value these days," Greg Brock, a senior editor at The New York Times, wrote in a 2008 issue of Nieman Reports. "By ignoring readers' pleas for accuracy and accountability, journalists are losing the most valuable asset: their credibility."[15]

And the problem is significant, according to Silverman. Citing research conducted by Phil Meyer and Scott Maier, Silverman said that between 40 and 60 percent of newspaper news stories have some type of error. Meanwhile, research from Maier published in 2007 found that only 2 percent of factual errors were corrected.

"So, we have a relatively high error rate, and that is compounded by an anemic correction rate," Silverman told Scanlan. "Errors are not being prevented, and they are not being corrected."[16]

And digital publishing has only made the problem worse. Many news organizations now publish separate versions of a single story, so correcting errors is a complex and cumbersome process. If a news story is posted to the main Web site or a blog, by e-mail, to a mobile phone, in a podcast, with a video and through RSS feeds, Twitter and other social networking sites, correcting a simple error becomes an arduous task.

The New York Times struggled for more than a year to develop a system for correcting and acknowledging online errors, according to Brock.

"From a practical standpoint, correcting every error that flashes on our Web site for even five minutes is a logistical nightmare. Nor does merely correcting what was wrong in a given article appease readers. They want us to acknowledge that we made the error," Brock wrote.

Many news organizations, including the Times, do this by adding a note at the top or bottom of any article that has been corrected. Silverman, meanwhile, advocates for every news site to feature, in one place, a list of all of its online articles that have been corrected.

---

[15]Greg Brock, "Correcting the Errors of Our Ways," Nieman Reports, Fall 2008. www .nieman.harvard.edu/reportsitem.aspx?id=100427.

[16]Scanlan, "We Stand Corrected."

NEWSROOM INNOVATOR

Credit: Photo courtesy of
Sona Patel

SONA PATEL

▶ **STAFF EDITOR FOR SOCIAL MEDIA** | The New York Times (@sona)

Most news outlets rely heavily on engaging audiences on myriad platforms, including social networks. And as audiences grow, readers begin to play a more critical role in shaping coverage.

Let's consider three primary ways that readers engage with the news: reader comments, Twitter and Facebook. Once an article is published online, readers immediately start sharing their opinions and, depending on the topic, their personal experiences. Many journalists argue that article comments are often futile, but when used effectively, reader participation can add valuable perspective to journalists' reporting.

I'll give you an example from The New York Times, where I am a social media editor. I worked with a team of health care reporters as they prepared to write about Americans who received health insurance for the first time under the Affordable Care Act. Part of that discussion included what role readers might play in shaping our coverage. We had access to some federal data and scores of contacts at insurance companies, hospitals and government agencies. But we needed to hear from people across the country, with diverse backgrounds, who could share their perspectives of what it was like purchasing and using their insurance.

Our reporters had already found some potential sources, but many of them were referred through—and possibly affiliated with—lobbying groups. We needed ordinary people, who could tell unbiased stores. We worked with our Interactive News team to build a suite of tools that allowed nytimes.com readers to share their stories privately on our site. We collected hundreds of personal experiences. Many of those submissions informed front-page articles. And many of the submissions seeded new story ideas. These reader contributions were invaluable. And we continuously informed our readers on how their experiences were being used in our reporting.

One principle of crowdsourced reporting is to establish two-way communication between journalists and readers. The more journalists are willing to engage and interact with readers, the more readers will be willing to participate in conversations with journalists and contribute to reporting. For example, The New York Times often invites readers to ask questions or chat with reporters online. The primary goal in doing this is to provide readers with access to our journalists while sharing useful, service journalism.

I'm not advocating that crowdsourced reporting is the only way to add valuable perspectives to coverage. It should not replace traditional methods of reporting. In fact, I encourage journalists to think about the most effective methods of crowdsourcing. When should you use it? What's the most effective way to reach the people you want to hear from? Those are just some of the questions journalists should consider before deciding whether to solicit stories from readers online.

[*Source:* Written by Sona Patel at the request of the author.]

Staff reductions at news organizations mean fewer resources for such additional tasks. But credibility remains an important commodity for news companies in the constant battle for audience and, therefore, business viability. Journalists need to compete for credibility by maintaining high standards and educating the public about why they matter, not sinking to a lower level because others do. This means that it's in the best interests of news organizations to standardize a work flow for error correction and to create the expectation that all journalists are to be accountable for their mistakes.

"Put simply, errors erode credibility," Silverman said. "The public notices mistakes, and they notice when we don't correct them. They don't expect perfection; they expect us to work hard to prevent errors and to correct any that occur. When we don't do that, they punish us by tuning out."

The best way to handle corrections is with a direct, transparent approach. Today's savvy readers understand that news is fluid in the digital age and will give news organizations credit for owning their mistakes.

"When a mistake is made or information changes, I'm honest about the process. I apologize and make corrections," Montano says. "I lay out the process of the information we're receiving and publishing so the community knows how, what and why a story develops as it does."

What is it?   What's *Next?* | **Summary** |

☆ COLLABORATIVE PUBLISHING, SOCIAL MEDIA ARE HERE TO STAY

Collaborative publishing, whether defined as journalism or not, is not a fad that is going away anytime soon. Wikipedia, craigslist, YouTube, Facebook and Flickr are all forms of collaborative publishing that did not exist before the digital age.

Now that the door is open, news organizations and journalists have an opportunity to collaborate with the audience and do better work.

"Crowdsourcing is one of the main roles in the daily news-gathering process," Montano says. "It goes beyond the editorial meeting. It should be a part of as many stories as possible each day."

Jay Rosen of New York University is famous for a blog post in 2005 that coined the expression "the people formerly known as the audience."

While editors and journalism professors will continue to debate the degree to which an audience should participate in journalism, the new information ecosystem demands that news organizations harness the power of the crowd to become more efficient, more transparent and more effective.

"It's risky and scary, maybe even threatening. Ultimately our journalism will only be as good as the leaps we are willing to take," says King.

Any journalist who is adept at using social media has a distinct advantage in terms of source development over journalists who still think it's not for them.

I've heard stories of newspaper reporters fighting against having to use e-mail for reporting when e-mail first became widely available, saying they didn't have time and didn't want to hear from all those crazy people on the Internet. Now some editors I know wish their reporters would not rely so heavily on e-mail and would actually get out of the office and go out and meet people in their communities. You know, do some of that old-fashioned "shoe-leather" reporting.

Social media, used correctly, connects journalists and reporters to people and information. Just as the telephone didn't replace the face-to-face meeting over coffee and e-mail didn't replace the telephone, social media doesn't replace other forms of connecting with people. It adds to them.

As Roland Legrand noted on the PBS MediaShift blog, "If we journalists want to survive, we will have to learn to come out from behind our institutions and to speak in a human voice—to engage in genuine conversations."[17]

GET GOING Checklist ✔

☐ Visit three or four of the sites mentioned in this chapter and find the best examples of collaboration between reporters and editors and their audiences.

---

[17]Roland Legrand, "Journalists Should Customize Social Networks to Maximize Experience," MediaShift, June 1, 2009. www.pbs.org/mediashift/2009/06/journalists-should-customize-social-networks-to-maximize-experience152.

☐ Create an account at Storify and use it to build a "story" about a specific topic, selecting the best pieces of information from social media and Web sites to demonstrate how you would link journalism for your beat or your class.

☐ Visit the community sites discussed in this chapter to see how newspapers are working with readers to provide deeper, more local coverage of their communities.

☐ Participate in the conversation online by placing a comment on a traditional news story and another on a blog that is not affiliated with a news organization. Compare and contrast the experiences.

☐ Join or follow the social media channels (Facebook, Twitter, etc.) for a handful of news organizations; include at least one local organization, one national and one topical.

CHAPTER 4

Going Mobile

The world has gone mobile. And so has journalism.

Just a few years ago, a reporter who wanted to be prepared for anything would have had to cram a backpack with a laptop computer, a wireless Internet card, a DSLR camera, a video camera, an audio recorder and, oh, by the way, a mobile phone.

Now, that same reporter can simply stick a mobile phone in a pocket.

The dizzying pace of innovation in mobile phones has had a huge impact on live coverage of news events and reporting from the field. Not long ago, the only way to cover a live event was to send a multiperson news crew to broadcast on TV or radio. Now, a single reporter with a smartphone can do almost anything an expensive television news crew can, and maybe more.

"Mobile technology is the ultimate liberator in modern journalism: the one thing that allows us to leave the desk journalists have too often been tied to," says Paul Bradshaw, a professor at City University of London and co-author of "The Online Journalism Handbook." "With a mobile phone, tablet or laptop we can take and make phone calls, follow updates on social media and RSS readers, and find the information we need online."

It's only natural that a device that has changed the way we live and think about information would also change the way we do journalism. In fact, many technology analysts believe that mobile computing will have the same level of impact on our world as the Internet did in the late 1990s (if it hasn't already).

The revolution has already hit journalism and created a whole new field: mobile reporting. From a scene where news is happening, mobile reporters do it all—write and update constantly, and take and transmit videos and photos directly to their audience. It no longer matters whether a reporter is working for a company whose primary focus is print, online, radio or TV. Mobile reporters can report in any medium, from anywhere, anytime.

Their deadline is always the same: right now.

In this chapter, you'll learn how the new mobile journalists do it, what makes good mobile reporting and what pitfalls to avoid. You'll also learn how to serve and engage an audience seemingly glued to mobile devices. The chapter will include explanations of the following:

- What kinds of stories lend themselves to mobile reporting

- What equipment and technology you need for mobile reporting

- How to use selected mobile publishing services for text, photographs and video

- How professional news organizations use mobile to complement their existing publishing platforms

- How to best serve news and content to an audience that only consumes on mobile screens

What is it? | What's *Next?* Summary

② MOBILE JOURNALISM

How old were you when you received your first phone? A 2011 survey conducted for Verizon Wireless and Parenting.com found that the average age for a first mobile phone has fallen to 11.6 years. And it looks as though this trend is set to continue: 10 percent of parents report that their children were between the ages of 7 and 9 when they received their first phones.

As of 2012, about half of Americans of all ages owned smartphones, according to a report from the Pew Internet and American Life Project. The phenomenon is not limited to the younger generations, nor is it limited to certain demographics. African Americans and English-speaking Latinos are more likely than white Americans to use nonvoice data applications on their cell phones, according to a 2008 Pew report.[1]

---

[1] John Horrigan, "Mobile Access to Data and Information," Pew Internet and American Life Project, March 5, 2008. www.pewinternet.org/PPF/r/244/report_display.asp.

News organizations in the United States have only recently begun to give mobile the attention it deserves. The Web presented a more obvious disruption to the traditional publishing or broadcasting model for news because of how easy it suddenly became for anyone to publish online. At first, mobile audiences in the United States were constrained by the major telecommunications companies, which controlled application development on their services. A publisher trying to release a new application for mobile audiences had to go through Verizon, then AT&T, then Sprint (and so on) for approval to get on each company's devices.

Although this practice created a bottleneck, it also bought news publishers time to catch up. Now, since the advent of the iPhone and application development for it (plus Google's Android and the BlackBerry family of devices), the mobile landscape is wide open, and innovation is occurring at breakneck speed.

Every news organization is looking for ways to leverage this exploding technology. Mobile reporting is only the beginning. Since journalism can't be journalism until it's published, mobile technology is emerging as a powerful means for publishing multimedia to mobile audiences. And, since more and more users are creating their own content on the go, journalists are also experimenting with using those audiences for mobile crowdsourcing.

"Whenever I talk to journalists about the mobile shift, they're quick to defend the Web over mobile apps," says Cory Bergman, general manager of BreakingNews, a mobile-first company operating within NBC News. "After all, the Web is what the news industry knows best after years of playing digital catch-up."

Today, mobile devices are like electronic Swiss Army knives, arming anyone and potentially everyone with all-in-one media tools that can view, capture and publish or broadcast. Mobile phones can take photos, video and audio and publish them all, plus text, through a connection to the Internet or a high-speed digital cellular network. They can also receive and display all forms of media. And they're cheaper, smaller and more portable than other devices that can do the same things, such as laptops, video cameras and digital still cameras.

The audience is going mobile, so journalism should too. This transformation doesn't mean mobile reporting and publishing will replace in-depth reporting, compelling writing or professional photojournalism. But mobile journalism can be an important complement to news reporting, especially in a breaking news situation where time is critical and others arrive on the scene before the professional journalists.

Ron Sylvester, who has been a journalist for more than 30 years and was one of the first reporters in the United States to report from a courtroom using Twitter, urges his fellow reporters to welcome technology, not fear it.

"I worked through decades where TV and radio reporters gave people the news, and I came along the next day to try and give them depth and understanding," says Sylvester, who is now assistant managing editor for local news at the Orange County Register. "The Internet has put us back in the game. Now the reporters formerly known as newspapers are breaking news live. People are coming to our sites to find out the news first, then coming back to get the depth and understanding. We really have the best of both worlds.

"Others my age who are resisting learning new tools, or are intimidated by them, sound starkly similar to the 'old guys' I heard at age 19 whining about having to give up their typewriters."

There was a time (not so long ago) when someone who shot a picture with a smartphone or uploaded a story to a Web site while out in the field would have been called a "backpack journalist" or a "mojo" (mobile journalist). Those labels are less buzzworthy today because so many reporters have integrated mobile technology into their normal workdays.

What is it? | **What's *Next?*** | Summary

⤓ MAKING MOBILE JOURNALISM

Advances in mobile technology, both devices and services, make it easier than ever before to cover a news event on location. Let's take a look at the gear, gadgets and services that journalists are using to make mobile a part of their daily routines.

When it comes to choosing the right equipment for mobile reporting, you have options from laptops to smartphones, audio recorders and video cameras, and many different ways to connect to the Internet no matter where you find yourself reporting. The range of options can be confusing and overwhelming at first. But remember, there are no "industry standard" tools to use in mobile reporting. The right choice is whatever works for you.

At a minimum, all you need is a tool to capture or produce content and a way to connect to the Internet so you can publish it. That could be through the use of one device, such as an iPhone or a smartphone powered by Android or Windows Mobile. Or it could be a full backpack kit with a camera, tripod, audio recorder, microphone and laptop with a 4G wireless Internet card.

The bottom line: Keep it simple. Don't lug more equipment than you need for a given assignment. And don't ever try to use a new device in the field before you've practiced enough to get comfortable with it.

The motto for backpack or mobile journalism could have come from the Boy Scouts: Be prepared. The idea is to equip a journalist with the tools to do reporting in any medium—text, photo, video, audio—from anywhere. Then it's up to the journalist to go somewhere interesting, find some news and start reporting.

▶ Choose your story

Why bother with the technological hassle? First, a reporter on the scene doing eyewitness interviews and making firsthand observations simply produces a better story. Second, today's news audience expects to see and hear that story now, as it's happening—not just tomorrow morning.

When you're trying to decide whether to go mobile on a particular story, ask these questions:

Will the audience benefit if we can take them there?

Will the journalism be better if it's done on location and with urgency?

Can this event be effectively communicated in small chunks over time?

Will sound reporting or video footage, turned around quickly, help people understand the story?

In many situations, the answer to this last question is yes. Here's a starter list of the kinds of assignments that create opportunities for reporting and publishing from the field:

Criminal and civil trials, especially when key witnesses are on the stand or a verdict is being read

Important speeches or announcements by public officials, celebrities, sports figures and business leaders

Breaking news events of all types, including fires, shootings, natural disasters, wilderness rescues, plane crashes and auto accidents that tie up traffic

Public gatherings such as protests, celebratory parades and activist and political rallies

Sporting events

Grand openings of popular consumer destinations such as shops and restaurants

It's important to remember, however, that the journalism should come first, the technology second. In other words, let your news judgment about what's important and what your audience will find interesting drive your decisions for mobile reporting. New tools change your tactics but not your standards. "Cool chance to use my new camera," you may recall, does not appear on the list of factors that determine whether something is news.

"A mobile editor needs to be a mobile user," says David Ho, who became the first mobile editor at The Wall Street Journal in 2009. "A serious mobile user. Simply owning a smart phone isn't enough. Because if you don't live it, you don't get it. If you're not using apps and mobile websites and mobile tools yourself in your own life, it's all but impossible to do a good job serving that audience."[2]

Sylvester says using mobile technology shouldn't change how journalists collect information—just when and how people see it. "Now I take notes and distribute them live," he says. "Twitter not only becomes my news stream for the trial, it also becomes my notebook. The difference is, my notes now come in complete sentences. At the end of the day, I can take my tweets and use them as the basis for the print story."

Reporters don't have to go all out right from the start. Mobile reporting can be done in small steps, such as filing the outcome of a news event as soon as possible to give an audience the headline while working on the story in a more traditional manner.

▶ Gear up and get out: Reporting on the go

First, think about where you fit on or between these two ends of the equipment spectrum:

Gearhead: A dedicated mojo whose job is to be out and about and report from the field all day, every day. This person is telling multimedia stories and publishing them from anywhere. This kind of journalist wants the best and coolest equipment.

Light packer: A more traditional journalist, someone who occasionally needs to report or publish immediately from the field. This person needs just enough equipment to get the job done.

---

[2]David Ho, "News in Motion: Six Ways to Be a Good Mobile Editor," Poynter Online, March 25, 2014. www.poynter.org/news/media-innovation/244675/news-in-motion-six-ways-to-be-a-good-mobile-editor.

Here's a suggested list of equipment and technology that people in each category usually want to have. But realize this is not an either-or situation: A journalist can easily pick and choose from both lists to assemble a preferred set of tools. And these tools and services are not the only options, either. They are simply examples of what has recently been used successfully for journalism.

DRILLING DOWN

Equipment Specs For specific brand and model suggestions, see chapter 6 (pages 198–199) for audio equipment and chapter 7 (pages 231–236) for video equipment.

CHAPTER 4

▶ ▶ *If you're a gearhead*

If you're planning to carry multiple devices, start with a goal of making sure they all fit into one backpack or case. This will keep things simple while you're traveling or in the field. As a result, compact versions of the following items are strongly recommended:

Laptop or tablet computer: A small laptop, with a screen no larger than 13 inches, or a tablet is all you need. Don't worry about big horsepower; having something portable is more important. You may use it for live blogging, microblogging and importing and editing audio, video and photos. (If you plan to use a tablet, make sure it has a keyboard so you can type fast.)

Internet connection: A portable wireless hotspot or a mobile Internet card that inserts into the USB slot of a laptop computer are the best options. Less expensive options include using a smartphone as the modem. If you can't afford any of those, get familiar with coffee shops and libraries that offer free Wi-Fi connectivity.

Camera: A point-and-shoot camera with video mode will allow you to carry one device instead of both a still camera and a video camera.

Video camera: If you have a smartphone that takes good pictures but less-than-great video, you can add a low-priced, compact video camera for less money than a full point-and-shoot camera costs.

Tripod: Use only a compact model that folds and stores in a small space. If you try to use a full-size model, you'll end up leaving it behind because it's too much of a hassle.

Audio recorder: A digital audio recorder that records to a memory card or easily interfaces with your laptop will allow you to add audio interviews and ambient sound to your coverage.

Headphones: Again, look for portable models that fold and store in a small space. But make sure they cover your ears. Noise-canceling capability is not necessary.

Microphone: Find one that's durable and has some type of windscreen.

Mobile phone: If you have all the other capabilities on this list, all you need your phone for is to make calls (crazy, I know). But, as we will see in the next section, a smartphone can take the place of much of the equipment on this list.

▶ ▶ *If you're a light packer*
A smartphone. That's it.

Well, OK, a smartphone that has the following things:

A camera that shoots good pictures and captures good video, preferably one with a flash

A full QWERTY keypad (or touch screen) for easy text inputting

Mobile Internet capability, preferably with full-featured e-mail

The right mobile apps for discovering, capturing and publishing information (covered later in this chapter)

▶ Publishing options

In the early days of mobile reporting, the major hurdle to clear wasn't recording audio or video or typing a story on a portable computer. Laptops, after all, have been around since before the Internet became popular. The problem was publishing content online from the field.

Today, the information economy has produced a multitude of middleware services (so called because they sit between the content creator and the publishing destination) that make it easy to publish any type of content online from anywhere. And the best part is that most of them are free.

This has led to a new model for mobile journalism, one that is constantly changing and progressing. Here is a look at some of the ways journalists have gone mobile, including some of the more popular services being used for each of the different tasks of a mobile journalist.

Remember that the companies providing many of the services listed in this section continue to push out new innovations at a rapid pace. The competition is fierce, and new companies and new products and services are constantly hitting the market, so don't assume that those listed here represent some kind of industry standard. These just happen to be services popular with mobile journalists in 2015. It's quite likely something better will turn up next year, and the year after that, and the year after that.

▶ ▶ *Mobile microblogging*

As long as Twitter remains the standard for microblogging, it will also be the standard for mobile microblogging. Twitter is easy to use on everything from a laptop to a mobile phone, where the Twitter app (and popular third-party apps such as Hootsuite and TweetDeck) makes it easy to publish and consume. Plus, a feed from the updates can be posted to any Web site, immediately connecting the journalist in the field to an online (or mobile) audience.

"We can be where things are happening," Bradshaw says. "This means more than just reporting from the ground, but also being able to react to what is being said there. As a mobile journalist you might be streaming video, filing audio, images and text from the ground—but the networked nature of modern communication means that journalists cannot merely be looking at what is in front of them: They must be monitoring everything that is being said about the event taking place—and reacting to it."

At first, sharing what are essentially notes with an audience makes some journalists uneasy; news judgment and quality control, after all, are what separate real journalism from the rest of the information flooding the Web. But with practice and an open mind, many journalists eventually find that the public note-taking aspect of microblogging keeps their attention focused and actually improves their reporting.

"I don't really see any downside," says Sylvester, who covered trials in Kansas live on Twitter for several years and whose court-coverage blog for Kansas .com was called What the Judge Ate for Breakfast. "I really don't think I'm sacrificing anything through Twitter. I think I'm gaining an advantage. People get the news as it is happening, and my stories for the next day's editions are easier to write."

Tumblr is another platform for micropublishing (with heavy social network capabilities) that can be used for microblogging. It's even possible, and just as easy, to use Facebook's status updates on assignment if you or your news organization has set up a Facebook profile for news reporting.

"One reason this works so well is because I use a Bluetooth foldable keyboard with my smartphone," Sylvester says. "I don't think I'd be able to do this, typing with my thumbs.

"That's also why Twitter works so well: I can send all my updates via text message. I don't have to juggle equipment. If I wanted, everything would fit in my pocket."

Like most experienced reporters, however, Sylvester has a backup: He carries a legal pad. "I jot down details I may not want to include in my tweets but may fit into my story later," he says. "Plus, I have a fallback if the electronic technology ever fails."

▶ ▶ *Live blogging*

If you have a laptop and Internet access, you might want to offer your audience a fuller experience than is possible with microblogging and its 140-character limit. Live blogging is the practice of covering an ongoing event with constant updates; it can be done with standard blogging software or with an add-on service such as CoveritLive or ScribbleLive.

If you plan to use a standard blog, remember to use a single post for all of your updates. In other words, don't create a new post for each new entry. Create one entry and keep adding to it. You'll make a cleaner experience for your audience while you establish a permalink for the coverage that can be archived and linked to by others. Simply add an update time stamp to a new paragraph each time you add new information. It can be as simple as "Update 12:14 p.m." or just "12:14 p.m." Updating the single post instead of creating a new post each time makes it easier for readers to follow along.

TechCrunch, one of the most popular blogs in the world, set the standard for live blogging years ago with its coverage of Steve Jobs and his keynote addresses at the Macworld conferences. By posting every minute or two with time stamps and adding ample photos, TechCrunch was able to provide the most timely coverage available anywhere. News organizations such as The New York Times took note (probably because they lost some of their audience to TechCrunch) and now live-blog similar events in a similar fashion. Imitation is still the sincerest form of flattery.

Next-generation news start-ups like The Verge and BuzzFeed have taken this to a new level by building live-blogging capabilities into their customized content-management systems. If you do not have access to such tools, then add-on services such as CoveritLive and ScribbleLive can help. Each company offers a module that embeds onto any Web page and gives a mobile journalist a blog-like interface. It provides several feedback features not found in a traditional blog, allowing the audience to comment and ask questions or participate in polls in real time. And everything is easily archived for later access online.

Reporting while on the go has also changed with the "real-time Web." Chris O'Brien, a veteran business columnist and reporter who has covered Silicon Valley for more than a decade, says, "Twitter is like radar," and that he can monitor "thousands of conversations" with an application such as TweetDeck or Hootsuite. "This becomes particularly vital when news breaks."

> ## DRILLING DOWN
>
> **Power Trip** The worst thing that can happen to a mobile reporter is to lose power. Pack an extra battery for every device you carry. If you have an iPhone or other device that doesn't have a removable battery, use a case that has an extra battery included (such as those offered by mophie). Make sure you also have the appropriate car-charging accessories. And consider adding to your arsenal a car power inverter, which turns the power outlet in your car into a regular power outlet you can plug into.

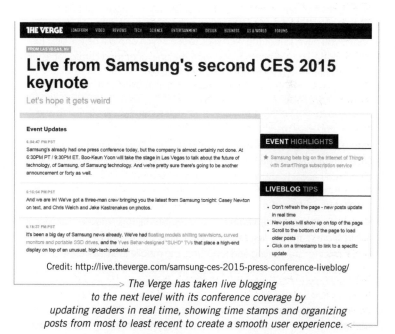

Credit: http://live.theverge.com/samsung-ces-2015-press-conference-liveblog/

The Verge has taken live blogging to the next level with its conference coverage by updating readers in real time, showing time stamps and organizing posts from most to least recent to create a smooth user experience.

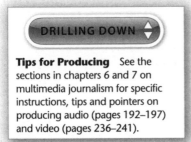

DRILLING DOWN

Tips for Producing See the sections in chapters 6 and 7 on multimedia journalism for specific instructions, tips and pointers on producing audio (pages 192–197) and video (pages 236–241).

▶▶ *Mobile video*

Several services make it easy to stream video live from anywhere on a cell phone without an Internet connection. These services run on the mobile network that connects your cell phone to the world, no Internet connection needed. This is super convenient—as long as it works, of course. If your service drops your calls regularly, don't expect to be able to stream video reliably from your phone.

With a reliable connection, you can broadcast video from your phone to the Web, either on the service's site (for example, ustream.com) or via a video player you can easily embed in your Web site or blog. As far as the audience can tell, your news organization has a whole camera crew on the scene. The services also have features that allow your audience to ask questions through chat or make comments during the broadcast. (Are you ready for some multitasking?)

The services, which include Ustream, Skype's Qik and Livestream, only work on phones that can shoot video. The various services have slight differences, and each has certain advantages, depending on your needs and the type of phone you have. Check the Web sites to see which one will be the best for you, and then start experimenting, with the goal of getting comfortable with the tools before you try to use them for journalism.

Another technological advance that could offer important opportunities for mobile journalists is the new wave of wearable cameras. While GoPro and other companies market their products for outdoor recreation enthusiasts, it would be easy for journalists to incorporate their devices into field reporting. Other companies are making over-the-ear cameras that look similar to Bluetooth headsets and are relatively inconspicuous.

▶▶ *Mobile multimedia*

As you've probably noted from the services listed above, mobile reporting is about more than text. Just as digital journalists should not be constrained to one format for storytelling and reporting, the mobile journalist should not be limited either. The only difference is the deadline. For a mobile journalist, the deadline is now.

While some reporters are still nervous about doing multimedia journalism in the newsroom, technology is already moving on. Combining photos, video and audio with text is definitely more challenging from the field than from the office. But publishing each format is not.

A good way to approach mobile multimedia reporting is to concentrate on the elements of the story independently. If these separate elements can be pulled together to make a cohesive package later, it's great. If not, it's no big deal.

The phrase "I'm there, you're not, let me tell you about it," coined by New York University professor Jay Rosen, provides a good framework for mobile reporting. Rosen goes on to describe how this process leads the reporter to a level of authority on a specific topic at a specific moment.

Text is critical, and it's the easiest to publish. Microblogging and live blogging are simple methods for continually updating an audience with many short bites of information. Either can also serve as the hub for links to the other forms of content, such as photos and video, that you are producing.

In a mobile setting, photos are likely to be complementary content unless you are a gearhead and can build a slide show with ample caption information on your laptop and publish it to a Web site. If you are not, then create that sense of "being there" for your audience by providing whatever photos you can, even if they are camera-phone pictures taken from too far away.

Of course, you need to work to get the best photos you can, but don't stop yourself from publishing photos because the composition or lighting isn't perfect. The standards for mobile reporting are different: Instead of "good as it can be," as you should aim for with your other work, think "good enough" for mobile reporting. Publishing any photo at all is especially important in situations where no TV coverage or other visuals are available. Photos are also crucial when you're microblogging, because it's difficult to provide rich detail with 140 characters at a time.

You can apply the same "good enough" standard to mobile video. Obviously, it's not possible to produce the same quality video story with a live stream from a cell phone that a professional could produce with a high-definition camera and Final Cut Pro. But, in many cases, immediacy trumps production values. A video that takes an audience to the scene of a police standoff or a protest that has gone wrong will have incredible power because of its relevance, not because of its editing and composition.

DRILLING DOWN

Accessorize Your Smartphone   A number of companies make add-on lenses for smartphones that can enhance your iPhone with telephoto or wide-angle capabilities. The Owle Bubo, for example, is a combination tripod/camera lens/external microphone for the iPhone.

ETAN HOROWITZ

▶ **SENIOR MOBILE EDITOR** | CNN Digital (@etanowitz)

Credit: Photo courtesy of Etan Horowitz

Throughout my career, I've always been drawn to jobs at the intersection of journalism and technology. When I was a newspaper reporter and columnist, I reviewed the first iPhone, the first Android phone and the first Kindle, and was an early advocate of using social media for journalism.

My role as senior mobile editor for CNN Digital is a natural extension of that path. As the editorial lead for all of CNN's mobile platforms, I work with writers, producers and editors to make sure we are serving mobile readers with the best headlines, photos, videos and coverage we can. I also work closely with product managers, designers and developers to take advantage of new technology as we enhance CNN's mobile Web site and apps.

Mobile usage has exploded since I started this job. At the end of 2011, only 22 percent of CNN's global digital traffic came from mobile devices. At the end of 2014, it's 50 percent, and on weekends mobile routinely accounts for more than half of our traffic.

Working in a digital newsroom where half of your traffic comes from mobile devices requires changes in tools, work flow, staffing and, most of all, thinking.

To make sure our staff is keeping a close eye on mobile, we installed big screens in our newsroom that show the home pages of our mobile Web site and mobile apps. During editorial meetings, we make sure to show mobile screens, and when writers preview their stories in our content-management system, they see a preview of the mobile Web version of the story alongside the desktop one.

CNN's coverage of the November 24, 2014, St. Louis County grand jury's decision not to indict police officer Darren Wilson in the August 9 shooting death of Michael Brown in Ferguson, Mo., is a good example of our mobile mind-set in

NEWSROOM INNOVATOR

action. CNN's coverage of the Ferguson decision was one of the highest mobile traffic days of the year.

The decision was announced at about 9 p.m. eastern time, falling squarely in the part of the day when traffic to CNN's mobile Web site and mobile apps is the strongest.

With a big breaking news story like this one, there are three main ways that news coverage from CNN will reach people using a phone or tablet.

The first is through push alerts from our CNN mobile apps. We sent our first app alert moments after the St. Louis County prosecuting attorney's announcement, and we sent three more in the hours following the announcement. Each alert offered up new developments, like a description of photos from the grand jury evidence or an update on violent protests.

The second way is through our mobile Web site or app home pages. These readers likely have heard the initial breaking news but want to know more. In a fast-moving story like Ferguson, we make sure to update the headlines and photos often. This is important on all platforms, but it is especially important on mobile platforms, where people have the mind-set of "What did I miss since I last checked?" A live blog pulls in the latest reporting and images from reporters on the ground, and a live video feed of the protests themselves lets users feel like they are on the ground. Finally, for users who want analysis of the decision, background about the case or perspectives about how it fits in to race relations in the United States, we have a special section on our mobile Web site and mobile apps where we have curated all of CNN's best coverage on Ferguson.

The third way CNN breaking news reaches people on phones and tablets is through social media. When you tap on a link to a CNN story from Facebook or Twitter on your phone, you come to CNN's mobile Web site. The live blog and live video stream are great tools to bring people to our mobile Web site through social media. Throughout the night and into the next morning, we post updates on Facebook or Twitter with developments, like the use of tear gas by police, and then link to the live blog or live video stream in our messages.

While the entire CNN Digital staff is responsible for producing and programming all platforms, it helps to have staffers dedicated solely to mobile during a big breaking news story like this.

[*Source:* Written by Etan Horowitz at the request of the author.]

▶ Mobile crowdsourcing

Now that you're equipped with mobile publishing capabilities, it's important to remember: so is your audience. The ease of publishing with mobile devices makes it that much more important to include your audience in your coverage plans.

Think about it: Broadcasting video from a mobile phone using Ustream is so much easier than shooting with an expensive camera, editing with expensive software and uploading to a special streaming server. The same goes for photos, which means anyone can do it.

DRILLING DOWN ⬆⬇

Apps for Journalists As smartphones have become the indispensable tool for journalists, many have found myriad mobile apps to assist them in their work. Here is a short list of apps to start with (with thanks to Damon Kiesow, senior manager for mobile initiatives at McClatchy):

- Twitter, TweetDeck or Hootsuite

- Filterstorm or Photoshop Express (professional-quality photo editing)

- Reel Director or iMovie (basic video editing)

- Ban.jo (find people nearby using social media)

- Storify (curate social media posts)

- Audioboo (record instant podcasts)

- VC Audio Pro (three-track audio editing)

- Dropbox (share files with your main computer and other users)

- Evernote (save notes, photos and audio to the cloud)

To wit, as of 2012, about 100 hours of video were being uploaded to Ustream any given minute, according to the company's co-founder Brad Hunstable. Ustream has 170,000 active broadcasters per month, sending out 1.5 million broadcasts. Hunstable told an audience at the 2012 SXSW Interactive conference that the average length of a broadcast is 2.8 hours.

Hunstable said 7 million people tuned in to Ustream to see the rescue of the Chilean miners in 2011. Millions also watched live coverage on Ustream of various uprisings and protests from the Arab Spring that same year. If you are at a news organization that wants to provide live coverage of world events like these but can't afford to send someone there, consider adding a stream from a "citizen broadcaster" on a service such as Ustream.

Cell phone photos submitted by the audience have been a staple in breaking news coverage for years, starting with the terrorist attacks in the

London Underground train tunnels in 2005. Every news organization should be prepared to accept photos from mobile devices—for breaking news, especially, but also just for interesting local event coverage.

Some news organizations already do this, but many are still asking their audiences to e-mail photos. A mobile solution, allowing the audience to upload photos directly to a Web site from mobile devices, will increase the timeliness and very likely the response rate on such requests.

You can also include the audience in covering an event, or get their comments and observations, by using a service such as CoveritLive or Twitter. Invite audience members to use a specific hashtag (for example, #flood) for a news event. Then post a feed from all the tweets with this hashtag for display on your Web site. Or mine the feed for the best tweets and republish them on one of the news organization's Twitter accounts.

After you understand the capabilities of mobile publishing, you'll find countless opportunities to include your audience in your coverage.

What is it? What's *Next?* | **Summary** |

☆ MOBILE FUTURE

We live in a mobile, global world. With mobile technology and adoption changing so quickly, connecting to an audience requires you not only to keep up but also to keep looking ahead.

Think about your first camera phone. It wasn't all that long ago, in the grand scheme of things. At the time, it was a cool feature that many of your friends might not have had yet. Nowadays, you can't even buy a cell phone without a camera.

In addition to still and video cameras, mobile devices now have GPS, or Global Positioning System, technology—another game-changing technology for journalism. With GPS, your mobile device knows exactly where in the world you are at any moment. News, information and even advertising are now being automatically served to you depending on your location.

GPS is also changing the way people contribute information. As it has become standard for mobile devices to attach latitude and longitude information to photos, video and text, it has become possible for people to quickly and easily publish to sophisticated Web sites that organize content geographically.

The portability and relatively small size of current and coming smartphones is also altering the relationship between reporters and the people they interview. Many print reporters originally balked at the idea of bringing a video camera to an interview because it compromised the personal feel of a conversation far more than an unobtrusive reporter's notebook. TV reporters have always faced the challenge of big and bulky equipment intimidating interviewees. Smartphone-enabled reporters don't have that challenge.

"It is a great, crazy time for mobile news," says Ho of The Wall Street Journal. "Innovation is nonstop and crops up everywhere."

Many smart people predict that mobile technology will change the media landscape more than the mainstream adoption of the Web did in the 1990s—if it hasn't already.

Get a jump on it now.

"There's no stopping the numbers: mobile is where people are and where they will be—at least for a while," says Ho.

Fortunately, with so many new services available, you don't need the resources of a big news company to connect with a mobile audience. Your penchant for publishing relevant, timely information will serve you well once you make mobile part of your daily routine.

GET GOING Checklist ✔

☐ Get started with mobile journalism by experimenting with the following assignments:

    ☐ Shoot photos of a news event with a mobile device and post them online—even on a social network like Twitter—as quickly as possible.

    ☐ Report from a news event with real-time text updates, using a laptop computer or smartphone and a standard blog, CoveritLive or Twitter.

    ☐ Broadcast video from a news event using Ustream, Qik or Livestream.

    ☐ Find a way to invite your audience to contribute by sending you photos shot by phone from a news event or providing text updates you can track and republish on a microblogging service such as Twitter.

CHAPTER 5

Visual Storytelling With Photographs

"Are we using 1,000 words where a picture should be?"

—Matt Thompson[1]

Visual storytelling, documentary photography and even just the basic illustration of information used to be reserved for serious technicians only. The process of making photographs, with its chemicals and darkrooms, conjured a sort of black magic atmosphere and erected a significant barrier between those who could and those who couldn't. One can argue that the digital age has had a greater impact on photography than on any other single skill or ability. The ability to publish to a global audience for free, with just a few clicks, opened up the world to a cacophony of new voices. But digital photography, including the ubiquity of cell phone cameras, lowered the bar on capturing images to the point where anyone and everyone is a photographer.

How many photographs were captured, and published, on New Year's Eve around the world? Countless.

Journalism without photographs is like writing without verbs. Writers have long been told to "show, don't tell" with their words. Thanks to digital photography, a journalist can easily replace words with images, improving the experience for the audience and improving the efficiency of the journalist. But doing it well takes patience, practice and preparation.

"Photographs, moving pictures, natural sound and the spoken word are all critical elements of telling news stories," says Stokes Young, executive

---

[1]Matt Thompson, "Ten Questions for Journalists in the Era of Overload," Newsless.org, December 31, 2008. www.newsless.org/2008/12/ten-questions-for-journalists-in-the-era-of-overload.

producer for multimedia at nbcnews.com. "At the most basic level, they allow storytellers to convey facts through their viewers' senses. Not to take anything away from a great written yarn, but readers can 'only' read how a scene looked or what it sounded like. Viewers, though, have more receptors open: They can actually see and hear the broad sweep, compelling details and central characters of a story."

"Photography is all about moment," according to Colin Mulvany, a visual journalist at The Spokesman-Review in Spokane, Wash., and author of the blog Mastering Multimedia. "Being able to quickly capture fleeting moments is what separates the professional photojournalist from the amateur photographer."

Even if you don't have aspirations of becoming an artist with a camera, you should understand how digital photography works. At a minimum you will handle digital photos and need to shoot a basic picture such as a mug shot. But once you experience the ease and power of digital photography, you will probably want to take it much further and explore the possibilities.

> *"This image is a favorite of mine because it captures Obama in an honest and telling moment," says Val Hoeppner, former manager of multimedia education at the Freedom Forum Diversity Institute. "I think great photographs show you things you don't see every day. It isn't every day that you see a politician like Obama working, feet up and the soles of his shoes worn."*

Credit: © Callie Shell/Aurora Photos.

Barack Obama at a campaign stop in Providence, R.I., in 2008.

"You need to know the basics . . . composition, how to operate the camera, how to work with a subject so you can make them feel comfortable," says Deb Cram, director of photography and multimedia for Seacoast Media Group in New Hampshire. "Being a good photographer isn't just about the craft of making a good image but about knowing how to relate to people. You must be able to be a fly on the wall yet be able to talk with all levels of society, making them feel like you can be trusted. You form relationships, even though they are brief."

There is an ocean of information online for those who want to get serious about digital photography and photojournalism. Following is a starter course (with references to further instruction) to help anyone who wants to become proficient in the basics. This chapter provides an introduction to digital photography, with specific explanations of the following:

- How to capture solid photographs

- How to edit and manage digital photos on your computer

- How to publish photos, including compelling slide shows that really tell the story

This chapter is *not* about smartphone photography, which we touched on in Chapter 4 in the discussion of mobile journalism. It's important to distinguish one kind of photography from the other. It's also important to remember, as Young reminds us, to balance these skills with others that are required for today's journalists.

"It's hard for individual journalists to be really good at multiple things: research, reporting, interviewing for broadcast, shooting, recording, editing, writing for broadcast, tracking and, ultimately, producing (bringing those multiple elements together, on deadline, in a way that tells the story efficiently and well for the target audience). So, it's important for journalists to focus first and foremost on building expertise in their communities and beats and finding great stories, second on the specific areas of expertise they can bring to bear to tell those stories and finally on collaboration with others whose skills complement theirs," Young says.

| **What is it?** | What's *Next?* | Summary |

⚿ DIGITAL PHOTOGRAPHY

Digital camera sales have slowed as mobile phones have improved their built-in cameras in recent years. The convenience of digital cameras versus traditional film cameras and now the wide availability of smartphone cameras have led the practitioners of many professions, including police officers, firefighters, real estate and insurance agents, scientists, doctors and dentists, to make taking photographs part of their work routines. That's because with a digital camera you can:

Essentially take as many pictures as you want, instead of being limited by the amount of film remaining.

Immediately see whether you captured the image you wanted.

Upload pictures to the Web and share them with friends and family anytime, anywhere.

Avoid having to purchase film—and you don't pay to print photos you don't want, so you save money.

Easily edit the pictures on a computer, including cropping and toning the images.

These advantages have actually been improved by the amazing cameras built into today's smartphones.

The key to understanding how to work with digital photographs is all in the pixels. "Pixel" is a mashed-up word meaning PICTure ELement, and a pixel is usually imagined as a tiny square on a matrix overlay on a computer image. A pixel is the visual representation of data in a digital image or graphic. To picture this in your mind, think of a photograph as a mosaic composed of hundreds or thousands of tiny squares.

Just a few short years ago, if you were shopping for a digital camera, the first measurement you would use to narrow your choices was the megapixel. Now, camera manufacturers have pushed the megapixel level on even the most basic cameras past the point of concern for most shoppers.

A megapixel represents 1 million pixels. It is used to measure the power of digital cameras with some simple math. For example, if a digital camera is rated at 3.2 megapixels, that means the largest photographs it can capture are 2,048 pixels wide and 1,536 pixels tall, and $2,048 \times 1,536 = 3,145,728$ (and the manufacturers round the number up for marketing purposes). If you used all the information in a 3.2-megapixel image, you could print a photograph that is roughly 11×14 inches.

This was more important when users needed to choose among cameras rated at 2.0, 3.2 or 5.0 megapixels. Now that entry-level cameras—and many smartphone cameras—start at 8.0 megapixels or higher, it's less of a factor.

A digital camera stores photographs as digital files on a memory card. The more pixels in a photograph, the more bytes needed to store the picture. Cameras can be adjusted to lower the number of pixels captured to save space on the memory card, but now that large memory cards of 4GB and 8GB are relatively inexpensive, this is rarely necessary. Cloud storage systems such as Dropbox, Google and Microsoft's OneDrive have created additional options for photographers.

Now that you understand pixels, you can begin to get your head around resolution. When it pertains to the display of electronic data, resolution is a measurement of pixels that are available to the human eye. Computers have displays that can be adjusted to show more or less information on the screen. (A common display setting is 1,024 × 768.)

When it comes to photographs, resolution refers to the number of pixels in an image. Because all computer monitors display 72 pixels per inch (ppi), photographs on Web sites need a resolution of only 72 ppi. Photographs in printed newspapers are usually 200 ppi, and glossy magazines use images at 300 ppi.

A photograph will be much larger in bytes at 200 or 300 ppi, and therefore will eat up more computer processing time to upload or download. Yet it will not display any sharper on a 72-ppi screen. Therefore, there's no reason to make users wait longer to download the higher-resolution image. This becomes a problem when a newspaper reporter finds a photograph on a Web site and would like to include it with a story in print. The low-resolution image doesn't scale to 200 ppi and will look blurry, especially if it is enlarged.

Conversely, if you have a high-resolution image for publication on a Web site, it should be compressed. Compressing an image means using software to squeeze the image, omitting the pixels that aren't necessary and making the file smaller (in bytes) without sacrificing the overall quality.

▶ **Ownership, copyright and fair use**

While it's easy to publish photographs on a Web site, it's just as simple to download and copy photographs that others have published. But just because you can doesn't mean you should. And when it comes to "borrowing" others' photographs without permission, you definitely should NOT.

"In this day and age of photo manipulation, students new to photojournalism must understand and adhere to the ethics of not creating images that lie or are deceptive to the viewer," Colin Mulvany says.

Before we go further with digital photography, it's important to recognize the potential ethical dilemmas involving ownership, copyright and fair use.

Do you remember the saying that everything you need to know you learned in kindergarten? It applies here.

Don't steal. If you want to use something that belongs to someone else, ask first.

This is a tricky new landscape, of course. Google, for example, has copies of billions of photographs on its servers that don't belong to the company. Google uses them to help people find photographs and Web sites through search by displaying thumbnail images (reduced versions about as big as your thumbnail). Google's offerings are protected by the fair use clause of the U.S. Copyright Law. Of course, this law applies only in the United States, and the Web extends globally. Much of this new world is governed by ethics and etiquette instead of laws and enforcement.

And because sharing is part of the culture of the Web, an effort called the Creative Commons project emerged in 2001. The project aims to provide legal protection to those who wish to share their work. Photographers, artists and others can mark their work with a Creative Commons license, which can range from "all rights reserved" to "some rights reserved," allowing others to use their work as long as they are given credit.

The Licenses

Attribution
CC BY

This license lets others distribute, remix, tweak, and build upon your work, even commercially, as long as they credit you for the original creation. This is the most accommodating of licenses offered. Recommended for maximum dissemination and use of licensed materials.

View License Deed | View Legal Code

Attribution-ShareAlike
CC BY-SA

This license lets others remix, tweak, and build upon your work even for commercial purposes, as long as they credit you and license their new creations under the identical terms. This license is often compared to "copyleft" free and open source software licenses. All new works based on yours will carry the same license, so any derivatives will also allow commercial use. This is the license used by Wikipedia, and is recommended for materials that would benefit from incorporating content from Wikipedia and similarly licensed projects.

View License Deed | View Legal Code

Attribution-NoDerivs
CC BY-ND

This license allows for redistribution, commercial and non-commercial, as long as it is passed along unchanged and in whole, with credit to you.

View License Deed | View Legal Code

Attribution-NonCommercial
CC BY-NC

This license lets others remix, tweak, and build upon your work non-commercially, and although their new works must also acknowledge you and be non-commercial, they don't have to license their derivative works on the same terms.

View License Deed | View Legal Code

Attribution-NonCommercial-ShareAlike
CC BY-NC-SA

This license lets others remix, tweak, and build upon your work non-commercially, as long as they credit you and license their new creations under the identical terms.

View License Deed | View Legal Code

Attribution-NonCommercial-NoDerivs
CC BY-NC-ND

This license is the most restrictive of our six main licenses, only allowing others to download your works and share them with others as long as they credit you, but they can't change them in any way or use them commercially.

View License Deed | View Legal Code

Credit: Creative Commons

Creative Commons licenses are less restrictive than traditional copyright; copyright owners can choose one of six licenses shown above to determine the rights they want to retain.

In 2012, the number of Creative Commons–licensed photographs on Flickr topped 200 million.

▶ Digital camera basics

Today many different devices can capture digital photographs. Everything from mobile phones to video cameras to tablet computers—and even most laptop computers—can take still images, and the traditional forms of still cameras commonly have the ability to shoot video. Given this overlap, it can be difficult to focus on one form compared with another.

▶ ▶ *Two kinds of digital cameras*

Following is a look at basic features and operation for standard point-and-shoot, consumer-grade cameras. Much of the information also applies to digital single-lens reflex (DSLR) cameras—cameras with detachable lenses—because they are often made by the same companies, so there is a bit of standardization among the features.

But first, let's look at the differences between the two primary types of cameras:

- A point-and-shoot, or all-in-one, camera is more compact, easier to use and more affordable. Its lens and flash are built in, and most are equipped with a video mode.

- A DSLR camera will capture better photographs because its image sensor is commonly 10 times larger. But it is more complex to use and usually costs two to three times more than a point-and-shoot. Accessories such as lenses and a flash cost extra, and video mode is not as good.

That said, camera manufacturers continue to improve the quality of point-and-shoot cameras while they make DSLRs easier to use and more affordable. So what may be true today in this comparison might be less true tomorrow. Most DSLRs have a green button, or easy mode, that turns all settings to automatic, allowing a user to take photos with the camera as if it were a point-and-shoot.

Using the automatic settings is a good idea for anyone just getting started. Today's digital cameras are built with sophisticated automated settings. Try these first and see if they work. If not, make adjustments.

▶ ▶ *Basic camera functions*

Camera modes: A dial on the top of the camera will control the shutter speed. Choose the icon that represents the moment you are trying to capture. Options usually include sports or action, portrait of a person or people, landscape photo and low-light or night photo.

Zoom: Most point-and-shoot cameras have two types of zoom: digital and optical. Be careful to use only the optical zoom. If you zoom beyond the range of the optical zoom, the digital zoom kicks in and basically just begins cropping the outside of the image to make it look like you're getting closer. Optical zoom is provided by the lens and does not affect the image quality.

Flash: A function with a lightning bolt icon, probably on the back of the camera, will allow you to toggle through several flash settings. Auto flash means the camera will determine whether flash will be used. You can also turn off the flash or "force" the flash, making the camera flash even when it doesn't think one is needed (this is helpful when bright backlighting leaves shadows on a subject's face). There is also a red-eye reduction mode for the flash, which will likely fire a preflash to compensate for the beam bouncing from the back of the subject's eyes into the camera lens. You can also try changing angles or having the subject look slightly to the side of the lens to avoid red eyes in photos.

View/delete: Find the function that changes your camera mode from shooting pictures to viewing pictures already captured. Every camera also has a trash-can icon for deleting images. Make a habit of viewing photographs on your camera as you shoot and deleting the ones that you are certain will not work. If you've ever worked with professional photographers, you've probably noticed them doing this constantly.

What is it? | **What's *Next?*** | Summary

⬇ SHOOTING BETTER PHOTOS WITH A DIGITAL CAMERA

The greatest advantage a digital camera provides you is the ability to review the photo on the camera's screen immediately after you snap a picture. Use it! If something is wrong with the photo, try again. The more you shoot and the more adjustments you make based on what you're seeing in the camera, the more you'll improve the chances that you'll get the photo you want.

"Beyond moment, composition is high on my list," Colin Mulvany of The Spokesman-Review says. "How you frame a photograph comes down to a decision of what not to show the viewer. Good composition cuts away the unimportant elements that distract the viewer from the message of the photograph."

Remember to consider several factors before hitting the button to take a photo. Nothing is more important than lighting. It is critical to account for the lighting in whatever situation you find yourself, and you can shoot a photo in, essentially, one of three ways:

1. With natural (or ambient) light only

2. With a flash as the primary light source (in a low-light situation)

3. With a mixture of flash and ambient light

The best photographs are shot in the first situation, when nature provides the correct light. But be careful not to shoot in harsh, bright sunlight, especially if you're photographing people. If the sun is in front of the subjects, it will create face shadows and make people squint. If the sun is behind the subjects, their faces will be dark.

You can compensate by forcing the flash in this situation, meaning you can use the flash setting on the camera to override the automatic function and make the camera use the flash.

Cloudy and partly sunny days actually provide the best light for outdoor photography.

▶ Shooting mug shots

The mug shot is one of the most likely assignments for journalists who are not photographers. Although it seems like this would be a no-brainer assignment, you need to consider several things when framing a head shot.

Use the right lighting. Try to avoid using a flash if possible; a flash can add shiny spots to the person's face. Move the person outside or near large windows to take advantage of natural light, and then make sure there are no weird shadows on the person's face.

- Avoid high-noon sunlight and strong backlight.

- Try to photograph when the skies are overcast, or try to photograph in a situation that replicates overcast skies.

- Use a flash as a last resort.

- Pick the right background; make sure it's as neutral as possible and simple, not busy; and darker is usually better than lighter.

- Position the subject away from any walls; if you don't, you'll end up with flash shadows behind the subject.

- Make sure there isn't anything like a lamp or pole "growing" out of the person's head.

Val Hoeppner, a trainer and consultant who managed multimedia education for the Freedom Forum Diversity Institute in Nashville, Tenn., says the biggest mistake amateurs and beginners make is that they don't get close enough to their subjects or to the action happening in front of them. During training sessions, Hoeppner uses a quote from photojournalist Robert Capa to reinforce her point: "If your pictures aren't good enough, you aren't close enough."

"I tell non-photojournalists that if they think they are close enough to a subject they should take 10 steps forward and then take the photo," Hoeppner says. "That might sound like an exaggeration, but filling the frame with all the information you want the viewer to see (and none that you don't) is one of the most important things you can do to improve your photography."

Take Better Photos   Here are some additional tips to help your shooting, courtesy of Craig Sailor, former photo editor at The Olympian and The News Tribune newspapers in Washington State:

- **Hold the camera steady:** Dig your elbows into your body or place them on something. Use two hands. Lean against a wall. Do anything you can to be still when shooting.

- **Fill the frame:** When photographing people, don't leave too much headroom, that space above their heads. The subject's face should be near the top of the picture, not in the middle.

- **Focus on one thing:** When shooting a person or group of people against a busy, complex background, focus on the person's eyes. The automatic focus function can focus on only one thing in the image, and a person's eyes will make the photo look the sharpest.

- **Get closer:** Most amateur photographers fail first by not changing their positions. They see something they want to capture in a photo and take out their camera and shoot without moving around. A professional photojournalist, in contrast, will move all over the place to get the right angle.

- **Go vertical:** If the subject is vertical, turn the camera into a vertical position to shoot it.

- **Shoot action:** Capture the moment whenever possible, and avoid posing people. Find the setting on your camera that snaps the shutter at 1/500th of a second or faster to shoot anything really fast, such as sports action.

The second-biggest mistake that new photographers make, according to Hoeppner, is that they don't take enough photographs.

▶ More time leads to better photos

The goal of these instructions is to help journalists who are uncomfortable with cameras to start learning how to take better pictures. One of the most

> "This is a great image because it gives the viewer a ton of information," Hoeppner says. "This is a simple image, with simple composition. Photographers often forget to change their point of view . . . getting high and looking down on this scene is the only way to show the expanse of this disaster."

Credit: David J. Phillip-Pool/Getty Images

A single home is left standing among debris from Hurricane Ike on September 14, 2008, in Gilchrist, Tex. Floodwaters from Hurricane Ike were reportedly as high as eight feet in some areas, causing widespread damage across the coast of Texas.

important factors to consider is time, because it's difficult to capture great photographs in a hurry. If you want to improve your photography skills, your first step should be to find more time when you go out to shoot.

"The biggest mistake I see when non-photographers try to do documentary photography is that they are impatient," Colin Mulvany says. "The best documentary shooters let the events and moments they are photographing unfold in front of their camera lens. Doing this type of work takes an investment of time, but the difference between a real image and a manufactured one is huge."

Mulvany says that when he is working on a long-term project, his goal is intimacy in his photographs. A photographer can't achieve this unless the subjects have formed a trust bond with the photographer. So, be honest with your subjects about the story you are trying to tell.

Mulvany recalls photographing a middle school student for her entire year in seventh grade. He told her up front what he needed to see and shoot—both the good times and the bad moments. Knowing that he had "cut the deal" with her allowed him to feel comfortable with being around at awkward moments—like when she was kissing her boyfriend behind the gym after lunch.

In addition to spending more time with subjects or assignments, it's important to take more photographs. It's a simple numbers game: The more shots you take, the better chance you have to get the one you want.

"Shoot a lot, not just one or two," says Deb Cram, director of photography and multimedia at Seacoast Media Group. "It makes things easier on the editing end plus increases your odds that you'll have a good image."

DRILLING DOWN ⬍

Capturing Audio and Images for a Slide Show   Val Hoeppner recommends doing the A-roll—the main audio interview—before shooting photographs. "The interview will put the subject at ease, and it will give the photographer ideas for images that will highlight good audio," she says.

Here is the rest of her checklist:

> Make sure you know how to operate both the audio recorder and the camera before you go out on an assignment. Test both to make sure you are getting sound and images.

Wear your headphones so you can hear what the microphone hears. Don't be afraid to stop an interview if there is too much background noise. Move to a quiet place and ask your question again.

Shoot plenty of images; for every minute of audio you will need roughly 20 photographs.

Listen closely during the interview, and shoot photographs that will complement the audio.

Shoot wide, medium and tight shots. You will need a variety of images to move your slide show story along.

Shoot plenty of detail shots; these tight shots will help you transition from one thought to another without confusing the viewers.

Record plenty of natural sound; as you are making photographs you should be listening for natural-sound opportunities.

Remember that you are telling a story. Multimedia is more than a buzzword; it is a powerful storytelling tool.

What is it? | **What's *Next?*** | Summary

⬇ WORKING WITH DIGITAL PHOTOGRAPHS

Once you have captured images on a digital camera, you are ready to experience the real power of digital photography: editing on a computer. The ability to crop, tone and resize any photograph quickly and easily will significantly improve your chances of having the right photograph for your journalism.

But there can be too much of a good thing. Most photo-editing software is equipped with many more features than are necessary for everyday use. Naturally, some people get carried away with all the interesting things they can do to a photograph instead of limiting themselves to what they should do to a photograph to make it better. I'm talking about using filters in Photoshop to posterize or crystallize your photographs. It's fun to explore the possibilities of this cool technology, but converting documentary journalism into art was probably never your goal (and probably never should be). The same goes for mobile apps on smartphones such as Instagram and Camera Plus.

In reality, before editing photographs you should submit yourself to that well-known precept of the physician's Hippocratic Oath: First, do no harm.

And remember to use your values and judgment when editing photographs digitally. Altering photographs by adding or removing objects is strictly forbidden in documentary journalism.

"Editing should maintain the integrity of the photographic images' content and context," says the Code of Ethics of the National Press Photographers Association. "Do not manipulate images or add or alter sound in any way that can mislead viewers or misrepresent subjects."[2]

▶ **Edit your take**

Because you will have taken more photographs than you can use, you will need to learn to select the best ones to edit and prepare for presentation. Like capturing compelling photographs, this is a skill that takes thoughtful consideration to master.

Another word of caution before we get started, however: New digital tools have made it much easier not only to improve a photo but also to make it lie about reality. And because the audience knows that, it's more important than ever for anyone publishing a piece of photojournalism to make sure it reflects the scene accurately.

Mulvany says good photo editors help photographers separate themselves from the emotions that went into finding and capturing images. They view photographers' images strictly from a storytelling point of view. Photo editors always ask: "What image best illustrates the story? What image captures a moment that will best communicate the message of the story with clarity to the viewer?"

---

[2]Code of Ethics, National Press Photographers Association, n.d. www.nppa.org/professional_development/business_practices/ethics.html.

Photo editing is more than just picking one image out of a hundred taken, Mulvany says. It involves the ability to "see a picture within a picture," he adds. "Many times, when I have sat down with a photo editor, they have found crops or moments within pictures I've passed over in my own edit."

If you can, enlist someone else in your photo editing. A cold eye on your photos, with your description of the story, may yield surprising feedback. Or it may simply reinforce your own direction.

"Editing skills result in the end product, which should be clean and easy to read; not filled with clutter and confusion," Deb Cram says. "You only have the audience for a brief time, so if the image has impact—having emotion or an interesting graphic element—that helps."

▶ Manage digital photos on your computer

First, you need to learn how to move photographs from your camera to your computer and organize them once they are there. The standard method of getting pictures off your camera is by connecting a USB cable from the camera to the computer. After you plug in the cable, any modern computer will recognize this new peripheral and automatically walk you through the process of downloading the images.

Organizing photographs is essential, especially if you plan to be a prolific photographer. There are, of course, software programs that will help you. If you are using a Mac, iPhoto is already on your computer and is a good basic solution for both organizing and simple editing of photos. Windows Photo Gallery offers the same functionality if you're using a PC. Because both programs are free and already on your computer, they can be good places to start.

If you have been using either iPhoto or Windows Photo Gallery for a while and feel as though you're outgrowing their capabilities, consider Google's Picasa or Yahoo's Flickr for online photo storage and organization. Both offer free accounts with generous limits on the number of photographs you can upload, and both offer professional accounts with small annual fees if you need more storage.

First, create a master folder on your computer where all your photos will live. You will create subfolders within this master folder, but it's important to have one "home" for all your photos. For one thing, it will make it easier to back up your photos to an external hard drive, a USB flash drive or a cloud storage system like Dropbox.

Next, determine your system for naming photos and folders. The obvious options are by time and by subject. If you follow the time format, you would create a subfolder for the year and then subfolders within the year for each month of the year. From there you can create folders for specific subjects, which is a good idea if you consistently shoot photographs of the same things (hiking or sunsets, for example).

Photos coming off your digital camera will have file names like IMG_0239.jpg. This, of course, tells you nothing. Most modern operating systems allow you to override these file names with something more intuitive as they are copied to your computer. You will find it easier to manage your photos if you take this opportunity to change the generic file names to something you will recognize. A combination of date and subject is usually the most powerful. For example, an IMG_0239 and the rest of the series of photographs taken on July 4, 2014, from Liberty Lake could be named 20140704_libertylake_0239.jpg. Notice that the date is written numerically, starting with the year (2014) and followed by the month (07) and day (04)—this method will keep your photos in chronological order on your computer.

Spaces in file names may limit a file's compatibility with some computers or operating systems, so use underscores (like_this) to separate words.

Of course, continuing advances in technology are making all this easier. Flickr and Picasa have powerful tagging functions that make it easy to classify your photographs without messing with the file names. iPhoto has facial recognition tagging and geotagging, allowing you to search your photo collection according to the face of the person you are looking for or where the photo was taken.

▶ Edit digital photos on your computer

There are many different ways to edit a photo on your computer. (See Table 5.1.) You can use free software that is already on your system, such as iPhoto or Windows Photo Gallery; a free online service, such as PicMonkey, or a paid online service, such as Pixlr; a photo-hosting solution such as Picasa or Flickr; or the more traditional way, with a commercial editing program such as Photoshop.

Because so many options exist, and the object of this lesson is to help you get up to speed as quickly as possible, we will use Photoshop Elements as our example. Elements is very likely all the Photoshop you'll ever need, and it costs less than $100 (compared with $600 for the full version of Photoshop).

The basic photo-editing tasks outlined in this chapter with Photoshop Elements will work similarly in other programs as well. For example, cropping a photo is the same whether you're in Photoshop or iPhoto or Picasa. The actual tool icon might look a little different from one program to another, but the basic function will be the same.

No matter which program you use, it's a good idea to follow a few simple steps when preparing an image for online publishing:

DRILLING DOWN

Advanced Photoshop Guidance If you are comfortable with basic photo editing in Photoshop or Photoshop Elements and want to learn more advanced techniques, check out www.photoshopessentials .com/photo-editing. It's one of many quality sites online offering free Photoshop assistance.

Table 5.1 QUICK GUIDE TO SOFTWARE AND ONLINE SERVICES TO USE FOR DIGITAL PHOTOS

On your computer	iPhoto, Windows Photo Gallery	Good for basic photo editing, especially when you don't have an Internet connection
Online full-featured	Picasa, Flickr, Pixlr, PhotoBucket	Good for managing and organizing your photo collection, sharing your photos with others, basic editing functions
Online editing only	Photoshop Express, PicMonkey, FotoFlexer	Good for quick and basic editing of photos, even on a smartphone
Value-priced software	Photoshop Elements, Paint Shop Pro	Good for advanced photo editing without an Internet connection for less than $100
Professional	Photoshop	Good for serious photographers and Web designers who need all the functionality that comes with the $600 price tag

1. **Edit a copy of the photo—never the original:** When you open a photo in an editing program, do a **Save As** and change the file name by at least one character. This will give you an exact copy of the original, just in case your editing goes awry.

2. **Crop the photo:** Few, if any, photos are perfectly composed when the camera makes the image. Use the program's cropping tool to omit unnecessary information in the photograph. Cropping a photo should answer this question: What's the most important information in the photo?

3. **Resize the picture:** If you are posting a picture to a blog, for example, all you need is a small, low-resolution image. Not sure how big? To find out how many pixels wide to make your photo, find a photo somewhere on the Web that is approximately the target size you want to achieve. Right-click (or control-click if you use a Mac) and select **Properties.** A pop-up box will display the measurements of the image in pixels.

4. **Modify the resolution:** Computer monitors, as we discussed earlier, display images at 72 ppi, so reduce the resolution of any image you publish online. This significantly reduces the file size, which means it will load faster.

5. **Tone and color correct the picture:** Most photo-editing software can quickly improve the quality of a photograph by automatically adjusting the tone, contrast, brightness and other features. Because it's so simple, there's no reason to skip this step. Simply try the functions, and if the photo looks better, save your work. If a particular function doesn't improve the photo, **Undo** the function.

6. **Save a Web version:** Because photos displayed on computers need to be only 72 ppi, and because people don't like to wait for long downloads, it's important to compress your images, squeezing out unnecessary data that won't be used by a Web browser anyway. The goal is to reduce the file size as much as possible without lowering the quality of the photo.

7. **Keep it simple:** If all you need is to crop or resize a photo, try one of the online services such as Pixlr or FotoFlexer. It takes only a few moments to upload a photo and crop it down to the part you really need.

Of all the online photo-editing services, including Adobe's Photoshop Express Live, PicMonkey is probably the easiest to use. The functions are labeled clearly on the left of the editing screen, so if you want to crop a photo, you click **Crop**. It really couldn't be easier to use.

Credit: PicMonkey

> PicMonkey is a free online image-editing tool
that is extremely easy to use. <

You will find the same basic level of photo editing on other online services, such as Picasa, Flickr and Photobucket. If you want to do more, however, Photoshop Elements offers professional-level features, is relatively easy to learn and costs less than $100.

▶ ▶ Using Photoshop Elements

Photoshop Elements has several advantages, including the ability to do cutouts and create collages, which is helpful if you're creating graphics for a Web site. Photoshop products also usually do a better job than other software when it comes to automatically correcting the color and tone of photographs.

Elements comes with an organization tool called Adobe Bridge, which helps categorize and classify photos and makes batch editing a breeze.

Let's go through each of the primary steps (with a few variations) from the list above for editing a photo for online publication and take a look at how each works in Elements.

1. Edit a copy of the photo—never the original: When you open a photo in Photoshop Elements, select **Save As** under the **File** menu and change the file name by at least one character.

To manage a group of photos, launch Adobe Bridge with the maroon folder icon in the top left corner of the Photoshop Elements interface. When you are working in Bridge, group-select a series of photos (use the Apple key or Control key to select multiple photos): then select **Batch Rename** under the **Tools** menu.

2. Tone and color correct the picture: Color correction is one of the most daunting processes for amateur photo editors. And the full version of Photoshop can be intimidating because it has much more power and many more features for color correction than most people will ever use. Elements offers the best of both worlds: an easy process and powerful software.

On the right side of the screen is a tool window with three tabs on top: **Edit, Create** and **Share.** Click **Edit,** then select **Quick**. This will change the window (and the tools set on the left) so it is limited to just a few basic, essential functions. **Red-eye fix, Levels, Contrast, Color** and **Sharpen** are displayed, each with an **Auto** button providing one-click automated correction on each of the functions. (There are also precision controls for each function if you want to control the details.)

3. Crop the photo: Using the **Crop** tool, click and drag across the image to select the part you want to keep. Then hit **Enter** or click the green check mark to activate the crop.

4. Resize the picture: Under the **Image** menu, select **Resize,** then **Image Resize**. Enter the desired width in pixels, and the software will automatically calculate the height as long as the **Constrain Proportions** box is checked. You can also reduce the resolution to 72 ppi, if necessary.

5. Save a Web version: One of the best features available in Photoshop and Photoshop Elements is the **Save for Web** function under the **File** menu. This will launch a new window that displays the current version of the photo you are editing on the left and a new, compressed version on the right for easy comparison. Adjust the settings on the far right to minimize the file size, which can be viewed below the compressed image, while you maintain the same level of quality you see in the uncompressed image.

For photographs, use the JPEG compression algorithm. Or you could also use PNG. If you are editing a graphic with text, then the GIF format is the best option.

▶ ▶ *More advantages of Photoshop*
In addition to offering better image manipulation and photo management that is still easy to use, Photoshop also offers several functions that Web-based or standard image-editing programs do not.

Photoshop has been used as a graphics program since it first hit the market more than 20 years ago. Tools that allow you to create shapes or text, combined with its **Layers** and **History** features, make it an indispensable tool for any Web designer. But you don't have to be a professional to find benefits.

You can batch process many photographs simultaneously with Photoshop or Photoshop Elements.

Photoshop Elements makes it easy to edit a photograph.

Create graphics: Shapes or text, or shapes with text and images, can be created easily with Photoshop. Because each element has its own layer, it's easy to edit and modify one part of the graphic at a time.

Modify screenshots for design: Capture a screenshot of a Web page you want to redesign, then slice it up in Photoshop and move elements around

→ *Cropping photos is like editing stories: Keep only the most important content.* ←

Image Size

Learn more about: Image Size

[OK]

[Cancel]

[Help]

┌─ Pixel Dimensions: 2.06M (was 22.9M) ─┐

Width: `980`   pixels ▼

Height: `735`   pixels ▼

┌─ Document Size: ─┐

Width: `13.611`   inches ▼

Height: `10.208`   inches ▼

Resolution: `72`   pixels/inch ▼

☑ Scale Styles
☑ Constrain Proportions
☑ Resample Image:

Bicubic (best for smooth gradients) ▼

→ *Be sure to "constrain proportions" when resizing an image.* ←

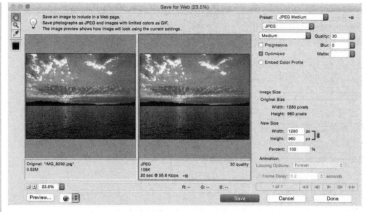

Save for Web (23.5%)

Save an image to include in a Web page.
Save photographs as JPEG and images with limited colors as GIF.
The image preview shows how image will look using the current settings.

Preset: JPEG Medium
JPEG
Medium   Quality: 30
☐ Progressive   Blur: 0
☑ Optimized   Matte:
☐ Embed Color Profile

Image Size
Original Size
    Width: 1280 pixels
    Height: 960 pixels
New Size
    Width: 1280 px
    Height: 960 px
    Percent: 100 %

Animation
Looping Options: Forever
Frame Delay: 0.2 seconds

Original: "IMG_8292.jpg"   JPEG   30 quality
3.52M   105K
                            20 sec @ 56.6 Kbps

23.5%   R: --   G: --   B: --   1 of 1

Preview...   Save   Cancel   Done

> Photoshop's Save for Web feature makes image preparation
for Web sites easy. <

and change colors and fonts. This is an easy way to test and communicate ideas around design.

Create cutouts and collages: Use the **Magic Lasso** tool to create a cutout photo quickly, eliminating the background to enhance a professional-looking design. Or combine several photos to make a collage for your Web site or blog. Photoshop's **Layers** makes this simple to do.

What is it?   **What's *Next?***   Summary

⬇ PUBLISH YOUR PHOTOS ONLINE

After you've decided which photographs to publish and you've prepared those images for publishing, you're ready to consider another important step in the process: how to present those images for maximum impact.

Photographs published in newspapers and magazines receive serious thought by page designers, presentation editors, photography directors and other creative staff. Since you probably don't have that luxury, you'll need to learn how to make a few basic decisions quickly that will maximize the impact of your photographs online.

"Presentation is all about first impressions. It tells the viewer what you are showing them is or isn't important," Mulvany says. "A photograph needs only simple presentation to be effective—especially in photojournalism.

Clean design, proper image size and selection is all that is needed to give a photograph the showcase it deserves. Bad presentation just wastes the viewer's time."

Photographs, and especially slide shows, can attract huge audiences online. Most news Web sites publish slide shows on a regular basis to attract, and keep, digital audiences. When the Seattle Seahawks won the Super Bowl in 2014, our team at KING 5 made shooting and publishing photographs a priority, which might seem counterintuitive for a TV station, given the amount of video we routinely produce. But, during the run-up to the big game and subsequent celebrations in the city, it was the photo slide shows that captured the lion's share of the audience on king5.com.

▶ Publish photos on a blog

Size matters, especially when you are publishing photos online. As you work through the primary steps for editing photographs outlined earlier, remember to select a size in pixels that will provide the most bang for your buck—or, in this case, power for your pixel.

It's important to discover the maximum possible width in pixels for display on your blog. If you don't know HTML well enough to view the source code and find the information, try uploading a test photo in several different widths until you find one that fits. Most blog designs accommodate images with a maximum width of 700 to 900 pixels.

After you know the maximum width you can use for a horizontal photograph, you know how wide to make your best horizontal photos and how tall to make your best vertical photos. Not all your photos, mind you. You will publish only the best 20 to 30 percent of the photos you take. You should reserve the largest display size for the images you hope will have the most impact. If you publish all your images the same size, your audience will become numb to the large format, and the photos will lose their impact.

Adding a photo to a blog post is simple with any modern blog platform. Simply place your cursor in the blog post where you want the image to go and click the icon or menu item that allows you to add an image. Then browse to the location on your computer where your Web-ready image is stored and select **OK.**

A few items to remember:

1. Wrap text around the photo: Use the **Align** function for any photo that doesn't span the entire column and set the photo to display on the right. The HTML code to make this happen is *align="right"*; this will wrap the text under the photo after it moves it to the right side of the column.

2. Use intuitive alternate text: Since search engines can't read photos, the way that Google and Yahoo and others learn about a photo is through the alternate text you enter through the blog software when adding a photo. This also helps sight-impaired readers who rely on voice-powered browsers to read Web pages to them. So, in the alternate text, make it clear in a few words what the photograph is about. The HTML code for this is *alt="kids play in Lake Park."*

3. Remember that it's only a link to a photo: When adding a photo to a blog post, you are merely adding a link to the photo so that a Web browser knows where to find it. The browser will then make a copy and display it with your blog post. The photo has to be available on the Internet—it can't live only on your computer.

Most modern blog software programs account for this by allowing you to upload your photos to their Web servers when you're adding photos. Other options include using an online service such as Flickr, Picasa or Photobucket, which can be configured to display a larger image when someone clicks over from your blog.

4. Use a screenshot and a link: If you don't have a photo to use with your blog post and you're writing about another Web site, make a screenshot of the Web site's home page and include a link to the site when uploading the image on your blog. This helps your audience get a feel for the site you're discussing and provides an easy way for them to click and visit that site.

▶ Create and publish compelling slide shows

Even if you are just starting out with digital photography, you should consider publishing slide shows and photo galleries when one or two photos just won't do justice to the subject.

Although there aren't any hard-and-fast rules about how many images to use in a slide show—it all depends on the subject and the quality of the images—a good rule of thumb is to create a slide show if you have a minimum of six to 10 good-quality images. Many news sites create slide shows with dozens of photographs in each one, so realize how much shooting you will have to do to build a comprehensive slide show—after you edit out the bad photos.

How to Build a Good Audio Slide Show

Limit the slide show to two to three minutes in length: A slide show longer than three minutes risks losing viewers' attention.

Use the right amount of photos: Too many photos crammed into one slide show usually means each photo appears for only a second or two, barely enough time for viewers to take each one in. Too few photos means each photo remains on-screen way too long, making the slide show feel drawn out and boring.

Match the photos to the audio: If the subject is discussing a cat, don't show a duck. Whenever possible, include a photo of the speaker at the beginning of the talk so the viewer knows who is speaking.

Use captions: Write a clear and concise caption for each photo, including the people, places or things being shown and the photographer's name; this takes the guesswork out of a slide show.

Avoid awkward transitions: Soundslides and some other slide-show editors allow the user to adjust the length of time each slide is on the screen. If the slide show has narration, tweak each slide to fade in or out during natural pauses and breaks to lessen the chance of awkward transitions.

Avoid using overpowering music: Many slide-show editors add royalty-free music to their projects to support the narration and heighten the drama. If they forget to adjust audio levels, however, the music may drown out the narrator or interviewee.

[*Source:* Based on Mark S. Luckie, "5 Common Photo Slideshow Mistakes," 10,000 Words, February 25, 2009. www.10000words.net/2009/02/5-common-photo-slideshow-mistakes.html.]

It's important to think about any slide show as another version of the story you are trying to tell. Order the images so the show is both logical and compelling. Your best image should lead the series, even if it doesn't come first chronologically. It is considered the opening of the story and can be followed by the rest of the images in an order that builds the story from a beginning to an end.

"Nowadays, in photojournalism for a newspaper, you can't just think of the still image," says Cram. "It's about multimedia storytelling using various tools to reach people."

Most blog software platforms make it easy to add a photo gallery. To create a slide show, especially one with audio, additional software is needed. Photoshop Elements offers easy slide-show creation through its Bridge platform. But if you want to add audio to your story, Soundslides is the tool of choice for most multimedia journalists, although some prefer video-editing software such as Final Cut.

Of course, to create a compelling slide show you need to begin planning it before you get to the publishing step. To present the most effective package, you will need to have been thinking about it while capturing the images. A good rule to follow if you plan to create a slide show is to take wide (far-away) and medium shots plus lots of tight shots (close-ups).

It's critical to have all the shots you need when building a slide show. Whether created with just photos or photos and audio, your slide show should have all the elements of a good story:

An attention-grabbing opening

A logical progression that builds to a climax

A walk-off or finish that provides a sense of summary

Once you have determined which photos accomplish this for a particular story, create a new folder on your computer and move the edited photos you have chosen to it.

▶ ▶ *Building a photo gallery in Photoshop Elements*
To build a photo gallery in Photoshop Elements, simply select **Create Web Photo Gallery** under the **File** menu and follow the instructions to determine which photos to use and how they should be displayed.

1. Under **Source Images** select **Folder** and then browse to the folder on your computer that contains the photos. Then select **Destination** and determine where the finished product should be created. It's a good idea to create a new folder as your destination because Photoshop will create seven different files when it builds your gallery.

2. Use the **Options** pull-down menu to modify the following settings:

   General: Decide between .htm and .html extension for the final product.

   Banner: Fill in the desired title, credit and date information.

Large images: Determine how big you want to display the images, the quality and the title.

Thumbnails: Determine how big you want to display the thumbnail images.

Custom colors: Modify the colors for the background, banner, text and links.

Security: Enter copyright information to protect your work or use this area to enter full credits for the slide show.

3. Click **OK.** Admire your work.

▶ ▶ *Building an audio slide show in Soundslides*

When you want to add audio to your photographs (see chapter 6 to learn how to gather and edit audio), using Soundslides is the way to go. It's not free, but the basic version costs $40 and the Plus version $70, and it's worth it if you plan to create slide shows with audio.

Without knowing any computer programming or Flash programming, you can create a dynamic movie of pictures and sound in just a few minutes by uploading a folder of photos and an audio file.

The user interface is ridiculously simple—just how it should be. The first screen asks whether you want to start a new project or work on an existing (or old) project.

DRILLING DOWN

The Big Picture   Veteran Web developer Alan Taylor launched a photojournalism blog called The Big Picture on The Boston Globe's Web site; see www.boston.com/bigpicture. It's a great resource for examples of quality news photography.

Other excellent resources are InFocus on The Atlantic's Web site (www.theatlantic.com/photo) and National Geographic (www.nationalgeographic.com/photography).

The next screen has only two buttons: Click **JPG** to browse and select the folder of images you will use; then click **SND** to browse and select the audio file you will use. You can also determine the output size, but the program allows you to do that later.

To build a slide show, rearrange the thumbnail photos to the desired order by clicking and dragging. Then drag the bars that separate the thumbnails in the project bar below to line up the

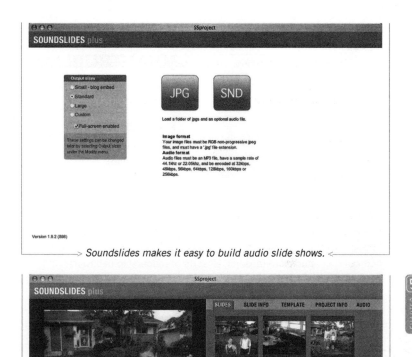

Soundslides makes it easy to build audio slide shows.

Soundslides lets you control the timing of the images to align them with the audio track.

image transitions with the audio file, so the timing of the audio matches the visual from the images.

After your timings are set, you can use the tabs along the top of the screen to add captions, modify the look and add headlines. When you're finished, click **Export**, and moments later you'll have a folder called "publish_to_web" that is ready for the Web. Upload it to your Web server and link to the "index.html" file.

JOSH TRUJILLO

▶ **PUBLISHER** |
SeattlePI.com
(@joshtrujillo)

Credit: Photo courtesy of
Josh Trujillo

Back when print was the leading local news and information delivery method, publishers would convene studies to research all sorts of readership behaviors. One thing that was almost always proven: Photographs were the top entry point that would draw readers into a story. Now in our digital world, online metrics show similar trends. Visuals are engaging, can be powerful and are a strong element to draw a viewer into your content. There is significant value to that, and it should not be overlooked.

Take social media: It is mostly photography based. Facebook found its biggest success as a stream for shared photos. Twitter—although often used for text and hyperlinks—can show photos, with those photo posts usually rising to the top. Instagram—well, that's obviously all about sharing images.

With a constant river of visuals being shared, the obvious challenge any street-level visual communicator now faces is rising above the noise, in a crowded space, where everyone has a camera in his or her pocket and the ability to publish. With dedication, understanding of the basics of your camera, knowledge of composition, understanding of the power of a moment and knowing what kinds of visuals can engage your audience, you can create visuals that rise above that noisy flow. The best visuals show viewers something they have never seen, or something they may see every day in a fresh, new way.

Something that has largely disappointed me about much of the photography I see in digital publications is that often it is static and kind of lifeless. If a story is about development, it will often include what I call a building mug shot. If it is about a person, it will sometimes include a picture only to show what the person quoted looks like. But visual communication has so much more potential than that. People are drawn to faces, expressions, moments, irony and a unique look at their community. Much of journalism is contemplating humanity, so why not show people in action? Your images can simply be used to show the reader what a static object looks like, or they can be crafted to engage, fascinate and communicate on another level.

The tools you can use to convey your information or observations are not limited to still photography. Digital publishing has the potential to make storytelling a completely immersive, exploratory experience for a reader. One of my favorite methods is to use Photosynth or some other kind of 360-degree panoramic tool to make images that a viewer can explore. If the goal is really just to show the viewer what a scene looks like—in some cases an important goal—why use a potentially mediocre photograph? Make it interactive. Allow your reader to explore. You can use Instagram's Hyperlapse to speed up and steady a scene. You can use slow-motion video to show small movements. As long as the method you are using maintains reality and is a truthful representation, why not try it? Just, please, leave the extreme filtered look out of your news-related photos—keep that in the 1970s.

I sometimes think of the success of a communicator as similar to that of a comedian. A comedian uses humor to call out things that are common and understood in our society. The magic and laughter there seem to happen when the audience realizes that the person on stage recognizes something funny or unusual in our world that they have also noticed. But the audience members perhaps haven't ever consciously thought about that before. It takes the comedian to trigger the audience's collective realization of the subject. Journalism (visual, text, etc.) can harness that same magic. Sure, your audience may not laugh, but when you can use visuals to show readers something that they may see every day but never really noticed before, you have achieved success. And it's likely your audience will grow to appreciate your work.

[*Source:* Written by Josh Trujillo at the request of the author.]

⚑ PHOTOGRAPHY IS A CRITICAL TOOL FOR JOURNALISTS

Taking good photographs is a matter of being in the right place at the right time. Often, reporters find themselves in the middle of something newsworthy or interesting, so basic photography skills are critical for anyone who considers him- or herself a journalist.

"The best photos happen when you least expect it," Colin Mulvany says. "Good documentary photographers understand this and are prepared to snap their shutters when the moment presents itself."

Because journalism is about providing readers and viewers with information, the addition of photographs is fundamentally just good journalism. Pictures are information, so if you're a reporter, you will become a better one if you learn to take photos on assignment. At a minimum, you can supplement your work by adding mug shots and other basic photos to all the stories that currently don't have accompanying art.

Today's digital world offers tools for consuming media in a way that is more beautiful, powerful and portable than ever before. From high-resolution tablet computers to large-screen smart TVs to bigger and bigger smartphones—at their best, they can be immersive.

"We need the ambition to tell really great stories really well in order to stand out. Our best work needs to be great," Young says. "If we can combine the power of immersive experience with great stories, great storytelling skill and the distribution power of these devices, we can realize a potential for telling news stories that has never existed before."

GET GOING Checklist ✓

☐ Get your hands on a camera and practice shooting with different types of light: natural, flash and a mixture of both. What differences do you notice?

☐ Practice filling the frame in your photos by shooting close-ups. If you don't have a lens that zooms, you'll have to move uncomfortably close to your subject.

☐ Create a slide show from a series of photographs using Photoshop or Soundslides.

CHAPTER 6

> ## Making Audio Journalism Visible

I t's an unlikely journalism success story: a 15-year-old murder investigation, told in 12 separate chunks over 12 weeks, without photographs, video or even text. It captured the imagination—and conversations—of millions around the United States, with each new episode sparking the kind of fervor normally reserved for a hit reality TV show or championship sporting event.

"Serial," a podcast series from the makers of "This American Life," launched in 2014 and quickly rose to number one on the podcast chart in Apple's iTunes Store. According to Apple, with more than 5 million downloads and streams, "Serial" is the most popular podcast in history.

The series explores the 1999 strangling death of a Baltimore high school student and the conviction of her 17-year-old former boyfriend for the crime; the young man, who is now serving a life sentence, became nationally famous almost overnight.

"It has sparked a following straight out of the golden age of radio," observed The Wall Street Journal. "It also has managed a rare trick in a noisy news and entertainment landscape driven by a lights-camera-action mind-set: It gets people to drop everything and just listen."[1]

The "Serial" story unfolds with good old-fashioned reporting and interviewing by Sarah Koenig and her team. It hooks listeners with a compelling "whodunit" feel of the case as the boy—now man—convicted of the crime maintains his innocence throughout numerous interviews with Koenig. The jailhouse phone conversations are the centerpiece of the series, which also includes new interviews and excerpts from the trial.

---

[1] Ellen Gamerman, "Serial Podcast Catches Fire," The Wall Street Journal, November 13, 2014. www.wsj.com/articles/serial-podcast-catches-fire-1415921853.

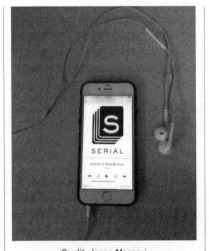

Credit: Janae Masnovi

The podcast series "Serial" launched in 2014 and quickly rose to number one on the podcast chart in Apple's iTunes Store.

Koenig guides the audience through the story with a personal, conversational tone unheard in conventional journalism. Listeners are provided with substance as well as style, however; the show reveals information that apparently neither the defense nor the prosecution had been aware of at the time of the trial.

"We wanted it to feel like a live thing . . . a *vital* thing in the sense of the word of being a living thing—as we went," Koenig told Terry Gross of NPR's "Fresh Air." "And we were still reporting last week for the final episode."[2]

People took to the Internet and debated each twist and turn, each fact discovered and each angle explored. Conversations on reddit, Twitter and many other digital communities lit up with "Serial" talk when each installment was released. Countless news articles were published about the "Serial" case, further analyzing the evidence and reportage.

"I look forward to every Thursday in a way that I don't remember awaiting the release of an episode of anything recently," filmmaker Jason Reitman, whose film credits include "Up," told The Wall Street Journal. "There's something very intimate about someone telling you a story that close to your ears."[3]

| **What is it?** | What's *Next?* | Summary |

ⓘ AUDIO JOURNALISM

Go back a few years and consider the financial meltdown of the U.S. home mortgage market in 2008 and 2009. It generated reams of text coverage and

---

[2]"Serial Host Sarah Koenig Says She Set Out to Report, Not Exonerate," "Fresh Air," NPR, December 23, 2014. www.npr.org/2014/12/23/372577482/serial-host-sarah-koenig-says-she-set-out-to-report-not-exonerate.

[3]Gamerman, "Serial Podcast Catches Fire."

hours of video. But some of the most compelling, informative reporting was delivered with audio.

"The Giant Pool of Money," a first-ever collaboration of NPR's news division and "This American Life," won a prestigious Peabody Award and was widely hailed as the best piece of journalism produced on the economic mess. The Peabody judges praised the segment for the "arresting clarity of its explanation of the financial crisis."

"Somehow audio has been considered the 'invisible' medium," says Karin Høgh, a podcasting expert based in Denmark. "However, if done right, audio can be as powerful in journalism as written articles or even TV and video."

With just a few simple tools—a microphone, recorder and free software (and a computer connected to the Internet, of course)—you can create full-featured segments that sound like radio episodes and distribute them as podcasts to build a loyal audience. Or, with a mobile phone, you can quickly publish a brief report from the scene of a breaking news event.

Journalists who didn't cut their teeth in radio reporting tend to relegate audio to second-tier status, figuring that text is more informative, photos and video more compelling. That kind of thinking makes less sense than ever now that the Internet gives every news organization and every reporter the option of producing audio journalism.

"Given the ease with which audio clips can be produced, it is surprising that their use is not more widespread," Jim Stovall, Edward J. Meeman Distinguished Professor of Journalism at the University of Tennessee, wrote on his JPROF blog. "Reporters and journalism students must stop thinking about sound as an exclusively radio format and adopt it as a reporting tool that can be learned and used to effectively deliver information to readers or listeners."[4]

As a form, audio is flexible enough to work in many different settings. Digital tools have taken a process that once required several people and made it easy for one person to master, from beginning to end. Years ago, radio reporters wrote cue sheets for the audio engineers to work with, alone or with the reporters. Today, with high-quality portable digital recorders, free editing software, free sound clips and music released under Creative Commons, all the phases of audio publishing can be handled by the reporter alone.

"Sound allows listeners to 'see' with the best lens of all, the mind," Stovall wrote on his blog. "A personal example: For years, I have shocked people

---

[4]Jim Stovall, "Audio Journalism II: Forms and Formats," JPROF, March 6, 2009. http://jprof.blogspot.com/2009/03/audio-journalism-ii-forms-and-formats.html.

Writing for the Ear Jonathan Kern offered these tips to journalists getting started with audio storytelling in the first and second editions of "Journalism Next":

- **Write conversationally:** Rely on the same vocabulary and syntax you'd use if you were talking to your peers—which may be quite different from the idiom of news writing.

- **Write simply:** Put just one idea in each sentence—and if the ideas are complicated or obscure, repeat them elsewhere in your story. Remember, people will only get one chance to grasp what you're saying.

- **Let people feel the tension and meet the characters:** And just as a joke will fall flat if it doesn't have a good punch line, an audio story will lose its audience if it isn't structured so that people stay tuned in to hear how it ends.

- **Be a performer:** Remember, when you're writing for the ear, you are not only a journalist—you're also a performer. Everything you do has to be geared to keep your listeners' attention and their interest. If that flags, you won't get a second chance.

by telling them that as a baseball fan, I would much rather listen to a radio broadcast of a game with a good announcer than watch the game on television. The reason: Video cameras are too confining; they do not give me a picture of the whole field or even a significant portion of it. If I am listening to it, however, I can 'see' everything, and the experience is much more enjoyable and fulfilling."

Painting sound pictures for listeners is a skill that takes practice, much like making real pictures with photojournalism. And as with photography, what you can accomplish is limited only by the time you're able to spend. Without text, without visual images, audio can produce a rich experience.

People often listen to audio journalism while commuting or otherwise spending time alone; they may use earphones for a more individual experience. "An audio journalist can create a more intimate and personal relationship with the listener and take advantage of that in many different ways," Karin Høgh says.

"Writing well for the ear is a lot like telling a joke or an amusing story," says Jonathan Kern, a longtime NPR producer and author of "Sound Reporting: The NPR Guide to Audio Journalism and Production." "Whether you've done an investigative report on police misconduct or an audio postcard on whitewater rafting, people won't pay attention unless you present it in a way that's engaging from start to finish."

▶ Why audio journalism is important

Capturing in words a story's particular sights and sounds has always posed a challenge for reporters. Photographs usually solve the visual end of this equation. Now, with the advent of cheap digital audio recorders and the ubiquity of smartphone apps, reporters can bring readers even closer to their stories by enhancing their reporting with audio clips. Or in some cases, such as "Serial," stories can be told better in audio than in other forms, especially on subjects that do not lend themselves to visual storytelling.

Interviews, unfortunately, are the most common form of audio journalism. Because most people are not compelling speakers, especially in extemporaneous situations, too many journalists end up producing lifeless audio reports that add nothing more to their stories than text or stand-up video interviews would.

Audio journalism is about more than just getting a sound bite. Even if an interview is the crux of the story you're trying to tell, audio can help you build a more textured, layered experience for your audience.

"I find audio journalism an excellent possibility to let people who are not so articulate get a voice and be heard," Høgh says. "By creating an atmosphere of confidence and relaxation, you can record the interviewee at such length that you afterwards, at your computer, can edit, add and mix the recordings."

Plus, as Høgh points out, audio journalism has characteristics that can't be matched by other forms of media:

Presence: On location, a reporter can literally bring readers to the story. The simple fact of being there boosts credibility and interest.

Emotions: Tone of voice, expressions, intonation and pauses—in the words of either the reporter or the sources—can enhance the message.

Atmosphere: Natural sound—the sound that's naturally happening around you as you report—helps pull the listener in close. Natural sound can be anything—weather sounds, crowd sounds, machine noises, whatever's happening in that particular setting.

"Using these assets, you can communicate your 'personal' perception of the events and add many facets and also take advantage of audio as a background medium," Høgh says.

By combining voice-overs, natural or environmental sound and sound effects (for transitions), you build a multidimensional story much like a compelling written narrative or a great documentary video.

▶ How news organizations use audio

Although radio is no longer the exclusive format for audio journalism, it's still the place to find the most consistent and best examples of the form.

NPR (formerly National Public Radio) sets the standard, and the audience knows it. NPR's audience grew 95.6 percent between 1998 and 2008 and hit a new high in 2013 with an average of 27.3 million listeners each month, according to the State of the Media report by the Pew Research Center.

Some might think "boring old radio" would be the first to get left behind now that people routinely watch TV shows and videos on their mobile phones. But NPR has made the most of its new-media opportunities.

The key to NPR's success stems, at least partly, from the connection to the audience its reporters and show hosts are able to make. Voice and audio are personal, allowing an intimacy and engagement that are rare in today's era of information overload.

How many other news organizations can talk about "driveway moments"? That's when listeners arrive at their destination (a driveway or a parking garage, for example) but can't turn off the radio because the story is too good. So good, in fact, that NPR has packaged and sold collections of these stories as CDs for years on its Web site and at Amazon.com.

NPR reporters are highly skilled and experienced. They expertly gather natural audio, conduct professional interviews and work with engineers to produce stories of the highest quality. Other news organizations that are not native to audio journalism, especially newspapers, have found that attempting to re-create the NPR experience is an unreachable goal.

Still, audio offers numerous opportunities even to journalists just getting started. Here are some ways to use it:

Reporter overview: Newspapers such as The New York Times routinely post quick, simple audio overviews by reporters that accompany their articles. The Times calls them "Backstory."

Podcasts: Regular episodes on a selected subject help build an audience but can be time-consuming and difficult to establish in the beginning.

Audio slide shows: Photojournalists have discovered the power of adding audio to their images to tell richer, more compelling stories.

Credit: National Public Radio

NPR has made an aggressive push beyond radio to capture Web and mobile audiences by providing digital users with an opportunity to listen to news, music streams, podcasts and other programs online.

Breaking news: With free services such as Utterli, a reporter can file a quick audio report from anywhere by mobile phone, to be published on a Web site.

"Audio collected in the field by reporters on a breaking story has an atmosphere that paints a picture quickly," says Marissa Nelson, senior director for digital media at the Canadian Broadcasting Company. "It's often powerful, and almost always lapped up by users."

Reporters love doing audio, Nelson says, because "if they don't have time to tap something out, they can call and leave an MP3 for us." (The proliferation of smartphones has led to more quick reporting with video than with audio, a topic we will explore in the next chapter.)

Most forms of audio journalism have just a few basic ingredients:

- Interviews and voice-overs
- Natural or environmental sound
- Imported sound clips, including music

But the recipe is different depending on the goal and the subject, from breaking news to audio slide shows to full, NPR-like stories where sound is not a supplement but the main way of conveying the message. Here's how to gather and edit each type of audio for use in any of these formats.

What is it?　**What's *Next*?**　Summary

⤓ GET STARTED WITH AUDIO

We all know how to talk, so it's tempting to think that improvisation is good enough when it comes to adding voice to a multimedia project. It's not. Whether you're interviewing a subject on "tape" or providing voice-over narration for video, preparation will make the difference between a professional-level project and something that sounds like amateur hour.

Invest a little more time to plan and prepare your voice contribution, and you'll make the rest of the effort worthwhile. For example, taking just a moment to decide where to record an audio interview can help you avoid ending up in a coffee shop with too much background noise. Here are some easy-to-follow directions on how to get ready for prime time.

▶ Recording interviews

As the cornerstone of audio journalism, successfully recording an interview is critical to incorporating audio in your reporting. While you may feel uncomfortable at first (or just want to avoid the hassle), there is real benefit to using this medium.

"A lot of print reporters are a little skittish about being on tape or performing in any way, but one of the things about audio is that you can't hide. You're there," said Amy O'Leary, multimedia producer for The New York Times, in an interview for the Nieman Journalism Lab Web site. "I mean some of the most revealing moments in an interview is not what someone says but the length of pause before they answer the question. And unless you have the question there in the tape, you don't get that interchange and the full richness of the interview."[5]

The advantage of mastering the audio interview in the digital age is being able to assess the number of different situations where it can be used.

---

[5]Zachary M. Seward, "Audio Tips for Print Reporters From NYT Sound Sage Amy O'Leary," Nieman Journalism Lab, March 26, 2009. www.niemanlab.org/2009/03/audio-tips-for-print-reporters-from-nyt-sound-sage-amy-oleary.

An interview recorded digitally can be used in many different ways:

- Stand-alone audio file with a news story (especially powerful if the subject matter is emotional or the subject is well-known)

- Podcast

- Stand-alone audio file for a blog post

- Audio to accompany a photo slide show (works best when mixed with natural sound)

▶ ▶ *Choose your location*
Ideally, you'll be able to record the interview face-to-face. If possible, pick a place that's quiet and has good acoustics. A person's home or office is a good option; a coffee shop or restaurant is not. If the interview needs to occur outside, make sure it is as far away as possible from traffic and crowds.

Although it's possible to record a phone interview, the lower quality of the sound that you will get makes listening difficult for long periods of time. If phone is your only option, try to keep the interview focused, and then edit it down to just the most salient points. One way of doing this is to ask some questions before you turn on the recorder; then start recording and ask a couple of the most important questions again.

▶ ▶ *Gather natural sound*
Natural sound is not the same as background noise. An interview should be done in a setting that allows the voices to be recorded without interruption. Separate from the interview session, however, it's always a good idea to search for those sounds that will help describe the setting. Are power tools being used? Is it a noisy office with lots of chatter and phones ringing? Is it an outside setting where you can hear the bugs and the birds?

If there is natural sound to be had, take just a few minutes and record it—without anyone talking. "You might feel silly just standing there holding your mic in the air, but when you get back to edit your stuff, you'll be glad you have it," said Kirsten Kendrick, a reporter and morning host on KPLU radio, an NPR affiliate in Seattle.

You should record natural sound in uninterrupted 15-second increments. That way you'll avoid the problem of not having enough to use in editing. You can always make a clip shorter by cutting it, but you can't make it longer, so make sure the material you're working with is long enough to cut from.

▶▶ *Prepare your subject*

The people you're interviewing deserve to know a few things before they start answering your questions, and you need to be clear on the basics yourself:

- What's the story, and what part will audio play?

- Who is the audience, and where will they go to hear this interview?

- How long will the interview be?

- What kinds of questions will you be asking? Consider sending a few to the interviewee in advance, so he or she can think about answers.

- How much editing (if any) will be done to the audio? Knowing that you'll have time to take out long pauses and "ums" and "ahs" helps your subject relax. Try to alleviate the interviewee's tension about being on the air and having to fill every second.

It's a good idea to have several questions prewritten. You may have years of interviewing experience, but this is a different kind of interview. You have to think not just about the speaker's words but about the equipment (is the microphone in the best place to pick up the voice?), the environment (is that air conditioner too loud?) and pacing the questions and your responses so it all sounds good later. You don't want to script every question, because the best questions come from an interviewee's comments, and the natural ebb and flow of conversation is an important quality of an audio interview that makes listening easier for the audience.

▶▶ *Watch what you say*

Your interviewee isn't the only one whose voice will be recorded. It's important to realize that some interviewing techniques commonly used by print journalists don't work well in audio interviews.

When interviewing for print, you've probably learned to rely on expressions such as "I see" and "Really?" to let the interviewee know you're listening and understanding. For audio, try to use nonverbal cues, such as nodding, instead. Though sounds like "uh-huh" can work to encourage your subject to keep talking, on tape they can distract listeners and may even cover up something the speaker is saying. So, remember, while the subject is talking, KEEP QUIET.

You may have also honed your skills researching before an interview, so you can establish a rapport with your subject by showing knowledge of his or her field. When working with audio, it's still great to develop a rapport; just try to do it before you start recording. Listeners want to hear from your subject, not from you. Your job is to ask questions. Adding some context after a subject's response—for example, spelling out an acronym the speaker used—can be helpful. But try to keep it to a minimum.

▶▶ *Try delayed recording*

If your goal is to produce an audio clip that will accompany a news story, consider waiting until the end of the interview to do the recording. You conduct the interview just as you normally would, but then ask the subject to speak again about a couple of the most salient points while you start recording.

Many interviewees find this technique reassuring because they can practice the wording of important answers earlier. Delaying recording also helps you as the reporter because you know which questions produce the best answers, which in turn helps you edit and process the audio. Instead of going over an hour of recorded material to find a few minutes worthy of publishing online, you'll have only a few minutes to edit. Of course, you'll also want to listen for happy accidents, where a seemingly throwaway question produces something you hadn't expected. In less formal stories, where you're not consulting an expert about a specific topic, letting speakers ramble on tape can often pay off.

▶▶ *Mark the best spots*

When you do record an entire interview, you'll want to mark the points where the speaker said the best stuff. Most journalists have little alarms that go off in their heads when they hear quotes or nuggets of information that will be especially useful. When that happens while you're recording, write down the time elapsed shown on your digital recorder. You'll save loads of time when you get back to the office, whether you're producing audio for the Web or just need to get to the best quotes quickly to write your story.

▶ **Doing voice-overs**

You can't control everything that happens when you are interviewing someone, but you do have complete control of the voice-over that you record to go with an audio slide show or a video story. Here's how to make the most of it.

▶▶ *Write a script*

Having a detailed script that you can practice a few times before turning on the microphone will greatly enhance the quality of the finished product. Crafting an effective script is quite different from writing a news story. The fewer words, the better; the purpose of voice-over narration is to amplify or clarify what may be obvious on-screen. Short, simple declarative sentences work best.

Audio scripts should not be written in the inverted-pyramid style. At a conference on narrative journalism at Harvard University in 2009, Amy O'Leary of The New York Times recommended enticing listeners with a compelling hook in the beginning and building up to the middle to make your main point (which would commonly be your lede in a print story).

O'Leary said that, based on responses to audio slide shows at the Times, people will listen to an audio piece for 15 to 20 seconds to test it. Once you get them past that point, they'll usually listen until the end. But you have to grab them immediately. Put your best quote up front and don't worry about explaining it, she said. You can backfill later.[6]

Avoid long, complex sentences and even long words. Choose words that are easy to say and have a good flow when put together—something that you can determine only by reading your script drafts aloud. Build in natural breaks for taking breaths. Allow some moments of silence—verbal white space—so the narration doesn't overpower the visual elements of the story.

▶ ▶ Warm up

It may feel weird, but stretching the muscles in your face and mouth and humming or singing will help prepare you to be recorded. Open your mouth as wide as possible and move your jaw back and forth. Then hum some deep notes and some high notes and sing a few bars of a familiar song, like "The Star Spangled Banner." Your facial muscles and vocal cords need to be ready to perform, just as your other muscles do before you go running or play basketball.

▶ ▶ Find operative words

Marilyn Pittman, who serves as a guest lecturer at the Berkeley Graduate School of Journalism, teaches journalists about audio and video performance. She recommends finding the operative words in your script— the words that are essential to telling the story—before you begin recording.

Which are the operative words? Pittman says they're the words that would convey the story even if you didn't put them in complete sentences. Usually they are the classic who-what-where-when-why-how words—nouns, adjectives, adverbs, titles, names.

---

[6]Lois Beckett, "Amy O'Leary: Writing for Audio," Telling True Stories in Turbulent Times (a blog covering the 2009 Nieman Conference on Narrative Journalism), March 21, 2009. http://ncnj09.blogspot.com/2009/03/amy-oleary-writing-for-audio.html.

▶▶ *Keep it conversational*

While focusing on operative words is helpful, don't allow yourself to be too distracted by them. It's more important to be natural and conversational as you speak. If it sounds like you're reading a script and deliberately choosing specific words to emphasize, the entire project will suffer. Aim for a flowing, conversational reading of your script first, and then add the more complicated technique of emphasizing operative words. When you're getting started with voice-overs, it can help to mark places in the script where you should take a breath. Pittman recommends finding places within sentences, not just at the ends.

Box 6.1   PUNCHING UP YOUR VOICE-OVERS

Marilyn Pittman, a San Francisco talk-show host and stand-up comic, coaches journalists on audio storytelling. In her workshops, she recommends that you first identify the most important words—called operative words—in your script. Then, as you read, practice emphasizing those words in four ways:

Volume: Increase or decrease the volume of your voice when saying an operative word. Emphasizing a word by making your voice louder is also called "punching" it.

Pitch: Change the pitch of your voice when you say an operative word, going up or down the scale, high to low, falsetto to baritone.

Rhythm: Change the rhythm of your voice—the space between the words. Pause before the word, or after the word, or both, to emphasize it. A pause is especially effective before a word that's complex or highly technical in nature. A pause is also effective when you're introducing a new idea in a script.

Tempo: Change the tempo or speed of your delivery to emphasize an operative word. You might pick up the tempo where the copy is less important, and then slow down when you hit a section with more operative words, to emphasize them. Or you might stretch out a vowel in an operative word.

⬇ GEAR UP AND GET OUT THERE

If you are a reporter, interviewing people is what you do. Sure, you can transcribe the best quotes for print, but does that really provide a complete report? Did one of your sources elaborate on an important topic, but then you paraphrased to avoid a long quote? Did someone say something with emotion, or in a way that you can't quite convey in print?

Most news stories can be improved with the addition of audio clips. Based on subject matter alone, a newspaper reporter could easily produce audio clips on more than half of the stories turned in. That may sound too ambitious if you haven't edited and published audio for the Web before. But after you do it a couple of times, it will become second nature.

The first step is to find the tool that's right for you, whether it's a smartphone app or a digital recorder. No one uses a typewriter for writing now that laptops and personal computers are affordable, and don't think you can use an analog recording device to do audio journalism in the digital age.

▶ Choose a digital recorder

As with most digital tools, the market offers plenty of options. Deciding which one is right for you starts with a basic question: How much can you afford to spend? You can buy a digital recorder for as little as $30, but even a little bit more will help you progress along the continuum from entry level to professional. You can find inexpensive devices calling themselves digital recorders, but unless you can transfer the files from the recorder to your computer, you'll be unable to edit the files or get them onto a Web site where readers can listen to them. That's like writing a story on a computer and not being able to send it to your editor.

When you choose a recorder, key points to consider include audio quality, digital file format and compatibility with your computer, ease of use and ease of transferring files. You should consider only recorders that have external inputs for mic and headphones. Here are a few options at different price levels.

▶ ▶ *Under $100*
Olympus WS-400S (see www.olympusamerica.com).

Recording is one-touch and easy. The recorder is tiny, so it's very portable. Reviewing recordings with fast-forward or rewind is a bit clunky; this can be done more easily on your computer. Files can be quickly downloaded onto a Windows or Mac computer through a USB 2.0 port. No additional software needed, which is nice.

▶ ▶ *$100–$250*
H1, H2 and H4 Handy recorders (see www.samsontech.com); Olympus LS-12 and LS-14 (see www.olympusamerica.com); Tascam (see www.tascam.com).

Arguably the best value in digital recorders on the market as of this writing, the H2 and H4 offer professional quality and advanced features at about half the cost of other devices. Both recorders have multidirectional microphones built in, allowing you to record in more situations without plugging in an external mic.

▶ Smartphone apps and SoundCloud

Another popular option in the age of do-everything smartphones is to download an app for audio recording and use the built-in microphone on the phone. This allows you to carry (and buy) one less gadget. This works great if you simply want an audio record of an interview to transcribe later, but realize the quality of the audio will not be as good as what a stand-alone recorder can produce. If you are planning to publish the audio, you will need to weigh the convenience of using one device against the quality of sound you can capture and offer your audience with a stand-alone digital audio recorder.

If you don't have a digital audio recorder, you can look into using your mobile phone or MP3 player. The Apple iTunes Store, for example, features more audio recording apps than you could ever hope to try on an iPhone or iPod Touch. These devices also come equipped with a Voice Memo app that is a decent place to start.

The mic quality is not as good as you'll find on a dedicated device, of course. But for many situations, a free or 99-cent app on your smartphone could be all you need. Here are some apps to try:

- iTalk (free)
- Audio Memos (free)
- DropVox ($1.99)
- iProRecorder ($2.99)

The key to capturing quality sound with your smartphone is using an external microphone. There are many options available for iPhones, Android phones and Windows phones. Some plug into the headphone port, some into the charging port and some can be connected via Bluetooth. Regardless of how you connect a mic or which mic you use (try to find the best mic available, of course), you will greatly improve the quality of your audio recording simply by using one.

The ubiquity of smartphones and social networking has logically led to the creation of an audio-driven social network. Enter SoundCloud, a social audio-sharing service that drew 175 million unique users per month in 2014. Musicians and remixers first discovered SoundCloud in 2007, when it launched in Sweden. The founders moved the company to Germany the next year and have been guiding one of the most successful social networks on the Internet not born in Silicon Valley.

SoundCloud has opened a door to a massive audience online and an effective distribution network for audio content. Think of it as being like Facebook or Twitter for links to online news, but, instead of text, photos and video, it's audio journalism that is being shared.

"The range of usage by journalists is quite broad," SoundCloud's Manolo Espinosa told ReadWrite. "Some use it to help fuel the online distribution of terrestrial programs, others for additional content that is of interest to their listeners."[7]

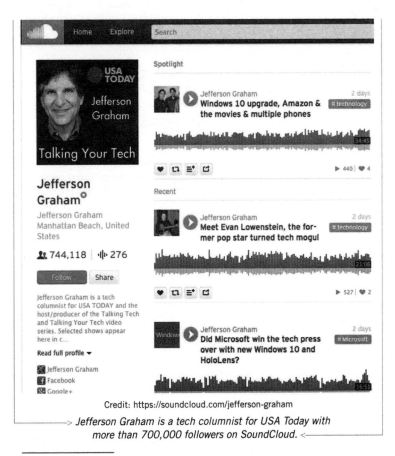

Credit: https://soundcloud.com/jefferson-graham

Jefferson Graham is a tech columnist for USA Today with more than 700,000 followers on SoundCloud.

[7]John Paul Titlow, "How Journalists Are Using SoundCloud," ReadWrite, September 28, 2012. http://readwrite.com/2012/09/28/how-journalists-are-using-soundcloud.

The primary function of SoundCloud is the sharing of audio files, but the company's smartphone apps have been upgraded to include editing features as well. News organizations have experimented with both aspects of the platform. Jefferson Graham, a tech columnist for USA Today and the host/producer of the "Talking Tech" and "Talking Your Tech" video series, has more than 744,000 followers. The Guardian of London posts a weekly politics interview show that has more than 1 million followers. In 2012, The Huffington Post used SoundCloud to allow readers to submit robocalls they received from political campaigns.[8]

Try using SoundCloud for your audio reports. With a free account, you are limited to 180 minutes of uploaded audio and can see only some of your stats. You can get more upload hours by paying for a Pro or Pro Unlimited account, which also comes with more extensive analytics.

As with Twitter or Facebook, it's simple, easy and quick to get started on SoundCloud. Log in with Facebook Connect or create an account, upload your first audio file and you're off. (See Drilling Down: Getting Started With SoundCloud for next steps.)

▶ Record with your computer

To record a phone call digitally, you'll need another piece of equipment: a telephone recording control unit, available at RadioShack and elsewhere for around $25. (You can also download an app on your smartphone such as Recorder to do this.) Journalists have used a version of this unit for years to record phone calls to their analog microcassette tape recorders. And those same journalists have drawers filled with jungles of tapes in which they can never

---

DRILLING DOWN ▲▼

Getting Started With SoundCloud Once you've logged in or created a new account on SoundCloud, follow these steps from Mashable's guide to getting started to get a full tour of the audio social network.

1. Set up your profile.

2. Upload a new track.

3. Make a playlist.

4. Share and download sounds.

5. Explore and follow other users.

[*Source:* Denise Lu, "The Beginner's Guide to SoundCloud," Mashable, November 10, 2013. http://mashable .com/2013/11/10/soundcloud-beginners-guide.]

---

[8]Titlow, "How Journalists Are Using SoundCloud."

find what they need. That's one reason to go digital—organization. With the control unit device you can record directly to your computer, which makes it easy to store files in an organized fashion. And listening to an interview is easier on a computer (or smartphone) than with tape because most playback software programs have slider bars that allow you to move through sections on fast-forward.

Your hardware is ready. Before you use it, check your state law. In about a dozen states, it's illegal to record someone without that person's permission. So it's safest to get into the habit of starting interviews by asking, while the recorder is running, "OK if I tape this?"

Next you need software to manage and edit the sound files on your computer. There are literally hundreds of options for audio software, ranging from Adobe Audition (the choice of most radio professionals, it costs about $300) to Audacity and JetAudio, popular free downloads that work great.

DRILLING DOWN

Digital Audio Formats

MP3: The best known of the digital audio formats, compressed MP3 files play on just about everything (Mac, PC, iPod, mobile phone and more) and have an .mp3 file extension.

WAV and AIFF: Completely uncompressed audio files that are high in quality but too large to transfer quickly across the Internet; they end in .wav and .aiff.

WMA: This is a common format for Windows users; this compression-decompression software was developed by Microsoft as part of its Windows Media suite. The abbreviation stands for Windows Media Audio.

[*Source:* CNET.com.]

No matter which audio software you use, before you start you need to learn about a few basic settings on your computer:

> **File name:** You will either need to select **File—New** and create a file or choose where on your system this new file will be created. Either way, you need to think about what to call your file. This is a good time to come up with a standard file-naming convention that will serve you for months and years to come. Include the date and the name of the person you'll be talking to—so an interview on Valentine's Day with Bill

Gates would be named "150214billgates." It's also helpful to create new folders by year or month for more organization.

Format: If possible, you should record in WAV format so your files are uncompressed and, therefore, of the highest quality. You can convert the files to MP3 (both Audacity and JetAudio can do this) once they're edited for publishing on the Web. You need to worry about this only when recording directly into your computer, not when using a digital recorder.

Input/mic level: Make sure the software is set to capture data via microphone input. Then find the setting that adjusts the microphone level, and set it to about 70 percent of the possible level. This will help you record audio that is neither too quiet nor too loud.

▶ **Use an external mic**

Using an external mic can be an extra nuisance during an interview, but the added sound quality is well worth the effort. Two types of external microphones are on the market: a standard mic with a cord and a wireless or lavalier mic. Let's take a look at the advantages of each.

A standard mic with a cord is helpful if you are interviewing more than one person at a time or you want to include your own voice on the audio clip so listeners can hear the full interview instead of just selected quotes. It is also the best way to gather natural—or environmental—sound, which can be spliced into the audio segment to enhance the listening experience.

A wireless or lavalier mic is most helpful when you're in the field and your goal is to capture the voice and words of one person. Although they might seem intimidating at first, wireless mics are really very simple. They have two halves: a battery pack and miniature microphone on a cord that clips onto the person you want to record (this sends the signal), and a battery pack and cord that goes into your recording device (this receives the signal).

Here's how to get started:

Clip the mic on the interviewee's lapel and give your interviewee the battery pack to put in a pocket. Don't forget to turn the device on!

Connect the receiver pack to your recording device, turn it on and put it in your pocket, purse or bag. Then operate your recorder as you normally would: Hit the **Record** button when you're ready and the **Pause** button if there's a break in the action.

Credit: ©iStockphoto.com/iceninephoto

A lavalier mic system has a wireless base station and a clip-on microphone.

▶ Use headphones

The only way to be sure you're recording good audio is to plug in a pair of headphones and listen while you record. That's why, if you're serious about quality, you should use only the type of digital recorder that has an external headphone jack.

The best headphones cover the ears and block out other sounds so you can hear an accurate representation of the audio your device is recording. It's not necessary to have a noise-canceling feature on your headphones.

It may seem awkward at first to hear your voice through the headphones while you're interviewing someone. Practice with a friend until you're comfortable, before you do it while on assignment.

▶ Prepare before you go out

As with all electronic equipment, it's important to test everything thoroughly before you try to use it on assignment for the first time. After you understand how everything works, you still need to be prepared for those worst-case scenarios that will, inevitably, happen.

"As a journalist your focus should mainly be on the content—the person you are talking to, the environment, the setting and the event you want to convey," advises podcasting expert Karin Høgh. "So, the better you know the interface of your recorder, the reach of your microphone, the volume, the more relaxed and focused you can be during recording. And the less time you will have to spend in postproduction."

What is it?   **What's *Next?***   Summary

⬇ EDITING DIGITAL AUDIO

It's helpful to have an understanding of digital file formats as you get started. For both video and audio files, the goal is to record with the highest quality possible and then edit the files before compressing them to publish and distribute them online. Compressing makes the files smaller so they download faster.

If you download or listen to audio on a Web site, it is probably in a compressed format. You're probably familiar with some of the formats, such as MP3 and Windows Media.

It's important to keep file size in mind when editing audio files, even if compression algorithms will magically shrink your files and make them download faster. From a content standpoint, you want to leave only the most important and compelling pieces in. Everything else should be removed. This will speed up downloads and streamline the listening experience for your audience.

▶ Understand digital formats

Digital audio comes in several different formats. Each uses a different "codec," which refers to the compression-decompression software enlisted to pack up a file for transfer over the Internet and unpack it for playback on a user's computer or device. Codecs discard unnecessary data, lower the overall quality and take other steps to make the file smaller. Different codecs also create specific types of files, which work only on specific players or devices.[9]

Your goal should be to provide audio clips for your audience in MP3 format for one simple reason: Virtually any computer can play an MP3. Programs such as iTunes, Windows Media Player and Real Player can play them, but those programs can't play the other proprietary formats. For example, you can't play a Windows Media file in iTunes or a Real Media file in Windows Media Player. But you can play an MP3 on any of them.

MP3 also strikes the best balance between high quality and low file size.

▶ Get ready to edit

It's unlikely you'll ever publish an entire recorded session online. You wouldn't publish an unedited interview transcript as text, and the same guidelines go for audio: You need to edit to make sure the best stuff is not obscured by content that's less compelling, less important or repetitive.

---

[9]Tracy V. Wilson, "How Streaming Video and Audio Work," HowStuffWorks, October 12, 2007. http://computer.howstuffworks.com/streaming-video-and-audio.htm.

Most journalists will do what they know first—use the audio to get quotes so they can write their stories before editing the audio for online publishing. That's great. But think about the audio editing you will do next as you listen to the entire take. If you make a note of the time when a good quote plays, you'll save loads of time when you go back to edit the take for the good stuff.

All audio-editing software programs feature convenient time track marks, so if your interview's best quote occurred 10 minutes into the interview, you write "10:00" next to the quote in your notebook. Then, when you're ready to edit, go directly to the 10-minute mark on the track and you've saved yourself 9 minutes, 59 seconds.

Editing audio is remarkably similar to editing text, so you shouldn't be intimidated when you approach this task. First, acquire the audio file if it's still on your recording device. Connect the digital recorder to your computer through USB and drag the file(s) you need into a folder or onto the desktop so you know where they are and can work with them. Most digital recorders come with a USB cord to make this easy; simply plug the cord into the recorder; then connect it to the computer through a USB port. Some recorders plug directly into the USB port without a cord (convenient for those of us who lose things). The cheapest recorders, however, even if they record digitally, do not interface with computers at all—which is why you don't want to buy one if you want to produce audio your audience can enjoy.

Professional audio-editing software, such as Avid's Pro Tools, Adobe Audition and Sony's Sound Forge Audio Studio, is largely geared toward the music industry and is not necessary if you're just starting out. Professional programs offer more powerful features, but they can be quite complex and difficult for the beginner to master.

A number of basic programs are available that are fully capable of basic editing tasks needed for great audio journalism. And many of them are free—such as Audacity, which has become something of an industry standard for entry-level sound editors.

▶ Editing with Audacity

The top priorities for any audio-editing program are that it be easy to use and able to export files in MP3 format. Audacity and JetAudio (Windows only) are excellent free options. We'll use Audacity for our examples because it is available on both Mac and Windows operating systems.

To edit:

1. Use **File—>Open** and open the audio file.

2. Crop out the bad stuff: Think about how users would best appreciate the content—in one full serving or broken up into smaller bites. Highlight areas that represent unwanted "ums," "ahs," mouth noises and lip smacking. Then simply hit **Delete**. Also crop out silence and any small talk at the beginning and end.

   Record your own voice as a test. Slowly count from 1 to 10 into a microphone and capture it digitally. Then edit your take. Highlight the section where you say 3 and select **Edit—Cut**. Then move the cursor to after the 6 and select **Edit—Paste**. Repeat a few more times with other numbers. This will give you a feel for how the sound waves represent words and sounds, and it will also show you how easy it is to edit audio.

3. Make it stereo: Some files will be mono, not stereo; this means you'll hear the audio in only one side of your headphones. You'll want to make your audio report stereo so the sound file will play in both sides of speakers and headphones instead of just one. To make it stereo, select **Split Stereo Track** from the drop-down menu by clicking on the green area in the screenshot.

   Then copy the region that you've edited by highlighting it and using **Edit—Copy**. Then click into the lower window and use **Edit—Paste**.

4. Export the file: Convert your audio edit into a compressed, ready-for-online-publishing MP3. Just go to **File** and select **Export as MP3**. Ignore the metadata interface (author, description, etc.) unless you're doing a podcast.

▶ **Try advanced editing techniques**

After you have a basic understanding of how to gather and edit a single audio track, you can begin to think about how more than one track will build a more engaging experience for your listeners. Then, as audio content becomes as flexible to you as text or photographs that can be arranged in any order, you will be able to envision more textured stories and reporting.

"Students should have some basic understanding of mixing sound tracks," Jim Stovall, the journalism professor from the University of Tennessee, says.

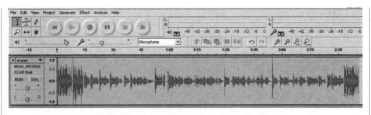

→ *Audacity makes it easy to edit audio files.* ←

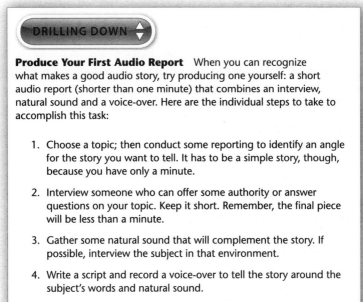

DRILLING DOWN

Produce Your First Audio Report   When you can recognize
what makes a good audio story, try producing one yourself: a short
audio report (shorter than one minute) that combines an interview,
natural sound and a voice-over. Here are the individual steps to take to
accomplish this task:

1. Choose a topic; then conduct some reporting to identify an angle
   for the story you want to tell. It has to be a simple story, though,
   because you have only a minute.

2. Interview someone who can offer some authority or answer
   questions on your topic. Keep it short. Remember, the final piece
   will be less than a minute.

3. Gather some natural sound that will complement the story. If
   possible, interview the subject in that environment.

4. Write a script and record a voice-over to tell the story around the
   subject's words and natural sound.

5. Edit the pieces together and publish the finished report online.

"The importance of beginning and ending, writing good introductions and
planning the sound story from beginning to end is basic to good audio
journalism."

Techniques to experiment with include the following:

Fade: A gradual increase or decrease in level of the audio

Cross-fading: A mix of fades with one track level increasing while
another decreases

Establishing music: Use of song clips to set the tone

Segue: Smoothly transitioning from one track to another

Transition: Connecting different tracks in a way that is smooth and natural

The best way to understand these techniques is to listen for them in other reports. Find the local public radio station near you or listen online from NPR's Web site (www.npr.org). Public radio broadcasters do a masterful job of weaving natural sound into their reports, in addition to these advanced editing techniques. And as a listener, you get a better sense of the setting for the story when you hear what it really sounds like.

What is it? | **What's *Next*?** | Summary

⬇ START PODCASTING

Podcasting has been around for many years now and has been considered "the next big thing" and an overhyped flop at different times. The "Serial" podcast in 2014 definitely brought the medium back to prominence.

Mignon Fogarty wondered if she'd missed the podcasting wave when, in 2006, she was trying to promote a science podcast she was hosting. As a science and technical writer, she knew that podcasting made sense, but she was struggling to get traction.

She grew frustrated with how much time and effort she was pouring into her podcast with little result and began looking for another path to podcasting success.

"Because I was working as a technical writer and helping science and technology people write, I would see the same mistakes over and over again," she said. "And so I got the idea of creating this simple, five-minute podcast with a quick tip every week that would help the kind of people I was working with their writing."

She named this new podcast "The Grammar Girl," and, unlike with her science podcast, she decided to make this one a hobby and made little effort to promote it. Yet in the first month it had reached the top 100 most-downloaded podcasts on iTunes, and within a couple of months it was at number two. Fast-forward a few years, and Fogarty has leveraged that initial success into a multimedia publishing company with a number of podcasts, a best-selling book and mentions in The Wall Street Journal and on "The Oprah Winfrey Show."[10]

According to the Pew Research Center's State of the Media report for 2013, the number of Americans who had "ever" listened to an audio podcast was down slightly, from 29 percent in 2012 to 27 percent in 2013. (That number will likely spike in the report for 2014 thanks to "Serial.")

Podcasting is the distribution of audio files over the Internet using RSS subscription. The files can be downloaded to mobile devices such as MP3 players or played on personal computers. The term "podcast" (iPod + broadcast) can mean both the content and the method of delivery. Podcasters' Web sites also may offer direct download of their files, but the subscription feed of automatically delivered new content is what distinguishes a podcast from a simple download. Usually, the podcast features one type of "show," with new episodes available either sporadically or at planned intervals such as daily or weekly.

▶ Vodcasting

Podcasting with video files is often referred to as "vodcasting" (video + podcasting). It works the same way but includes video. If you download a vodcast on an MP3 player that doesn't have a video screen, you will still be able to hear the audio.

In format, podcasts are similar to conventional radio programming, with a host or hosts interviewing a subject, playing music or introducing prerecorded audio stories. So it's no surprise that NPR produces some of the most popular podcasts online.

Broadcasters such as CNN, MSNBC and NPR as well as the Big Three networks compete for higher rankings on the iTunes podcasts home page. Newspapers such as The Washington Post, The New York Times and The Wall Street Journal and magazines such as BusinessWeek also publish regular podcasts.

▶ iTunes and podcasting

If you have iTunes, finding and listening to podcasts is simple. Just click the **Podcasts** link in the menu, and then click **Podcasts directory**. Search by

---

[10]Simon Owens, "How 'Grammar Girl' Turned a Single Hobby Podcast Into a Growing Media Network," Nieman Journalism Lab, February 17, 2012. www.niemanlab .org/2012/02/how-grammar-girl-turned-a-single-hobby-podcast-into-a-growing-media-network.

The iTunes store has thousands of podcasts you can subscribe to.

category or most popular. Click **Subscribe** if you'd like to add a podcast to your collection, and it will automatically update whenever new content is available.

If you know you will have regular audio files on a specific topic to offer to readers, setting up a podcast will make organizing and publishing the audio convenient for you and your readers. A good example is a sports beat writer who records interviews with coaches and players and wants to offer them to readers. Setting up a podcast will allow readers to subscribe to this podcast and automatically receive new files as they become available.

Creating a podcast that others can subscribe to is easy and free—if you have an RSS feed set up (see chapter 2 for how to set up an RSS feed). Go to iTunes and click on the **Submit a podcast** logo.

DRILLING DOWN

Podcasts on Android Since podcasts were spawned by the iPod (get the "pod" reference?) you might wonder if non-Apple users are left out. Nope. Here are some apps that will help Android and Windows phone users access this great audio content:

- Podcast Addict (free)
- Pocket Casts ($2.99)
- DoggCatcher ($2.99)
- TuneIn (free)

Credit: Photo courtesy of
Robert Smith

ROBERT SMITH

▶ **EDITOR** | "Planet
Money," NPR
(@radiosmith)

When telling a story in audio, there is one goal and
one goal only: Make sure the listener stays with you
until the end. No matter how many great facts and
interviews you have, none of it matters if someone
gets bored and turns it off.

So at "Planet Money," we try to grab listeners and
keep them entertained. And since we cover global
economics, we have to try really, really hard. No one
wakes up in the morning wanting to hear about trade
policy or commodity prices. But everyone wants to go
on an adventure. So that's what we try to deliver.

The first key to adventure in audio is to have a
mission. Tell the listener the question you are going
to answer and the story you are going to tell.

For instance, rather than say, "I want to talk about
how tariffs have shaped manufacturing around the
world," at "Planet Money" we said, "We are going
to make a T-shirt." We are going to follow the process
from the cotton fields in Mississippi to factories in
Bangladesh. It was a classic call to adventure. A
promise that we would take listeners around the
world and show them something remarkable.

That promise is the hook. But to keep someone
listening you need action. Something needs to
happen in front of the microphone.

The way we do this at "Planet Money" is to throw
ourselves into the scene. Every step in the process
of making a T-shirt had a reporter getting in close
with a recorder and interacting with the world. In

NEWSROOM INNOVATOR

the cotton fields, I walk with the farmer through the rows. We touch the cotton. I climb up the ladder into the harvester and make the driver give me a driving lesson. All of this is recorded. The listener moves with us.

We create a path for the listener to move through a complicated story. Our reporters in Bangladesh follow the women who sew our T-shirts from the factory back to their apartment. And later, we travel with the women back to their home village. We meet their parents and hear the story of how they left a life of poverty for a slightly better one in the city. The story moves.

Quest. Action. The only remaining secret to creating a compelling audio story is to tell the listener what it all means. We need the people in the story to reflect on what is happening and what it means to them.

In most "Planet Money" stories, you'll hear the reporter asking these questions on mic. And reacting to the answers. We ask the farmers if they ever thought about where the cotton goes and who is wearing their product. We ask the women in Bangladesh what their lives would have been like if they hadn't left their village for the factory.

The questions and answers create more than just facts in the stories; they are emotional moments. The listener hears the reporter and the subject in a real place interacting. And if done right, it creates a mini-drama. A moment when you can't turn off the story because you want to know the answer. You want to know what will happen next.

In print, a reader can skip to the end of an article or just stop reading. But in audio, you have to take the listener with you. Give the listener a reason to listen, a path to walk down and a satisfying end.

In this case, the end was the T-shirt itself. We sold it online. Twenty-five bucks. And listeners wanted it. By the time the series was over, the T-shirt wasn't just clothing but a character in the adventure. Someone you had gotten to known along the way.

[*Source:* Written by Robert Smith at the request of the author.]

⚑ AUDIO JOURNALISM—PART OF THE NEXT BIG THING

In chapter 4, we discussed mobile technologies for reporting and publishing. This is the area that many people think holds the most promise for audio journalism. In fact, it's important to think mobile when you picture the audience you are preparing for.

"Audio journalism is important because it is the dominant form of information distribution on The Next Big Thing in Journalism: mobile journalism," Stovall wrote on his blog, JPROF. "Despite all the current attention to texting, Web site scaling and video on cell phones and hand-held devices, people generally use these devices to talk and to receive sound, either from other talkers or from audio producers."

Even if you're not ready to create fully developed stories with different layers and advanced editing, audio journalism can be powerful as a simple and quick publishing format.

"It doesn't always need to be an edited piece," says the CBC's Marissa Nelson. "It can be, especially with news, a one-take wonder. That's what we've done, and it's worked well. If you fumble, just do a retake."

GET GOING Checklist ✓

☐ Record an interview, paying attention to the setting (background noise) and your interviewing (articulation and clarity).

☐ Test an online recording service such as Utterli from your mobile phone as if you were on a reporting assignment.

☐ Listen to at least one episode from each of five podcasts. Subscribe to those you find interesting or useful. Note the qualities that make one better than another.

☐ Explore SoundCloud. Download the app or visit soundcloud .com and find audio journalism—and music—that interests you. Follow others and think about which news and information accounts you find compelling and why.

CHAPTER 7

Telling Stories With Video

Charles Bertram was mowing his lawn on a sunny weekend in Kentucky when his assignment editor and good friend, Tom Woods, called. Woods was watching his nephew's baseball team playing and suggested that Bertram come to the park to see this remarkable kid playing on the other team.

"I was a little put off at having to go inside and get cleaned up on my day off, but I really love baseball," said Bertram, whose son was drafted by the Detroit Tigers and plays in their minor league system. "So I hustled to the park."

Adam Bender was 8 years old when Bertram showed up to his Southeastern Rookie League game at Veterans Park in Lexington. Having lost a leg to cancer when he was 1, Adam was competing with only one leg. Bertram, a photographer at the Lexington Herald-Leader, arrived too late to shoot photographs of the game, so he used the trip to meet Adam's parents and coaches and find out when the next game would be played.

Bertram came back for the next game and shot still photographs of Adam. Although the images of a one-legged boy competing with youngsters without similar disabilities were compelling, they didn't tell the whole story.

"After looking at the shoot, it was fairly obvious that I needed video to show his incredible ability to 'run' the bases," Bertram said.

So Bertram returned with a video camera and captured the action of Adam hopping to first base after a hit. The video shows Adam being handed his arm braces at first base and then rounding the rest of the bases quickly. From his catcher position, Adam blocks the plate but lets an opponent score on one play. Then he comes back on the next and records the out.

Credit: AP Photo/M. Spencer Green

Adam Bender, who appeared in Charles Bertram's viral video for the Lexington Herald-Leader, is shown here catching the first pitch at a Chicago White Sox game.

The two-and-a-half-minute video has no voice-overs. It has no titles. No interviews. No description of the setting, no context for the story. The images, the action, the emotion are so compelling the viewer is moved with inspiration. It's a powerful story of the human spirit that could be told best in video. No other form would do as much.

"I realized after one game of shooting that the only difference between Adam and his teammates was that he had only one leg," Bertram said. "His attitude was that of a baseball player—not a 'handicapped' baseball player. That's when I decided to shoot the video with no voice-overs and no interviews. I wanted the video to stand strictly on his athletic ability and without any additional attention drawn to his assumed handicap."

Published on June 1, 2008, the video went viral. At the time, the most popular video on the Herald-Leader Web site routinely received 500 views. Within a few weeks, Bertram's video of Adam had been seen more than 3 million times, with about half the viewers using the Herald-Leader site and the rest using YouTube and other sites, including Lance Armstrong's Livestrong.org.

"I had several comments from photographers who appreciated my approach to telling Adam's story," Bertram said. "In fact, I heard that after the story ran in the paper, several of his teammates were a little upset and wondered what was so special about Adam, that they were baseball players, too. I think I was prouder of that comment than anything else relating to the entire story. I knew then that I had accomplished a story on the human spirit and not just a story on a kid with a handicap."

After the story was published in the Lexington Herald-Leader and on www.kentucky.com, Adam was asked to throw out first pitches at home games for the Chicago White Sox, Cincinnati Reds and Houston Astros and was invited to a Garth Brooks benefit concert in Las Vegas. He was also profiled in a 10-minute story on ESPN and appeared on CBS, ABC and NBC and even in People magazine.

The tools have changed, but the game remains the same: Visual journalism is about telling compelling stories that connect an audience with subjects, people and issues. One of the most powerful types of visual journalism, video storytelling, is surprisingly easy to learn.

In this chapter you will learn how to use simple video equipment and common software platforms to produce basic video stories quickly. You'll find step-by-step guides and equipment highlights as well as explanations of the following:

- Capturing quick video highlights, not documentary projects

- Managing digital video on your computer

- Using common software to edit video

- Choosing online video hosting services

- Driving audience to your video

What is it? | What's Next? Summary

?, THE DIGITAL VIDEO REVOLUTION

The advent of cheap digital video cameras and free video-editing software has ushered in the video age. Instead of a $35,000 camera, an even more expensive editing station, a two-person crew and years of training, one person can produce high-quality Web video with a $200 camera and a laptop or desktop computer.

▶ Impact of digital video

The impact of the video age has been felt far and wide. For example, around the United States, thousands of high school and junior high students are receiving formal training in shooting and editing video at school. When those who go on to journalism school graduate, they will have a broader array of skills than most of the experienced journalists working today.

Digital video is so easy to produce that millions of amateurs worldwide are also publishing frequently. How about these overwhelming numbers:

- More than 1 billion unique users visit YouTube each month.
- Over 6 billion hours of video are watched each month on YouTube— that's almost an hour for every person on Earth.
- 100 hours of video are uploaded to YouTube every minute.
- 80 percent of YouTube traffic comes from outside the United States.
- Mobile makes up almost 40 percent of YouTube's global watch time.[1]

This chapter will help you understand the basic concepts of shooting and editing digital video, with enough step-by-step instruction that you will be able to pick up a camera and shoot footage and then edit it and publish it online. Is it that easy? Well, almost.

"The path to a career in broadcast journalism used to be: Get a job in an obscure small media market outpost, make your mistakes, learn the craft and move up to increasingly larger markets," says Doug Burgess, my colleague at KING-TV in Seattle who was named 2013 Photographer of the Year by the National Press Photographers Association (NPPA). "While variations of this model still apply, the playing field has been altered considerably. Instead of the limited exposure of a small-market TV station or print publication, with the development of Internet sites, a journalist now has the potential of worldwide exposure from day one of a career."

"The only way to learn video journalism is by doing it," says Angela Morris, a video journalist who worked as a multimedia producer for the San Antonio Express-News and published the Web site NewsVideographer.com. "It will take time and practice to master the fundamentals. But don't let that stop you from trying to learn, because you must just DO IT, over and over, to get good at it. The best thing you can do is attempt to make all your mistakes as quickly as possible."

▶ A versatile form of journalism

Now that video is easier for everyone to produce and to view online, any kind of journalist can participate. As a result, some TV news companies have broken up traditional news teams to create MMJs (multimedia journalists) or VJs (video journalists). Also known as backpack journalists or "one-man

---

[1] "Statistics," YouTube, January 2015. www.youtube.com/yt/press/statistics.html.

bands," they work solo and serve as both reporter and videographer on assignment. Nonbroadcast news organizations have also jumped in, publishing documentary video stories, breaking news, in-studio stand-ups and all manner of other features in video.

The quality varies greatly, of course. It's up to each news organization or individual journalist to determine how much time and energy can be devoted to a video project. Each project not only educates the audience about an important news issue but also helps develop an accurate level of expectation in terms of quality. When nonbroadcast news organizations first started doing video, it was assumed that each project had to look as close to a standard evening news broadcast as possible. The popularity of YouTube, among other factors, means those days are gone; all kinds of levels of quality are now acceptable.

▶▶▶ Two journalists, one goal

Let's take a look at two very similar video features, one by David Pogue, formerly of The New York Times, and one by Walt Mossberg, formerly of The Wall Street Journal. Interestingly, both men are popular technology columnists who have moved on from two of the most respected names in the news business to new ventures. Pogue is now with Yahoo, while Mossberg and partner Kara Swisher launched their own venture called Re/code in 2014. Both still regularly publish product and service reviews in video, but the quality and production values of the Pogue videos are significantly higher than those of Mossberg's videos. And because the differences are deliberate and the audience knows what to expect, that's OK.

Pogue is a former Broadway accompanist whose personality drives his video reports with humor and creative story angles. He has the benefit of producers from traditional TV news; the segments also air on CBS's news programs. Pogue's reports are shot in several locations and heavily edited, complete with dramatic production values, music and title overlays and grand transitions.

Other performers often appear, acting out stories that make points about whatever technology Pogue is featuring. For example, his report from the 2015 Consumer Electronics Show in Las Vegas was done as a mock musical. In fact, the video was titled "CES: The Musical!" and featured Pogue highlighting products and companies with an upbeat score and lots of action.[2]

"In the modern Journalism 2.0 world, good, entertaining video gets repurposed and rebroadcast," Pogue said in a comment on my Journalism 2.0 blog in 2009.

---

[2]David Pogue, "CES: The Musical," Yahoo, January 9, 2015. www.yahoo.com/tech/ces-the-musical-las-vegas-ces-the-annual-107639111709.html.

CES: The Musical!

C.E.YES!

David Pogue
January 9, 2015
🐦 Follow

LAS VEGAS — CES, the annual Consumer Electronics Show, is
staggeringly huge, crowded, and noisy. It's sensory overload. About
3,300 booths fill enough floor space for 35 football fields. Trying to

Credit: https://www.yahoo.com/tech/ces-the-musical-las-vegas-ces-the-
annual-107639111709.html

*David Pogue's videos on Yahoo.com are highly produced,
as you can see by this snapshot of CES: The Musical!, where David is
wearing a tuxedo and putting on a mock performance to cover the event.*

"My goofy video segments are on YouTube, iTunes, nytimes.com, CNBC.com,
CNBC television, TiVo (you can subscribe to them), and even JetBlue."

Mossberg, meanwhile, turns on an inexpensive webcam in his office and
records his two-minute reviews without even a script. The video is published
with only a lead-in (opening credits and music) and lead-out (ending credits
and music). Except for the variation of camera angles, there is little to no
editing of the content.

One of these video features looks like a TV show—because it is. The other
is just a guy sitting at a table and talking. So why does Mossberg compete
with Pogue and the countless other tech review videos on such a seemingly
uneven playing field?

One reason is that the audience for video has become extremely forgiving
and is now open to all levels of quality. Another is the bargain Mossberg

Walt Mossberg of Re/code takes a simple, low-tech approach to his videos, as he is shown here sitting at a desk and using an informal feel.

has established with his audience. He is an authentic voice who started writing a technology column in The Wall Street Journal in 1991. He produces his content in video as a supplement to his writing—a way to show his audience new technology while holding it in his hands.

▶ ▶ *Perfection not necessary*

The Pogue-Mossberg comparison shows there's no need for a debate about quality versus quantity to strangle news organizations. Some editors and photographers, unwilling to publish what they see as inferior products, painstakingly edit and produce high-level video work that, while great, often takes more time and effort than the stories deserve. Then, when the pageviews are modest (at best), the journalists start blaming video as a format and retreat to what they know best.

Meanwhile, the quick and less polished video content on news sites often draws bigger audiences. This discovery has led several newspapers to change their approach to video, broadening their definitions of what's publishable to include content such as video broadcast with cell phones from the scenes of news events.

Publishing these unedited video streams would have been unthinkable a few years ago in many newsrooms. Today, it's becoming common practice, illustrating how far some journalists have come in understanding their online audience. They can strike a different bargain with their audience on the Web. They can provide video that isn't perfect or in some cases isn't even very good. If it's authentic, if it takes a viewer to a news event or behind the scenes of somewhere important, it works.

Mara Schiavocampo became NBC News' first digital correspondent in October 2007 when the network started experimenting with one-man-band assignments, sending "digital journalists" to shoot, produce and edit stories by themselves. She has since moved on to ABC News, where she still brings a fresh approach to video storytelling.

Schiavocampo traveled to Detroit in 2009 to report on the economic calamity the area was experiencing because of the troubles in the auto industry. When anchor Brian Williams introduced one of her pieces on "NBC Nightly News," he called her "our digital correspondent" and said "she went there with her camera to see what's at stake"—thus signaling to the audience that the story would look and feel different. It did, but the lower production values didn't hurt the story's impact.

"It was intentionally shot shaky and without three or four lines of track and everything else," Schiavocampo told an audience at a May 2009 workshop sponsored by the National Association of Black Journalists in New York. "These were real people telling good stories. Why would I get in the way with a bunch of track and stand-ups and everything?"

Video that doesn't look just like the usual network story "is not *bad* news video," she said. "It's shot vérité style, which lends itself very well to the tools we are using."

What is it?   **What's *Next?***   Summary

⬇ PLAN YOUR VIDEO AND GO

The best way to build a solid video story is to think about it the same way you would think about writing. How will the video tell the story? After you've envisioned what the story should say, it's simply a matter of filling in spots with the most appropriate footage.

▶ Use different approaches for different projects

When you're starting out, you will undertake essentially two types of video assignments: a full documentary-style video story, and breaking news and highlights clips. Both forms require you to approach them with an attitude of more than "just getting some video."

If you are shooting a breaking news video, you rarely know in advance what the story will be. You simply know that news is happening, and you want to capture some essence of it on video. For a breaking news event such as a highway crash or a school shooting, you probably won't get to the scene in time to record the real action. But reactions from witnesses and investigators, as well as environmental footage of the scene, are well worth capturing.

Press conferences connected to compelling news events can make good video. They're also easy to shoot because you have a fixed subject and the lighting is usually good, especially if a lot of TV cameras are around.

Highlight clips, especially in sports, can be among the most popular content on any news site. Shooting sports video can be challenging, however. The constant movement of the subjects requires large capacity in the digital video file and can be difficult to follow when the video is downsized and compressed for Web display. Further challenges include lighting and zoom. As a result, isolating short clips of the best action is the way to go, with the clips either edited together with voice-over descriptions or linked to a news story as raw clips with caption information next to the link.

A documentary-style video story is different because you have more control. You can decide whom to interview, what footage to shoot and what not to shoot. Because this is a lot more work, it requires a lot more planning, for which many professionals recommend using storyboards.

The bottom line is to always be expanding your approach and experimenting with new methods of producing great video.

"It is also important to remember that learning is an ongoing process," Burgess says. "After 25 years of shooting and editing and storytelling, I'm still learning every day, every story."

▶ Try storyboarding

A storyboard is a visual sketch of the story, separated into different parts so it can be organized. The pictures help you define the scope of the project, given the time and resources available, so that you have realistic expectations for what you're hoping to produce. Storyboarding also forces you to think about the focus of the story: What's the one main idea you want to get across to the viewer? Make sure you answer that question first, so you can choose interviews and demonstration sequences (also known as A-roll), plus environmental footage (known as B-roll), to support and help explain that main idea.

The process of drawing out a storyboard is simple; no artistic talent is necessary. Find a whiteboard and start by writing the main idea at the top. Then draw boxes in a row from left to right, using more than one row if needed, with labels that represent each piece of the story. Imagine the boxes are the video viewer or screen and sketch a quick representation of what the viewer should see. (Yes, we're talking stick figures here.)

Even though this left-to-right format suggests a linear story form, you can rearrange the pieces to tell a more effective story. So, if the B-roll is the last footage you plan to capture but it is the best footage to lead off the story, you can still plan for it to be the first clip shown in the story.

While having a storyboard plan will help you organize your shooting, it doesn't mean you can't change your plan during the shooting process. It's important to adapt your shooting to what will make the most compelling video story. If a shot you planned to include turns out to be lifeless and boring but you discover another shot that is surprisingly interesting, by all means change your plan.

"Before you shoot, have an idea of what your story is," says Colin Mulvany, a multimedia producer at The Spokesman-Review newspaper in Spokane, Wash. "Sometimes I'm not sure what direction my video story should take until I get about a third of the way into shooting it. Make a mental list of shots and interviews you'll need to tell your story effectively. Look for shots that could be great openers or enders in your video. The bookends are really important in video storytelling. Don't pack up until you've made the mental checklist of all the video you'll need. Nothing is worse than being knee-deep in an edit and realizing you forgot to get a simple but crucial shot."

If necessary, you can do an update of your storyboard after you have shot the video and before you move on to editing. With a little more effort and planning, you can capture and produce great video, no matter the form.

▶ Mix your shots

The next time you watch a good video story, analyze it as a videographer would and pay attention to how many different types of shots are used. You'll notice that the videographer shot footage from different vantage points—some close, some far away and some in the middle. The best way to capture these different views is to think of them as separate shots and reposition yourself each time.

"Zoom with your legs, not your lens" is an old saying among photographers, but it's a new concept to many beginners.

"A big mistake I see by beginners is the overuse of zooming and panning while shooting," says Morris. "They're overwhelmed, they don't really know what pictures they're supposed to be taking, so they kind of try to take all the pictures, all at one time. They'll hold the camera and swing it back and forth over a scene, while zooming in and out. The resulting video footage makes the viewer feel sick to his stomach."

Instead, Morris urges shooters to focus their attention on collecting sequences of wide, medium and tight shots. At a minimum, shooters need to plan for those three different shots for each subject or situation. A good ratio would be 25 percent wide-angle, 25 percent close-up and 50 percent medium or midrange shots for the general footage.

Wide-angle shots, also known as establishing shots, give viewers a sense of the environment. For example, shoot the outside of a building before you go in. Once inside, back up and shoot the entire room.

Medium shots, somewhere in between wide-angle and close-up, are the ones you're probably most comfortable shooting.

Close-ups zoom in on the person talking or on what that person is talking about. Remember: Always zoom first, then record, instead of recording and zooming at the same time.

Although a mix of shots should be your goal when you start, don't let yourself stick so closely to a plan that you miss important action you didn't

Credit: ©iStockphoto.com/thinkomatic
> *A wide shot gives the viewer the full scene.* <

Credit: ©iStockphoto.com/befa

A medium shot gives the viewer a normal view.

anticipate. The concept of capturing interesting scenes is not that different from the way you'd work with a still camera.

"When I first started shooting video, I would get overwhelmed at all the multitasking I had to do—framing, sequencing, monitoring audio, keeping the camera steady," remembers Colin Mulvany. "Once all these things became second nature, I learned to slow down when shooting. I constantly reminded myself to use my video camera like I would a still camera.

"In many ways, I think still photographers make the best videographers. They already are able to see moment, have finely honed anticipation skills and understand composition. When I train a print reporter in video, these are the skills I have to teach the most."

Natural sound and environmental pictures are also important. Remember to record "blank" shots of a story's location or setting. Think of the standard "60 Minutes" piece: It shows the outside of a building where the subject works, then cuts to a shot of the subject walking up the street or answering phone calls in the office. These are called "establishing" shots because they establish the setting for the viewer.

▶ Build five-shot sequences

Of course, your video story should include something interesting actually happening—for example, someone doing a specific task as part of a daily

Credit: ©iStockphoto.com/LeoGrand

A close-up focuses on one subject.

job—that illustrates the main idea of the story you're trying to tell. Identify that task and then prepare to shoot it as a five-shot sequence.

The BBC Training and Development team recommends that such a sequence consist of these five elements: close-up on the hands, close-up on the face, wide shot, over-the-shoulder shot and then another shot from a different angle. For that last one, the BBC's training video urges you to be creative— "side shot, low shot, something from on high, up to you." (This video used to be available on the BBC Web site, but it can no longer be accessed there.)

The experts at the BBC suggest that you shoot the five elements in exactly that order. "We shoot sequentially because these shots always cut together," the video narrator says. "If you film in sequences, you will get usable material every time."

The video example provided with this guidance shows a man giving a woman a tattoo on one of her arms. Here's a breakdown of the five shots in the video:

1. **Close-up on the hands:** Shows the needle applying ink to the woman's skin

2. **Close-up on the face:** Shows the man's concentration

3. **Wide shot:** Shows the two together and a view of the room where this takes place

4. **Over-the-shoulder shot:** Shows the view that the tattoo artist has of the process

5. **Creative shot:** Shows the room from behind a table (another look at the main subject)

Five Shots, 10 Seconds For a closer look at this concept, visit this page from Mindy McAdams, one of the most innovative college journalism professors in the United States: www.jou.ufl.edu/faculty/mmcadams/video/five_shot.html.

Each shot is steady. There is no panning or zooming. The videographer stops shooting one sequence, gets in position for the next shot and then records again. But in the editing, the shots flow together seamlessly.

"Here's a true story that made me realize the importance of basic shooting and editing skills," says Angela Morris, recalling her time as a multimedia producer at the San Antonio Express-News. "I had the opportunity to spend about eight months, off and on, with a family whose father had been seriously injured in Iraq. My story came out in installments. About halfway through the time, my newsroom invited a TV photojournalist to teach us the basic shooting rules in a day-long workshop. If you look at the installments that came out before I learned these lessons, and compare them to the installments published afterwards, you can see a huge difference!"

Instead of simply shooting from some generic distance, Morris concentrated on mixing shots, getting close-ups and wide shots. As she says, the difference was "huge."

What is it? | **What's Next?** | Summary

⬇ VOICE IN VIDEO

Because most journalists are already comfortable with the practice of telling stories with words and interviewing people, these are the key building blocks you should base video stories on. It's also easier than learning the documentary video flair that someone like Ken Burns uses to show the audience instead of telling them the message he is trying to communicate.

▶ Learn effective video interviewing

One of the most basic forms of video journalism is the interview. It seems like a simple process, but it's also simple to mess up if you don't take a moment to plan.

DRILLING DOWN

Practice Makes Perfect Practice using a video camera to interview someone you know. Write a script first, then review it and listen to how well you manage the flow of the conversation. Listen for things you wish you had or hadn't done.

The first step is selecting the right location. Pick an environment where the subject will be comfortable and, if possible, one that complements the topic of the story. Remember to ask for permission to shoot video if the location you choose is on private property.

Whether you are on location or in your office building, think sound and lighting first. If the on-camera subject will be wearing a wireless mic, you can get away with some environmental noise (but not a lot). If you have some heavy-duty lighting equipment, you can get away with shooting anywhere indoors and even compensating for indirect sunlight outdoors. If you don't have good external lights, make sure you pick a location that fully lights the subject. You don't want any backlighting or shadows on the subject's face.

It's a good idea to have several questions prewritten. In some situations, it might help to send some of the questions to the subject in advance. Or you can discuss the questions with the person a few minutes before you turn on the camera. But in most news situations, you want to capture the first response, with all the body language that might come with it. That's the power of video, after all.

As we covered in the previous chapter, remember that the interviewer needs to remain silent while the subject is speaking. Instead of saying "Uh-huh" and "I see" and "Really?" to convey interest, try to use nonverbal cues such as nodding.

Reporters have a way of establishing a rapport with a subject by showing how much they know about the topic. Although this can be effective early in the relationship, a video audience wants to hear what the subject has to say. So, remember, your job is to ask questions. Some context following a subject's response, such as spelling out an acronym he or she has used, is helpful, but try to keep it to a minimum.

Refer to chapter 6 on audio journalism for other best practices for interviewing.

▶ Use a stand-up, even if you don't want to

The on-camera stand-up, a staple of the evening news, can be an uncomfortable experience for journalists not accustomed to being on camera. Occasionally, however, it may be necessary, especially in a breaking news situation or during coverage of a major sporting event. For best results, do some planning and remember the following tips:

Offer useful content: You want to keep it short, of course, but still provide something extra for the audience. Remember, it's what you will be reporting that attracts an audience, not your pretty face. So make sure you're on the scene in order to provide important or interesting details in your report, not just to be seen standing there.

Write a script and warm up: Even if you are reporting on location from a breaking news event, you can find a few minutes to run through a rehearsal before you start recording. If there isn't time to write a script, at least jot down an outline with the major points that you need to cover, so you stay focused after the camera gets rolling.

Be stable, breathe easy: Posture is important, so be sure you're standing up or sitting as straight as possible and that your chin is parallel to the floor. Relax your shoulders but try not to move them too much while you're talking. Breathe from your stomach and diaphragm, not your chest.

Don't be afraid to talk with your hands: The people who do best on camera are the ones who capture viewers with their personality, which is nearly impossible to do if you're not relaxed and conversational. Using some hand gestures is an easy way to look less formal and will feel more normal during the recording. But use gestures sparingly. Too much movement will be distracting to viewers.

▶ Control your story with voice-overs

You cannot control everything that happens when you are interviewing someone, but you can have complete control of the voice-over that you record for an overlay on a video story. Refer to chapter 6 for details on writing a script, warming up and using operative words while recording a voice-over.

⬇ GEAR UP AND GET OUT THERE

Those grainy home videos you watched as a child are long gone. Digital cameras have done to video what CDs did to old record albums (and what MP3s are doing to CDs). By storing video as digital bits on mini-DV tapes or on hard drives, compact and portable cameras are able to collect and store much more data than analog tape ever could, greatly improving video quality and making editing a breeze.

▶ Array of camera choices

As posited by Moore's law, digital storage and computing power have increased exponentially while prices have actually decreased, and this means the market is filled with ever more powerful digital video cameras at lower and lower prices. For example, a company called Pure Digital—which was bought by Cisco Systems for $590 million in stock in March 2009—released a new line of video cameras in 2007 that make shooting basic video as easy as recording a conversation on an old microcassette recorder. The Flip cameras sold millions of units and became a staple in the beginning video journalist's toolbox. Unfortunately, in 2010 Cisco closed the business down, but many other camera makers (including Sony, Kodak, RCA, Apitek and DXG) had already picked up on the simple style of the Flip cameras and had begun producing similar products.

These devices are small and basically idiotproof, since they have only a few buttons for play, record, stop, forward and back. They cost $100 to $200, depending on the make and model. They do come with some limitations, however. The audio often isn't great, so look for one with an external port for a mic. New models do have the ability to connect to a tripod, too, which is an improvement over the original versions. These cameras also offer very little zoom capability, so they're appropriate only for basic videography.

Most of the models come standard with a flip-out USB arm (which is why the original was named the Flip) and transferring software on the camera, so moving footage to your computer is quick and easy.

You can save money by using a point-and-shoot digital photo camera or even a smartphone, since many of them now have good video modes. Plus, if you're shooting primarily for the Web, quality is not much of an issue.

Anyone who spends considerable time shooting video will want a camera designed for that purpose as well as the accessories—memory, microphones, chargers, lighting—to help it do its job. All these gizmos and the terminology attached to them can make shopping for a video camera confusing. Here are some tips to get you started.

▶ Video camera shopping questions

High def or standard? CCD or CMOS? Tape or hard disk? These are just some of the questions you must answer when purchasing a digital video camera, which can cost anywhere from a few hundred to a few thousand dollars. Here's the first tip the experts will give you: Don't buy more camera than you need.

"A high-end professional camera can actually put an undue burden on an organization with limited resources and staff with limited technical ability," says Jeremy Rue, multimedia training instructor for the Knight Digital Media Center located at the University of California Berkeley Graduate School of Journalism.

> **DRILLING DOWN** ⬍
>
> **CCD Versus CMOS** When shopping for a camera, you will run into CCD and CMOS sensor technology. CCDs tend to be used in cameras that focus on high-quality images with lots of pixels and excellent light sensitivity. CMOS sensors traditionally have lower quality, lower resolution and lower sensitivity, but they are getting better and will likely match CCD quality in the near future, while still beating CCD cameras on price and battery life.
>
> [*Source:* "What Is the Difference Between CCD and CMOS Image Sensors in a Digital Camera?" HowStuffWorks, n.d. http://electronics .howstuffworks.com/question362.htm.]

"Some require the separate purchase of microphones and lenses that usually come standard with consumer-grade cameras. A news organization should be realistic about its needs and funding capabilities."

Rue has spent more time than most people ever will researching video camera options for journalists. He recommends making the decision based on four factors: media type, high definition or standard definition, software and accessories.

▶▶ *What media type?*
"This is often a difficult choice to make because there is no best answer," Rue says. "Most of the time the decision revolves around convenience, durability, capacity and longevity."

Cameras that record to a hard drive are popular because they make transferring the video to a computer simple. Unfortunately, this type of storage is "well known to be more fragile than tape and solid-state media," according to Rue. The same issue applies to cameras that record to DVDs (and they also have storage limitations). Solid-state media, usually in the form of memory cards, are another popular choice, but solid-state media limit the amount of footage you can capture at any given time.

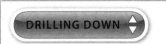

DRILLING DOWN

A Journalist's Buying Guide Jeremy Rue presents one of the most definitive explanations available on how to choose the right video camera in his "Tutorial: Video Cameras," on the Web site of the Knight Digital Media Center at the University of California at Berkeley: http://multimedia .journalism.berkeley.edu/tutorials/ video-cameras.

"We currently recommend purchasing a camera that uses either mini-DV tapes or a solid-state memory card, like SDHC," Rue says.

▶ ▶ *What software will I be using to edit this footage?*
Journalists shopping for video equipment often don't think about software, but Rue says they should. It's important to make sure the footage captured by the camera will be compatible with the software program you plan to use.

While most video-editing software can log tape footage, some programs will not work with DVD or the newer AVCHD format. Whether you find a software solution before or after purchasing a camera, make sure the two are compatible—and will work with your computer systems.

"Consider the work flow before you purchase the camera," Rue says.

▶ ▶ *What accessories do I need?*
According to professionals, accessories are often the most overlooked aspect of purchasing electronic equipment. You need the best ones for your purposes, compatible with your camera, so don't forget to include accessories when figuring cost, as many people do.

Many companies will price big-ticket equipment such as cameras at cost and make their money from selling accessories. In fact, the cost of the accessories can add up to half the cost of the camera.

Here are some tips on the accessories you're likely to be shopping for:

Tapes and batteries: Several hours before you need to use the camera, check to make sure the battery and backup battery (if there is one) are completely charged. Most cameras come with a standard battery that won't

WHAT'S IN MARA'S BACKPACK?

Mara Schiavocampo, the first digital journalist hired by NBC News, allows us to look inside her "backpack" (which actually has wheels and a pull handle):

Sony HVR-V1U HDV camcorder (about $4,000) with two add-ons: a Rode AA-battery-powered shotgun microphone ($250) and a Sony wide-angle conversion lens (about $500) that threads on the front of the camera

Lightweight Libec video tripod (7 pounds), as well as a monopod ($300 total)

Litepanels MiniPlus camera-mountable LED light ($800)

Apple MacBook Pro laptop with Final Cut Pro, and an extra charged battery ($3,000)

External hard drive for the laptop ($200)

Apple earbuds

Fuji point-and-shoot camera ("I almost never use it anymore") as a backup ($300)

XLR cables and XLR adapters that can input into a small audio jack on her laptop for voice-over

Two wireless lavalier microphone sets (about $500)

Array of white-balance cards in blues and greens, to either heighten the warmth of skin tones or adjust for fluorescent light

Bags of spare connectors and cables

Lots of spare tapes, in HD mini-DV format

Plug converters ("You need them if you're in another country on assignment")

And, though every ounce matters, the manual for every piece of equipment she has in the bag

The total cost is about $10,000—a fraction of the cost of a broadcast-quality high-definition camera.

[*Source:* Edward J. Delaney, "Profile of a Backpacker: Inside Mara Schiavocampo's Toolkit," Nieman Journalism Lab, January 12, 2009 (updated by Schiavocampo at the request of the author, June 2009). www.niemanlab.org/2009/01/mara-schiavocampo-backpack-journalist.]

cut it for many professional uses because it lasts less than an hour. If possible, purchase the largest-capacity battery available for your camera and then use the one that came with the camera for backup. Three-hour batteries are available for most cameras.

Also, check to make sure you have enough mini-DV tapes or storage capacity on cards or hard disk for the assignment (plus a backup plan in case you need more than you originally anticipated). Tapes and cards can be reused, which is nice because they're not cheap.

Microphones: A charged battery and ample storage are the most important accessories you'll need for your shoot, but you'll need to consider many others, including external microphones. See chapter 6 for more information on digital audio. Later in this chapter you'll find more tips on choosing the right microphone to get good audio.

Tripod: The easiest way to make your videography look professional is to use a tripod. A steady shot is essential for quality video, and even though many cameras these days have fancy image-stabilization features built in, nothing will provide a rock-solid shot like a tripod. That said, developing a steady hand is necessary if you're going to start branching out and doing different types of shooting.

All cameras have a round (usually silver) hole on the bottom with circular threads. All tripods have a round (usually silver) bolt-like stem on the top. All you have to do is place the camera on top of the tripod so the stem matches up to the hole and then turn the dial below the stem until the camera is tightly fixed to the tripod.

Headphones: As we will discuss later, audio is essential to video. And the only way to be sure you are recording good audio with your video is to plug in a pair of headphones and listen while you shoot. All cameras have a headphone jack; simply plug in the headphone cord.

If it's not practical to use headphones during the shoot, use a co-worker or the subject to test the audio level while you're setting up the camera. Simply talk to that person while you are wearing the headphones to make sure the mic and sound are working correctly.

Lighting: If you have ever "shared" an interview with a photographer from the local TV station, you probably thought, "Why do they have to use that spotlight? It's blinding the person talking."

There's a good reason. Just as still photographers need a flash in almost all indoor settings, powerful lighting is essential to shooting video.

There are several options for lighting, spanning various price ranges. Most clip into a "shoe" on the top of the camera. As with most photography equipment, the better products are more expensive. In this case, more powerful lights are brighter. So if you don't have access to the big, bright lights that TV people use, look for a more entry-level version for less than $100.

Credit: Photo courtesy of the Knoxville News Sentinel

Former Knoxville News Sentinel online producer Erin Chapin prepares to capture video at the University of Tennessee's basketball practice.

Remember that running a light—especially a powerful one—will increase the drain on your battery, so having a backup battery is even more important.

What is it? | **What's *Next?*** | Summary

⬇ SHOOTING GOOD VIDEO

All digital video cameras come with convenient automatic features as the default settings. Unless you're a "camera person," you probably won't ever switch to manual settings. And that's fine; let the camera do the heavy lifting for you.

Focus: The automatic focus feature means that when you turn the camera on, it will automatically focus on whatever you're pointing the camera at. This will suffice for most of your shots. The only time it might not be good enough is when you are shooting something complicated, where there are multiple subjects moving within the frame. Still, the automatic setting will probably produce a better picture than you could get using the manual focus dial, unless you already have photography skills.

Zoom: Most new cameras have powerful zooms that are easily manipulated with a rocker button on the top of the camera. Set the zoom before beginning to record and then zoom only when absolutely necessary—and as slowly as possible. If you are shooting someone talking, don't zoom at all. Ever. If you want to have different angles and compositions, do separate shots.

DRILLING DOWN

Create Great Video Stories   NPPA Photographer of the Year Doug Burgess offers these tips for creating great video stories:

Structure a story: Not just a list of facts, a story with a beginning, middle and end. There is a reason the "who" is first on the list. Any good story is, at its heart, about people, about someone. It may take place at an event, something may have happened, but at the heart of the story there is a person, or persons, to build the story around, someone to care about.

Consider the nuances: Composition, sequencing, focusing, sound engineering, lighting, screen direction, exposure, when to use a tripod, when to shoot off the shoulder, how to work in sometimes difficult situations—it all can be daunting to someone who has not given much thought to the process.

Grasp your gear: Learn everything you can about the equipment you are using. The availability of high-end equipment, such as high-definition cameras, means that you can create stunning professional images with some basic knowledge, but such equipment can also glaringly highlight poor lighting, exposure, and focus. The only way around these pitfalls is to know your equipment, have a basic setup, know how certain types of light look on your camera, and know your audio settings.

Use a tripod: If you think you are super rock steady, you're not. And smaller, lighter cameras don't help. Until the camera becomes an extension of your body, use a tripod as much as possible.

Keep your editing simple: Learn the basics and build from there. Don't get crazy with effects. While the editing can allow you to get really creative, it is important to remember that you can't edit what you don't have. If you don't have compelling video, you can't edit it.

Edit, edit, edit: Learn the ins and outs of your editing system like the back of your hand (or better). Edit, edit, edit, edit the same story in different ways. Watch stories or movies you think are exceptional and break them down. What specifically makes them exceptional?

7

CHAPTER

Exposure: Most cameras also come with automatic exposure, which will give you the appropriate lighting in most circumstances. If you are shooting in especially low light, try switching to manual exposure and allowing more light in (this will open up the iris). Check the manual for information specific to your camera.

▶ Aim for solid, not spectacular, clips

Be selective in shooting: There are two good reasons for this: You don't want to waste tape or space on your hard disk, and you don't want to waste time editing.

Avoid panning and zooming: When you're switching among wide, medium and close-up shots, stop recording. Avoid zooming and panning if possible. Simply shoot a shot, stop recording, then adjust for the next shot and hit **Record** again. If there is action in front of the camera (people walking by in a busy market, for example), keeping the camera steady and letting the action enter and leave the frame works much better than trying to follow the action.

Hold your shots: Because you can make a shot shorter in the editing process, but not longer, be sure to hold each of your shots for at least 15 seconds. Even if it's a wide environment shot that you'll likely use for five seconds, shoot the full 15 seconds. You'll be glad you did. (Use the counter on the camera to avoid the temptation to cut it short.)

Be silent when you shoot: The camera will pick up every sound you make—a sigh, a cough, a chuckle or anything you say. So keep your lips zipped when recording, because you won't be able to edit out the unwanted audio later.

Framing and composing: Follow the "rule of thirds" when composing your frame (deciding how much to zoom in). Imagine a nine-square grid overlaid on the frame, dividing the horizontal axis and vertical axis into three equal parts. Then compose the shot so the most important subject in the frame is aligned with one of the four axis points in your imaginary nine-square grid.

If you are shooting a person, leave some space—or headroom—above the person's head, but not too much or the person will look unnecessarily short. Once you master this basic concept, you can experiment with off-center composition as in the example here. Though not perfectly centered horizontally, the subject's face is lined up exactly on the right vertical axis. And it is centered perfectly vertically, with equal space above and below the subject's face.

Credit: ©iStockphoto.com/LeoGrand

Use the rule of thirds to compose your shots properly.

▶ Get good audio

One part of the equation that is easy to overlook when shooting video has nothing to do with the picture. The quality of the audio is critical to producing good video, even more so for online video, because the size of the video picture will be relatively small.

If the first mistake beginners make in shooting video is doing too much panning and zooming, the second is neglecting to get good audio, says Angela Morris. "Audio is almost more important than video in your story," she says. "If you can't hear what people are saying, there's no point in watching the piece. Shooters must make proper microphone choices and know how to use them."

The best way to ensure that the quality of the audio will enhance, not sabotage, your video project is to choose the best microphone for the assignment. Here are the options:

Built-in mic: All digital cameras have built-in microphones that will capture the audio sufficiently if you are shooting video and want natural or environmental sound. Think sporting events, fairs and festivals and the like.

Wireless mic: A lavalier, or wireless, microphone is an additional accessory that is essential to purchase if you want to capture interviews on video. Here's how to use one:

1. Clip the tiny mic onto the lapel of the subject. This mic is wired to a transmitter that can be clipped on the subject's belt or placed in a pocket.

2. Plug the receiver into the camera using the jack marked "mic" (or it might have a small icon that looks like a microphone).

3. Turn on both units—the transmitter and the receiver—and test the signal strength by using headphones and asking the subject a couple of small talk–type questions. If the signal isn't strong, turn up the levels on both devices. If that doesn't work, look for a better place to put the mic, one that's closer to the subject's mouth.

4. Remind the subject that the mic is sensitive, so he or she should avoid adjusting any clothing during the interview, as this will result in loud scratching sounds.

Shotgun mic: This is the best choice when you want to capture a conversation among several people. Placing wireless mics on more than one or two people will make the sound unrealistic and too "out front." (Plus, you may not have access to a half dozen wireless mics.)

Shotgun mics come in two types: smaller ones that attach directly to the camera and larger ones that attach to a boom. If you have the on-camera version, slide the mic into the shoe on the top of the camera. The camera will recognize the accessory and automatically switch from its built-in mic to the shotgun mic.

Credit: Flickr user philcampbell.
Image available under Creative Commons license.

> *Use a wireless mic for better sound quality in your video.* <

A larger shotgun mic will probably be wireless and have a transmitter and receiver. You will need a boom—an extendable pole with a microphone clip to hold the mic—and someone who can hold it near the subjects (you have a sound crew, right?). But not too close, or you'll end up with a

video that has shots
of the mic poking in
from the edges.

▶ Mix in still images

Most new digital
video cameras have
the ability to take
still photographs,
too. This can come in
handy for shooting
a screenshot or a
mug shot that can
be used in print to
tease to the online
video package or
on the Web site as a
promotional icon.

Switch the camera
mode to **Card Mode**
instead of **Tape
Mode** if your camera
has this option. This
will change the

Credit: Flickr user 4nitsirk.
Image available under Creative Commons license.

> *A shotgun mic focuses on specific
sound sources.* <

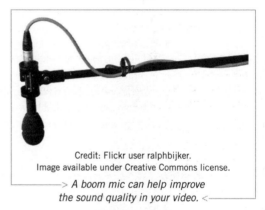

Credit: Flickr user ralphbijker.
Image available under Creative Commons license.

> *A boom mic can help improve
the sound quality in your video.* <

recording source from the DV tape to the portable storage card that your
camera uses, such as a secure digital (SD) or compact flash (CF) card.

To capture a photo, use the button marked **Photo** instead of using the red
(or other) button that is used to begin a recording. You can (and should) use
the regular zoom.

What is it? | **What's *Next?*** | Summary

⬇ WORKING WITH DIGITAL VIDEO FILES

The best video stories are composed of many short clips edited together,
and your job is to get the best short clips. The best way to understand
fully the array of clips you need to capture is to actually perform the

editing—or at a minimum sit through the editing process with the person who edits the video. That's the only way to see which of the clips you shot work best, as well as which clips you didn't shoot but should have. If you shoot video footage and hand it off to a Web producer or multimedia editor to await the final product, your video storytelling skills will never improve.

"I think editing my own work has been the biggest help to my shooting," Schiavocampo said. "Because when I'm cutting I always notice what I didn't get. You see your mistakes. You see where your composition could have been better."[3]

Whether or not you made a plan and drew a storyboard before you started shooting video, it's a good idea to take a few minutes before you begin editing the video to revisit the plan or draw up a new one. It may be helpful to review all the footage you have captured, just as you would review your notes for a story you're writing. Once you have a feel for the footage you'll be working with in editing, draw boxes on a whiteboard (yes, more stick figures) to represent different stages of the video story and give yourself some direction before you begin working with the software. You can always change the plan as you edit, but it's a good idea to remember the main point of the story you are trying to tell before you lose yourself in the editing process.

▶ Keep it short

Keep your video piece short, for two reasons. First, because video is stored in large files and large files take longer to download, the shorter the better. The second reason is that Web video is a separate genre unto itself; the audience expects short video stories.

Naka Nathaniel was an original member of the team that launched nytimes .com. On September 11, 2001, he filmed the second plane crash from his Brooklyn rooftop. (A sequence of shots from the videotape became the dominant images on nytimes.com during the day, and the footage was broadcast on network and cable channels.) He says when you think short, think of the Beatles. Most of their greatest hits lasted less than two minutes. So you don't need a longer video story than that.

---

[3]Edward J. Delaney, "Profile of a Backpacker: Inside Mara Schiavocampo's Toolkit," Nieman Journalism Lab, January 12, 2009. www.niemanlab.org/2009/01/mara-schiavo campo-backpack-journalist.

"A couple years ago, I read this New Yorker piece about Paul McCartney[4] and it made me curious about the Beatles. I went out and picked up all of their records and loaded them into my computer. I was struck by the running times of their songs—especially the early albums. Most songs were two minutes or less," Nathaniel said. "They got in, hooked you and then they got out. I thought about how that contrasted with a lot of the work I was seeing."

Nathaniel set most of his templates at 1:45 and tried to stay close to that time. He chose that number because it felt "to be about right" given his production limitations—he was usually out in the field and transmitting via satellite hookup—and storytelling needs.

"I always viewed multimedia as several parts working together, and no one medium should have to shoulder the complete story," Nathaniel said. "A lot of work I was seeing on sites felt bloated and pointless. Too much was being asked of the audience—and not in a good way. As an audience member, I like it when a piece challenges me on an intellectual level. I don't like to have my patience tested. I also don't like to have to decipher what the story is."

▶ Choose your editing software

You will realize the true power of digital video during the editing stage. It is remarkably easy to cut and arrange video clips with basic video-editing software; anyone can produce a package as a nonlinear story or series of highlight clips.

Most computers have a video-editing program such as Windows Movie Maker or iMovie already installed. Also available are several powerful programs

DRILLING DOWN

Changing Software Windows Live Movie Maker, Microsoft's video-editing software, is already installed on millions of computers worldwide. The company redeveloped its original Windows Movie Maker program and packaged it with the Windows 7 and 8 operating systems.

Apple updates its iMovie program every year or so, meaning there are several different versions. Even if you are comfortable working with previous versions of iMovie, once you upgrade you'll have a new interface and features to learn.

7

CHAPTER

[4]John Colapinto, "When I'm Sixty-four," The New Yorker, June 4, 2007. www.newyorker .com/reporting/2007/06/04/070604fa_fact_colapinto.

for $100 to $200 that will feel like professional editing suites to amateur video editors:

- Final Cut Pro ($300; Mac)

- Adobe Premiere Elements ($80; Windows or Mac)

- Sony Vegas Movie Studio HD ($50; Windows)

- Corel VideoStudio Pro X2 ($60; Windows)

▶ Practice visual storytelling

There's a reason most of this chapter focuses on gathering good stuff instead of on editing it. Digital video editing is not something you can learn from one chapter in a generalist's book such as this. But if you capture the right content with your camera, you'll be able to make a solid video story no matter how much or little experience you have with iMovie or Final Cut.

Just remember: Tell a story.

How? By arranging video clips in a coherent and interesting order. By running audio of an interview or a voice-over "under" the video so your story is not about talking heads. By keeping it short and to the point.

Here are some more lessons to learn:

- Define your story in the first 20 seconds; hook the audience.

- Make sure you have a beginning, middle and end.

- Don't let the viewer have a chance to be bored. Use short clips, the more the better.

- Focus on one central idea and stick with it.

- Remember that characters make stories. The better your characters, the better your stories will be.

Use the power of the medium. Visual storytelling is, of course, about what your audience sees. "Visuals that connect to your narrative are important," Colin Mulvany of The Spokesman-Review says. "When the fire chief says: 'We gave mouth-to-mouth to six kittens,' I don't want to see his face. I want to see the kittens. This is an import fundamental in video storytelling: show the viewer what your video subjects are talking about."

⬇ PUBLISHING VIDEO ONLINE

Even with the proliferation of broadband connections, most video files are too large to publish online unless they're compressed. Many video-sharing services solve this problem by compressing video files and publishing them online in the universal Flash video format. So publishing a video online is now simple.

Today the best approach is a content delivery network such as Brightcove or Akamai, or a free video-sharing service such as YouTube, Vimeo, Blip.tv or Metacafe. These services take your video files, in several different formats, and convert them to playable format across multiple platforms while compressing them so they are smaller in size and transfer faster over the Internet—meaning less wait time for your audience. The services also offer embed codes so that you can publish the videos on your Web site—and other people can publish them on their sites—meaning no one's users will have to leave a site to view the video content.

Most services even handle HD video files and serve them in their native 16:9 aspect ratio (think flat-screen TV shape).

Each of these services makes it drop-dead simple to publish video. You have to create an account first; then follow the clear instructions on each site to upload the video file. Before you upload, though, there are some steps you can take that will ensure the highest possible quality for your video after it is compressed by the robots at YouTube or one of the other sites.

Using iMovie, Final Cut, Premiere or other video-editing programs, you can generate files that can be easily uploaded onto the Web. Each program has an **Export** function, usually found by choosing **File—Export—Movie**, or something similar. In the resulting menu, find a link to the **Settings** and make the necessary adjustments.

▶ Do your own compression

It's still possible, of course, to do your own compression and publishing. However, you will need a Web server with ample bandwidth and storage. You will have to factor in any additional compression the file will receive before publication by a video-sharing site, too. If you use a site such as YouTube that does a lot of compression, you will want to upload less compressed (higher-quality) movies. But remember, the higher the quality, the larger the file size and the longer it will take to upload.

Credit: http://vimeo.com/create

Vimeo is a video-sharing site that aids users by offering music for their videos, explaining the ways they can license their videos, and providing a video school to share best practices.

If you need to send a video file to someone and it's too big to e-mail, use file transfer protocol (see chapter 1) or an FTP service such as Hightail.

▶ Seek viral video distribution

In addition to providing a simple means for publishing your video online, Web sites such as YouTube and Vimeo can help you distribute your video and get it seen by more people than if you were to post it only on your own Web site. These sites have much larger audiences and much more search engine visibility than your site, greatly improving the chances for more viewers. And the embed codes that allow others to publish the videos on their blogs and Web sites make it easy for others to help distribute your video, too.

"It's great to host videos on your own site, but you can greatly expand your audience if you seek out viewers at their own watering holes," Angela Morris says. "Distributing your videos on the popular video-sharing sites can only help you, especially if you brand your video with a logo in the corner and you include a note at the end telling people to find more coverage on your URL."

Morris recommends a Web service called OneLoad (formerly TubeMogul) that automatically uploads your video to as many as 20 different video-sharing sites, including YouTube.

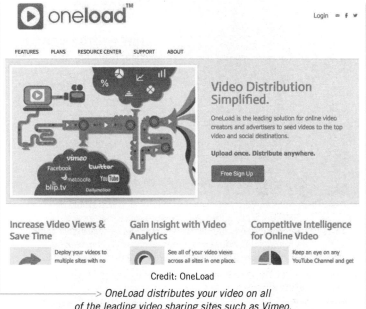

Credit: OneLoad

> OneLoad distributes your video on all
of the leading video sharing sites such as Vimeo,
Twitter, YouTube, Dailymotion, blip.tv, Facebook and metacafe. <

Watch Great News Video   The best way to learn how to produce great news video is to watch great news video. "You have to be able to recognize exceptional work before you can produce it," award-winning news photographer Doug Burgess says. "The process of storytelling is a lifelong journey, with a beginning, middle and end. The best advice I ever received was to learn all the rules and then learn how to break them."

Visit the following Web sites for great examples:

National Press Photographers Association, monthly multimedia contest winners: www.nppa.org

TV News Storytellers: www.tvnewsstorytellers.com

Interactive Narratives: www.interactivenarratives.org

B-roll.net: www.b-roll.net

Credit: Photo courtesy of
Matt Mrozinski

MATT
MROZINSKI

▶ **CHIEF PHOTOJOURNALIST**
| WTHR, Indianapolis

▶ **FOUNDER** | TVNewsStory
Tellers.com (@MattMrozinski)

When I leaped into the TV news business 10 years ago, I remember the old-timers telling me how much news had changed. You get that kind of commentary in any industry, because after all, the only constant is change.

Those "old-timers" had no idea what news would be in 10 years, and those stories were mere monikers of seniority. The truth is, the industry was virtually unchanged for decades. Today we're not talking about developing film versus cutting NLE or carrying less battery weight, but we are talking about the disruption of news platforms altogether.

There has never been a more turbulent time since the invention of TV. If you are looking around for something to anchor yourself to there is one thing that *is* constant, and that is the desire for great storytelling.

On every platform—Vine, Instagram, TV programming, stand-up comedy, commercials, movies and even music— the audience is screaming out for an incredibly well-told story with surprises, reveals and moments.

Quality video storytelling was quite common during the early days of TV news. I think back to Edward R. Murrow and Charles Kuralt, who are two iconic storytellers from a different generation. Over the last 15 years, we have begun to lose sight of what they symbolized to harness a demand for instant consumption of news headlines. Now that social media headlines stand alone, there is no longer a reason for TV to compete unless applicable during breaking news. Daily, we must separate ourselves with something not found in a headline, and that's (you guessed it) compelling video storytelling. Viewers turn to us for the experience, not the headline.

We have come full circle and I can tell you firsthand that our industry *significantly* lacks the writing and story-producing skills to support success in this rebounding endeavor. It is holding us back. If you can craft the skills to tell a great story it will carry a career far beyond what a pretty smile can attract you.

Understanding video storytelling is not exclusively upon the photojournalist. Every news professional, from producers, promotions people, Web producers and reporters up to the managers, must comprehend how to write with pictures and what constitutes an engaging story. Video storytelling is much more than pretty pictures, it is the organization of sound, moments and pictures that are coupled with a narrative that engages you from the beginning, takes you on a journey and unravels a story as if you were peeling back layers of an onion.

Compare it to your favorite movie. We should look at all news stories with this possibility. I strongly believe the success of our industry depends on this. We have to be creative educators; simply delivering the message is not enough: We must skillfully entertain.

My approach to video storytelling has always been one of purity. I don't consider myself a photographer; I'm a documentarian who captures life as naturally as possible. The wireless lavalier microphone has changed what is possible in news, and I use it to capture natural moments. We should document life and history as it happens, like a reality show, respectfully. Introduce us to, and let us understand, people outside of five-second sound bites. We must look to capture moments that define a person, or people, or society and the surrounding circumstances. This is a theory practiced by the best video journalists, and it can be recycled for spot, investigative, general assignment and, of course, in-depth news.

Not every day or every circumstance will lend you the opportunity to craft a great story. Sometimes simply getting the facts on the air is our responsibility, and occasionally live storytelling is the experience. Video storytelling is one critical element of what we do, and if we expect to stay relevant we have to engage our viewers creatively.

[*Source:* Written by Matt Mrozinski at the request of the author.]

Twice as many people, for example, watched Charles Bertram's video of Adam Bender because it was posted on YouTube than would have seen it if it had been published only on the Web site of the Lexington Herald-Leader.

Credit: Interactive Narratives

> *Interactive Narratives highlights best practices for multimedia journalism, organizing videos by those that excel in innovation, storytelling, design or all categories.* <

What is it?   What's *Next?*   **Summary**

☆ START SMALL, BUT MAKE SURE YOU START

Before you head out on assignment, it's a good idea to get comfortable with how to shoot and what to shoot.

Shoot some footage at home of your family or friends and experiment with different types of shots. Practice capturing a mix of shots, using different types of microphones and using a tripod and lighting. Shooting basic video is not difficult, but, as with most things involving new technology, it takes some getting used to. Your goal should be to capture stable shots with good lighting and good audio.

Then expose yourself to good video storytelling, and the pieces will fall into place.

"Experienced journalists are usually coming into this world from one of two directions: from the photographic side or the reporting side.

Both bring established skill sets to the job, but they have new areas to learn," Burgess says. "Photographers or videographers have to learn to think more about the story, how to tell stories in compelling ways while maintaining all of the standards of journalism: accuracy, ethics, newsworthiness, along with the who, what, where, when and why."

It's a lot to balance, but, when done well, the result is arguably the most powerful form of journalism.

GET GOING Checklist ✔

☐ Visit different sections of a news Web site and identify one story from each section that would have made a great video story.

☐ Create a basic video story, less than one minute in length, with at least three different shots and a separate audio track (voice-over or background music).

☐ Publish your video online with a service such as YouTube or Vimeo. Compare several different free services to determine which one you prefer.

CHAPTER 7

CHAPTER 8

> ## Data-Driven Journalism and Digitizing Your Life

Data, data everywhere. Now that we're deep into the information age, it's time for everyone to accept that the amount of information in our lives is only going to keep growing. As author Clay Shirky has stated repeatedly, "There is no such thing as information overload, only filter failure."

This onslaught of information has a double impact on most people, and we'll address both sides in this chapter. The first challenge is personal: taking advantage of digital tools and services to manage your day without drowning in e-mails, status updates, blog posts and other interesting information. The second is professional: seizing the opportunities that new technology—searchable databases, APIs that enable various Web sites to interact with each other and interactive maps—offers you as a journalist.

As chapter 1 asserted, we're all Web workers now. If you use a computer for a good chunk of every day, you are constantly connected to a wealth of information and large groups of people. How do you make the most of those connections? Although this book and many excellent blogs and Web sites (see the appendix for a reading list) focus on using technology to do better journalism, it's also incumbent on the people doing the journalism to tap into technology to improve their own productivity.

Thousands of smart people are out there working to streamline your life by creating services such as Evernote and Tripit. Meanwhile, new technology is continually being developed to make your journalism more meaningful to your audience. Why waste time longing for the old days, before that audience had so many claims on its attention? Better to spend the time exploring new opportunities—and you can do that by making sure you spend as little time as possible on mundane tasks such as e-mail and note taking.

Let's begin by digitizing your life. Then we'll work on digitizing your journalism.

| **What is it?** | What's *Next?* | Summary |

⚡ YOUR DIGITAL LIFE

Unless you are a so-called early adopter, you probably find it impossible to keep tabs on all the latest and greatest tools and services available online. Often you get the frustrating feeling that somewhere out there exists exactly the cool new thing you need to help you with your latest task—but it just doesn't seem worth the time and energy to try out new products from seemingly fly-by-night companies.

News flash: In most cases, the return is worth the investment. With so many tools and applications available for free (or as free trials), the barriers to testing new applications that could save you time and help organize your life have largely been removed. And because you're a journalist, you're innately curious and equipped with the skills and judgment necessary to make smart decisions.

David Allen spawned a movement in 2002 with his book "Getting Things Done." It has grown into a cult phenomenon, with "GTD freaks" launching and publishing blogs and Web sites tailored to the millions of people who have found Allen's lessons to be a perfect fit for their helter-skelter lives.

Allen does not rely heavily on technology; a foundation for his system is to write every idea or task on a piece of paper and file it in a labeled file folder. That's just too much paper for a digital denizen like me, but Allen's core principles (identify, capture, organize), combined with digital technology, can help streamline your professional and personal lives. Even I am willing to admit that technology can't do everything. But it can help.

▶ Organize your e-mail

If you take some time to use organizational tools such as filters and folders in your e-mail program, you can bring order where there is commonly chaos. But technology can do only so much. It's kind of like driving a car: No matter how cool the car or how many gizmos it has, it's still the driver who makes the decisions that matter.

Commit to following a few time-saving rules to manage an e-mail account (or several) that receives dozens of messages each day. The first is to limit

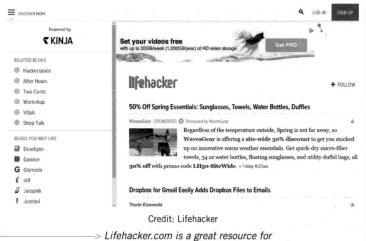
> Lifehacker.com is a great resource for
tips on productivity, offering blogs on money, work, food,
shopping and other topics in the left column. <

the time your e-mail program is up on your screen. Focus on other tasks
for an hour, or two, or four; then launch e-mail again and address the new
messages before closing it and getting back to your other duties. This will
prevent you from being distracted by each new e-mail that arrives in your
in-box and will keep you focused when you do start working with
your e-mail.

One of Allen's best GTD suggestions is to spend no more than two minutes
on each e-mail. If you can reply in less than two minutes, do it. If you can't,
file it. This system works only if you've set up an intuitive folder system so you
can move e-mails without losing track of them. Allen suggests a "Waiting On"
folder for storing e-mails that you can't reply to until you receive additional
information and a "Read This" folder for storing e-mails that contain
attachments or more information than can be read in two minutes. You can
go back to those when you have time, or print them out and take them with
you to read on a bus, train or plane.

The goal is to look at each e-mail message only once. This will save time and
thought energy.

This method is also referred to as "Inbox Zero" by Merlin Mann, who created
the popular personal productivity Web site 43 Folders (www.43folders.com/
izero). The goal is to have zero e-mails in your in-box after you finish an
e-mail session, much like clearing off your desk and putting everything away
before you head out for vacation or home for the night.

▶ Find the right personal productivity tools

E-mail, of course, is just the beginning. All professionals, including journalists and freelance writers, have to manage contacts, to-do lists, calendars and notes. Depending on your profession, the list could also include spreadsheets, presentations, images, databases, project management, Web or graphic design and collaboration with colleagues.

Fortunately, a bevy of slick, simple-to-use tools are available for doing all this—and more. The key is to find as few solutions as possible that do as many of the things on your list as possible. That way you will streamline your productivity and visit fewer Web sites as you get things done.

Manage your time by managing your inputs. If you use a system such as Google Docs or Evernote, for example, you can add notes and Web links while simultaneously managing a to-do list. Such systems also store any documents or images that are related to your projects, so you can keep all your stuff together. And you can access the material from anywhere, via the Web, and share it with others on your team.

An electronic system is better than a paper-and-pencil one because it makes it easy to edit and modify lists and change their order or priority. A shared calendar such as the one available on Google allows you to group items and serves as an archive. Unlike paper, it can't be lost; your system is always waiting for you online. And it is easily shared with more than one person from more than one location.

The virtual-office solutions available range from Microsoft's Office, which includes online versions of Word, Excel and PowerPoint, to free online solutions such as Google Docs and Zoho.

Storing documents and conducting all your business online is a form of cloud computing. By saving your stuff "in the cloud" (on servers accessed over the Internet) you gain the advantage of always having access to your files, no matter where you are—as long as you are able to access the Internet, of course, which is an important consideration when you're planning your personal productivity strategy. Some online solutions feature an offline mode that makes the system and your files available to you when an Internet connection is not.

Remember to keep copies of your important files. This advice is worth following whether you store files in the cloud, as do millions of other people, or store them in some system of your own. It's been said that computer users come in two varieties: those who back up their data and those who will. The first time your hard drive crashes and you lose important work, you'll know what I mean.

▶ ▶ *Develop a strategy*

Forming a personal productivity strategy starts with a simple equation:

What you need to manage + the right tools to manage it = personal productivity.

What you need to manage:

E-mail

Contacts

To-do lists

Calendars

Notes

Word processing

Spreadsheets

Presentations

Images

Databases

Project management

Web or graphic design

Collaboration with colleagues

Some variables to consider when choosing tools:

How much are you willing to pay? ("Nothing" is a viable answer, since many solutions are free.)

Do you need to integrate with other systems for your job or with a particular mobile device? (Outlook for e-mail and calendar, for example, or an iPhone.)

Do you need an offline solution? (This is important if you regularly spend time working somewhere that does not have an Internet connection.)

After you know the answers to these questions, you can begin investigating possible solutions. Here is a list to get you started, with at least one option for each of the tasks listed above.

Office suites:

Google: Contacts, e-mail, documents, calendar, sharing

Office Live: Word, Excel, PowerPoint

DRILLING DOWN

Top 10 Productivity Basics Lifehacker, a popular productivity Web site, recommends these 10 habits and techniques:

1. Text expansion
2. Keyboard shortcuts
3. Inbox Zero
4. Quick searches (local)
5. Quick searches (Web)
6. Timers and working in dashes
7. Ubiquitous capture
8. Remind your future self
9. Ninja-like search skillz
10. Doable to-do lists

For explanations, see Kevin Purdy, "Top 10 Productivity Basics Explained," Lifehacker, June 27, 2009. http://lifehacker .com/5303204/top-10- productivity-basics-explained.

Zoho: Full suite of productivity and collaboration tools, most of them free (Zoho provides tools for everything listed above, plus wikis, customer relationship management and much more.)

Specialized solutions:

Instapaper: Saves Web pages for reading later

Remember The Milk: To-do and task lists

Evernote: To-do lists and note taking; includes audio for use with a cell phone

Dropbox: Storage for files and documents that allows access from anywhere

Backpack: Information organizing and document sharing, plus notes, task lists and calendar

Basecamp: Project management system for teams

Socrata: Creation of dynamic databases from spreadsheets or from scratch

Tripit: Simple organization of travel itineraries in one place

And one more:

MindMeister: Mind-mapping software for brainstorming, for either groups or individuals

▶ ▶ *Bring order to your contacts*

If you are using a Rolodex with little cards to keep your contact list—STOP! This antiquated method is robbing you of precious time and preventing you from storing more pertinent data on each of your contacts. Learn to use the contacts function in your e-mail program (Outlook or Gmail, for example) or, better yet, a service such as Plaxo or even a basic spreadsheet.

You can become a better, more efficient reporter or editor simply by trading any of the paper-based information storage systems you're using and going digital. Your contacts, beat sheet of story ideas, source lists and more will be more sortable, more flexible and more useful if you store them electronically—in spreadsheets, databases or project management systems.

One of the best examples in digital journalism started in 2001, when The Spokesman-Review in Spokane, Wash., began using a database of e-mail addresses for something it called a "reader network." By organizing the contacts that already existed in the newsroom (contacts that

had been spread around and not centralized), the newspaper created a valuable resource for its journalists to use while conducting distributed reporting. This model has been copied by newspapers everywhere and used effectively in many situations, especially when new sources are needed for interviews on specific topics or feedback or reactions to current issues in the news.

Most reader networks began with e-mail addresses from readers who had contacted the newspaper, either by sending a letter to the editor or by asking a reporter about a news story. Through its Web site, a news organization can also build the database by advertising the network and inviting readers to join. By collecting as much information as possible on each contact, the news organization can slice the network several different ways and target specific subsets of the list for certain queries—people who live in a particular ZIP code, for example, or sports fans.

Some news organizations now have more than one reader network. It can make sense to create and manage separate contact databases for education stories (if you need direct contact with teachers) or business stories (if you need to get feedback from local business leaders only).

These lessons can be applied to an individual journalist or a small team of reporters. Every time you receive an e-mail from a reader or potential source, enter it into the contacts on your e-mail program or a separate spreadsheet. Fill out as much information as possible, including where the person lives or works, his or her occupation, interests and anything else that might be helpful the next time you're looking for sources for a story.

▶ *Bring order to your work*

Software developers usually work on projects in collaboration with other people. As a result, many of these developers have at one time or another wanted a better way to manage their projects. This is good for the rest of us because some of these developers have used their software programming skills to create elegant and easy-to-use programs that can track all kinds of projects, including news stories. These programs are especially helpful in the management of big, wide-ranging stories and ongoing coverage.

Project management programs allow you to assign tasks, share files, establish deadlines and include notes. This structure can bring order to an individual working on a big story with lots of moving parts or an entire newsroom attempting to hit daily deadlines.

The Daily of the University of Washington, which has more than 100 part-time reporters, photographers and editors on staff at any given time, uses Basecamp to track all the news stories, photographs and other elements that go into the newspaper and onto its Web site every day.

"I can't imagine how we'd get our newspaper out every day without it," former Daily editor Casey Smith said. "We are able to track reporters and what they are working on, assign photographers to stories and keep tabs on everything that's coming in. The system e-mails the people who are involved in a particular story so there's no more missed communication. It's all there."

While Basecamp requires a subscription (30-day trials are free), other services, such as Zoho, provide basic project management tools free of charge.

Project management is more than just software. It's a skill that is acquired and honed over time. You can take courses on it at your local community college or online. It can help you manage all the facets of work, no matter what kind of work you're doing. Get started at a Web site such as Lifehacker or with a book like "Making Things Happen," by Scott Berkun.

Credit: Basecamp

→ *Basecamp is a project management program that makes group collaboration easy.* ←

⎗ DATA-DRIVEN JOURNALISM

Swimming in data? Face it, every profession, every industry is going through this. Most are learning how to leverage all that digital information. Sophisticated databases are helping attorneys, baseball coaches and every profession in between. Smarter information is now more possible than ever.

What about journalism?

Opportunities abound for journalists to use databases, spreadsheets and other forms of structured or fielded data in news coverage and story development. Using data for writing some stories, about the census or the latest property tax valuations, for example, is obvious, but almost any assignment can be broken down into data points and organized for customized manipulation.

Think of all the information that passes through a news organization every day. Now think about how little of it is accessible to those who work there— or, more important, to interested members of the public. News organizations and journalists can fix this problem by storing information electronically in spreadsheets and shared databases.

A typical newsroom compiles and publishes various lists, some weekly, some annually. The first problem here is that the audience wants access to the information now, not whenever the news organization gets around to publishing it. The next problem is how much repetitive effort goes into building or updating these lists each time they are published. So, most daily newspapers have launched event calendar databases on their Web sites, where visitors can access the most recent information anytime. And event planners can log in and add their events directly into the database.

▶ Why is data-driven journalism important?

The above example is just one way that many news organizations are making their Web sites data destinations, as well they should. Computer-assisted reporting has been around for decades, but when it's restricted to the newspaper format, it can't realize its full potential. On the Web, it can sing—with depth, customization, searchability and a long shelf life. USA Today realized this years ago when it began loading the salaries of professional baseball, football, basketball and hockey players into searchable databases (see www.usatoday.com/sports/mlb/salaries).

RANK	NAME	TEAM	POS	SALARY	YEARS	TOTAL VALUE	AVG ANNUAL
1	Zack Greinke	LAD	P	$ 28,000,000	6 (2013-18)	$ 147,000,000	$ 24,500,000
2	Ryan Howard	PHI	1B	$ 25,000,000	5 (2012-16)	$ 125,000,000	$ 25,000,000
3	Cliff Lee	PHI	P	$ 25,000,000	5 (2011-15)	$ 120,000,000	$ 24,000,000
4	Robinson Cano	SEA	2B	$ 24,000,000	10 (2014-23)	$ 240,000,000	$ 24,000,000
5	Prince Fielder	TEX	1B	$ 24,000,000	9 (2012-20)	$ 214,000,000	$ 23,777,777
6	Cole Hamels	PHI	P	$ 23,500,000	6 (2013-18)	$ 144,000,000	$ 24,000,000
7	Mark Teixeira	NYY	1B	$ 23,125,000	8 (2009-16)	$ 180,000,000	$ 22,500,000
8	Albert Pujols	LAA	1B	$ 23,000,000	10 (2012-21)	$ 240,000,000	$ 24,000,000
9	Joe Mauer	MIN	1B	$ 23,000,000	8 (2011-18)	$ 184,000,000	$ 23,000,000
10	CC Sabathia	NYY	P	$ 23,000,000	5 (2012-16)	$ 122,000,000	$ 24,400,000
11	Felix Hernandez	SEA	P	$ 22,857,142	7 (2013-19)	$ 175,000,000	$ 25,000,000
12	Masahiro Tanaka	NYY	P	$ 22,000,000	7 (2014-20)	$ 155,000,000	$ 22,142,857
13	Miguel Cabrera	DET	1B	$ 21,843,026	10 (2014-23)	$ 292,000,000	$ 29,200,000
14	Adrian Gonzalez	LAD	1B	$ 21,857,142	7 (2012-18)	$ 154,000,000	$ 22,000,000
15	Matt Kemp	LAD	OF	$ 21,250,000	8 (2012-19)	$ 160,000,000	$ 20,000,000
16	Jacoby Ellsbury	NYY	OF	$ 21,142,857	7 (2014-20)	$ 153,000,000	$ 21,857,142
17	Carl Crawford	LAD	OF	$ 21,107,142	7 (2011-17)	$ 142,000,000	$ 20,285,714
18	Matt Cain	SF	P	$ 20,833,333	6 (2012-17)	$ 127,500,000	$ 21,250,000
19	Jayson Werth	WSH	OF	$ 20,571,428	7 (2011-17)	$ 126,000,000	$ 18,000,000
20	Justin Verlander	DET	P	$ 20,000,000	7 (2013-19)	$ 180,000,000	$ 25,714,285

Credit: http://www.usatoday.com/sports/mlb/salaries/

USAToday.com's salaries databases were among the first searchable database projects on a newspaper Web site.

Here are some other kinds of databases that news sites are building and publishing:

Public employee salaries

Property taxes and assessments

Top employers

Test scores

Summer camps for kids

Restaurant and movie listings

Vital statistics (births, deaths, divorces)

New businesses

Business hires and promotions

Guides to local ski areas, golf courses, hiking trails

Newsroom staffs have been entering data on each of these types of content, and more, for years, if not decades. Newspapers have found success in maximizing the value of this information by providing it to their audiences in searchable database formats while streamlining their own operations and cutting down on data entry.

Credit: http://www.baltimoresun.com/news/data/

Data Desk from The Baltimore Sun features searchable databases produced by the newspaper staff.

▶ Every story is a field of data

The term "fielded data" refers to information that is organized into fields in a spreadsheet or database. All news stories contain information, right? So, it's conceivable that any story can be broken into separate fields for analysis.

For example, a business reporter who produces a profile of a local company that recently expanded or won a prestigious award has begun the process of compiling a database. In the narrative form of the story are the following types of information that will fit nicely into a spreadsheet or database:

Company name

Location of headquarters

Address

City

Other locations

CEO/president/owner

Number of employees

Years in business

Annual revenue

Market segment

Awards

A reporter is going to gather this information (and more) while reporting a story. If the data are then entered into a spreadsheet or database, along with data about other companies, the reporter will soon be managing a dynamic and growing data set that can be published online for readers to search and use.

This kind of "evergreen" content is valuable to a news Web site because readers can use it to form their own customized reports. Now that many news organizations have figured this out, everything from casualties from the wars in Iraq and Afghanistan to votes in Congress has become material for searchable databases online.

BreakingNews.com, a subsidiary of NBC News, organizes all the news it publishes with structured data. This allows the site, and its corresponding mobile app, with more than 7 million downloads, to efficiently target its audience with the most relevant news possible, according to general manager Cory Bergman.

"We feel it's incumbent upon us to find people with the news they need," Bergman says. "This is a different approach from the just-publish-it-and-post-it-on-social-media approach. By attaching a metadata payload to each of our BreakingNews alerts, we have the capability to target news to the right people, mostly through push notifications, e-mail and personalized streams."

Bergman offers the example of someone traveling abroad when an explosion shakes a nearby hotel. "You are very motivated to know what happened," he says, and then describes how his team can send a "proximity alert" to everyone with the BreakingNews app in that city soon after the event. "Without the metadata attached to that alert—the location where it occurred, the geographic impact of the story, etc.—we would be unable to make that connection."

Bergman admits it is more work on the publishing side, but he says it is well worth it. "We've engineered our content management system to estimate the metadata—make intelligent guesses—and then our editors can quickly make tweaks on the fly. We're able to do this in a matter of a few seconds."

▶ Telling stories with data

The News-Press in Fort Myers, Fla., along with other news organizations, finally won a long legal battle in 2006 to gain access to a database of Federal Emergency Management Agency payouts to victims of the 2004 hurricanes in Florida. The news organization didn't take the database and spend days or weeks analyzing it before producing a one-size-fits-all report, however. The paper published the database—all 2.2 million records—on its Web site on the same day it acquired the information. Then it invited readers to search and discover for themselves.

In the first 48 hours, visitors to the site performed more than 60,000 searches. Each person wanted to know who got paid what in his or her neighborhood, and The News-Press was able to help each person find out without writing thousands of different stories.

The Washington Post has used databases to tell many stories that are based in its coverage of the federal government. For example, in 2005 Derek Willis and R. Jeffrey Smith used electronic and paper campaign finance filings to build a database of flights on corporate jets by members of Congress. They found that House and Senate leaders flew on corporate-owned jets at least 360 times from January 2001 to December 2004.

"We had to do a lot of work to make it into a coherent set," said Willis, who now works for The New York Times. "The information was there in public, but it wasn't simply a matter of downloading a file and—presto!—instant story. I think most good data-driven pieces share that aspect. The other reason I like it is that it took a common notion (members of Congress fly on corporate jets) and really attempted to define the scope of the activity."

Using databases can work on a local level, too. Think of city council or school board meeting coverage. If you were to create a database that stores all the pertinent data for each meeting (date of the meeting, top agenda items with a quick summary for each, the votes and maybe a field for analysis), you

Credit: ©iStockphoto.com/Stratol

Databases provided the foundation for reporters at The Washington Post for a story on congressional leaders flying frequently on corporate jets, found at http://www.washingtonpost.com/wp-dyn/articles/A38637-2005May5.html.

could pull from this to create an "alternate story form" for the print edition. Online, the audience (and your reporters) would be able to search and sort previous meetings.

Many newspapers have adopted such alternate story forms for basic news coverage, where a narrative is broken apart into easily digestible chunks with labels such as "What happened," "What it means" and "What's next." This new story form applies perfectly to databases. (At The News Tribune in Tacoma we called these "charticles" because they were mashups of charts and articles.)

You can apply this thinking to almost any set of information you collect as a reporter, journalist or blogger. Break down the information into its common parts—subject, location, date, action—and begin building an information resource that will grow as you gather more. It will be useful to you and, more important, to your audience.

Databases can also help you solve the problem today's journalists face with gradual, turn-of-the-screw news stories that can't find the light of day when competing with short, quick news of the now. Adina Levin compares slowly developing stories to "frogboiling," the urban legend in which a frog in gradually heated water gets accustomed to the slowly changing temperature and doesn't jump out—and so boils to death.

"The decline of the North Atlantic cod fishery or the Sacramento-San Joaquin delta are not newsworthy until the cod and the salmon are gone," Levin wrote on her blog. "Wage stagnation isn't newsworthy until the middle class is gone. Tens of thousands dead on US highways each year isn't newsworthy, though a traffic jam caused by a fatal accident is news. Many eyes hunting through financial data may find dramatic scandals, to be sure.

"With database journalism, perilous or hopeful trends and conditions can become worthy of storytelling and comment."[1]

▶ ▶ *Helping reporters do their jobs*

Bill Allison is a senior fellow at the Sunlight Foundation and a veteran investigative reporter and editor. In a 2009 interview with John Mecklin of the Miller-McCune online magazine, he said the notion that computer algorithms combing databases could do what investigative reporters had always done seemed "far-fetched." But they can help.

Computer algorithms can, of course, tirelessly sort through the huge amounts of databased information available online much more quickly than a human reporter could. A public interest reporter can use the power of database technology to discover potential story leads that otherwise might never have been found. But the reporter still has to cultivate the human sources and provide the context and verification needed for quality journalism.

"I think that this is much more a tool to inform reporters," Allison said, "so they can do their jobs better."[2]

One such example was published in 2008 by The New York Times. Andy Lehren, Walt Bogdanich, Robert A. McDonald and Nicholas Phillips used a computer analysis of federal records for a story about employees of the Long Island Rail Road. They found that virtually every career employee (97 percent in one recent year) applies for and receives disability payments soon after retirement. Since 2000, the data show, $250 million in federal disability money has gone to former LIRR employees, including about 2,000 who retired during that time.

"The smart use of data here takes this story from the anecdotal to the slam-dunk case that it is," Derek Willis observed. "Data makes the story airtight in a way that even the best anecdote cannot. It's also an example of what often leads to great stories—looking at information that few (if any) people have examined. The LIRR was unaware of the trends in claiming disability until our reporters brought it to their attention."

---

[1] Adina Levin, "Database Journalism—A Different Definition of 'News' and 'Reader'," BookBlog, March 23, 2009. www.alevin.com/?p=1391.

[2] John Mecklin, "Deep Throat Meets Data Mining," Miller-McCune, January 10, 2009. www.miller-mccune.com/media/deep-throat-meets-data-mining-875.

▶▶ Sharing data

Recently, several of the largest news organizations have built an application programming interface (API) to allow anyone to tap into their data and build tools and Web pages. The use of APIs is nothing new in the technology world; this is how Google made its maps the basis for so many mashups. But a news organization opening up its content through the use of APIs illustrates two important developments, one technical and one political. News organizations are closing the technical divide—it takes programming skills to develop an API—and are finally realizing that closed systems and absolute control over content don't work in the new digital information ecosystem.

The New York Times, the BBC, NPR and The Guardian newspaper in London all have developed multiple APIs for their data. This means other programmers and organizations can mash up the data and news stories on these organizations' Web sites for use on their own sites. (The New York Times

Credit: ©iStockphoto.com/demerzel21

New York Times reporters used databases to discover a high rate of disability pay for railroad retirees and write this story: http://www.nytimes .com/2008/09/21/nyregion/21lirr .html?pagewanted=all.

DRILLING DOWN

What's an API? An application programming interface allows one Web service to feed another. In other words, it's a connection of data and technology between two different Web sites. APIs have changed how Web-based companies interact on the Internet, creating new distribution channels and potential sources of revenues.

is allowing access to story excerpts only for nonprofit purposes, while The Guardian is allowing full text for all purposes, including commercial.) As of this writing, the Times has more than a dozen APIs available, on everything

from events to real estate to campaign finance (see http://developer.nytimes
.com/docs).

News organizations aren't alone in opening up data for others to use.
President Obama's Open Government Initiative led to the creation of Data
.gov, a catalog of federal data sets that anyone can download and mash up
and even display on their own Web sites. Launched in 2009 with 47 data sets,
the site featured 137,000 in 2015.

Another example of the U.S. government sharing data is a Web site at
USASpending.gov that, like Data.gov, is a playground for journalists. The APIs
and data sets allow Web developers at news organizations or independent
journalism start-ups to mix and mash all those data with other information
sources, according to their own specific focus. That means new Web pages
and database subsets built by industry, geography, voting trends or any
other slice of interest.

What is it? | **What's Next?** | Summary

⬇ BUILDING SPREADSHEETS, DATABASES

As more journalists go digital, sharing information becomes easier. That's
a good thing because most newsrooms are rivers of information, much of
which should be easily available to all the journalists who work there. Derek
Willis, while he worked at The Washington Post, wrote a series of essays on
his blog ("humbly titled," comments Willis) Fixing Journalism.

"Can you imagine another information-based business that permitted its
employees to build walls around their information? Can you imagine it
succeeding today?" wrote Willis. (Read the entire series at www.thescoop
.org/thefix.)

Ideally, newsrooms should create central databases containing information
on the sources used for reporting every kind of story. Such a database would
store each source's name and contact information, background information
and the file name and location of a mug shot if one exists. It should contain
personal information on each source, such as professional title and affiliation,
birth date, marital status and spouse's and children's names and ages.
Affiliations (schools, businesses, agencies) should be stored in a separate
table so each can be entered once and related to a source. Then anyone in
the newsroom can search by name, specialty or agency.

That's the key difference between a flat file spreadsheet and a dynamic relational database. If you have a database of all the contacts for a newsroom, you can easily view all the contacts who work for the city. In a spreadsheet, you would have to sort columns and scroll to the part of the list where city hall is listed as the place of work. Searching is just a lot easier in a database.

Even if you don't work in a newsroom, you can build such a database for your own use. It will make tracking the sources for your reporting, and other types of information, more efficient.

▶ Creating a spreadsheet is easy

Even though databases are more powerful than spreadsheets, it's often easier to use a spreadsheet as the first step toward creating a database. There are also times when a spreadsheet is all you need.

When you set up a spreadsheet to compile lists, always try to include as many fields as possible. Fielded data are the key to sorting efficiently and being able to group items.

For example, if you were to make a spreadsheet for all the books you own, you could create the following fields by entering the terms in the first row across the top:

Title

Author

Publisher

Year published

Number of pages

Fiction or nonfiction

Hardcover or paperback

Having this information in a spreadsheet would allow you to sort your list by each of these fields. You could choose to list your books by most recent to oldest, longest to shortest and so on. You could also create spreadsheets at home for your collections of DVDs, CDs and video games. As part of your professional life, you might use spreadsheets to track telephone calls, expenses for a project or lists of leads you maintain for finding a job or freelance assignments.

Launch Excel or log on to Google Docs and get started creating your own spreadsheets.

▶ Moving from spreadsheet to relational database

Now take that same "flat" list of books and turn it into a relational database. On a spreadsheet, you would have to list repeated authors separately each time you entered one of their books. In a database, you would have a separate table for information on the authors, meaning you'd have to enter "John Grisham" just once. That's why it's called "relational"—one type of information relates to another.

A database also allows you to view each record as its own page. Take the example discussed previously regarding a business reporter building a database of local companies: Each company could be displayed as its own page in the database. Or you could search for all companies in a particular market segment or all companies in a certain city.

A number of software solutions can help you build your database once you have information in a spreadsheet. Some are free, some cost a few dollars a month and some—designed for specific kinds of business solutions— cost hundreds or thousands. Popular options include Microsoft Access for Windows and FileMaker for Mac. But if you are just getting started and want to experience the process of building a dynamic database before purchasing software, you might try a free online solution such as Socrata, Zoho or Grubba.

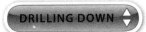

DRILLING DOWN

Discover More Databases To see examples of data-driven journalism and find links to more instructional resources, visit the NICAR (National Institute for Computer-Assisted Reporting) section of the Web site of the Investigative Reporters and Editors (in conjunction with the Missouri School of Journalism) at http://ire .org/nicar/database-library.

Another powerful tool for journalists is Google Fusion Tables, which can help you find data from different sources and bring them together. You can use this service to produce interactive maps and create Web forms to allow collaboration with users.

The Texas Tribune used Fusion Tables to build an interactive map to illustrate its state's congressional redistricting battle. The map was so popular with users that the Tribune revamped it, adding redistricting maps for the House of Representatives, the Senate and the state board of education. The map enables users to see where the current districts are located and allows them to push and pull the map to compare current boundaries with proposed boundaries under the redistricting plans.

For an overview and examples of how news organizations have used Google Fusion Tables, see the presentation provided by Google's Rebecca Shapely at the NICAR conference in 2012 at http://goo.gl/Wkm0f.

⁉ MAP MASHUPS

When Google decided to provide an API for its popular mapping program, it created a whole new category of information on the Web: the map mashup.

This is the product of taking physical location data, such as addresses or points on a map, and organizing them based on a category or information type. Paul Rademacher, a 3-D graphic artist from Santa Clara, Calif., created the first such mashup. He combined apartments listed on craigslist with Google maps to create a map that helped guide him on a hunt for a new place to live.

Since Rademacher's HousingMaps hit the Web, people have created map mashups with Google, Yahoo and Microsoft maps for everything from pub crawls to tracking buses in Bangalore. For a tour of some of the better projects, see http://googlemapsmania.blogspot.com.

▶ Map mashups tell stories, too

Murders happen. In Los Angeles County, they happen practically every day. Reporters at the Los Angeles Times are challenged to keep pace with the news of each new incident, let alone provide context and analysis for what it all means and discover any trends that might be important for the community and local police. So, in 2007, reporter Jill Leovy started the Homicide Report blog to chronicle each new death.

A year later, a team of developers and editors joined forces to build a corresponding database and map.

"[The blog] really wanted to be a database, but at the time we didn't have tech capabilities to do that," said Megan Garvey, deputy metro editor at the Times. "So, I think it was ahead of its time. Now, it definitely has a devoted audience."

While the content is sad and tragic, the execution is elegant and sophisticated. The data are displayed geographically, with each incident mapped to a precise location on a Google map, and are broken down categorically by age, gender, race, type and more.

Traditionally, a newspaper would cut a reporter loose for a couple of weeks each year to research and compile the statistics to go with a long narrative story about the past 12 months of homicides or other crime. But the Times' effort performs that same research and tells a story with maps and data for each new visitor, updated with the most recent information.

"It's heavy on manual labor, but once the work's done, we have a repository of everything we know in one place," Garvey said. "And that's hugely powerful."

Los Angeles homicides are an example of ongoing stories that benefit from the use of data visualization and the compounding power of capturing information and sorting it into the right buckets. If the structure for the data is done correctly, then computer software makes it easy to update and produce.

▶ **Applications in breaking news**

Databases and maps can also be used for breaking news stories. In February 2009, The Salt Lake Tribune used both after a magnitude 6.0 earthquake was felt throughout the region.

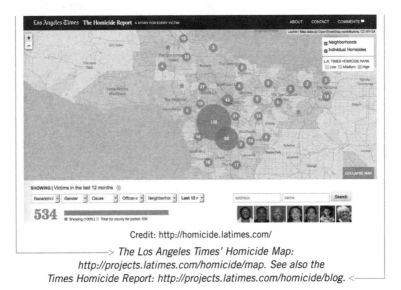

Credit: http://homicide.latimes.com/

> *The Los Angeles Times' Homicide Map:*
http://projects.latimes.com/homicide/map. See also the
Times Homicide Report: http://projects.latimes.com/homicide/blog. <

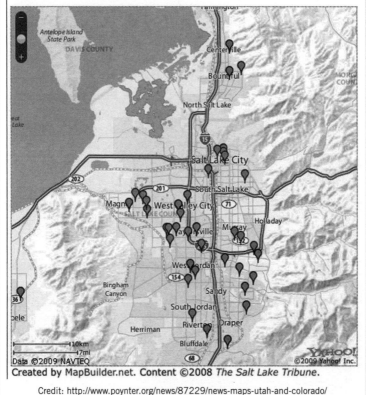

Credit: http://www.poynter.org/news/87229/news-maps-utah-and-colorado/

The Salt Lake Tribune built a collaborative map so users could share their experiences following a local earthquake.

Tribune Web producer Kim McDaniel told The Poynter Institute that the Tribune immediately put a story online and solicited reports and photos from readers. "As those started to come in, I repurposed a map we had built in MapBuilder, along with our admin pages and existing database from a holiday light display map we had done back in November." The Tribune relaunched it as an earthquake map, with a form for readers to submit where they were and what they felt, heard or saw during the quake.

"I also went through and added the accounts from our updated stories and those submitted via e-mail before we got the form up," McDaniel said. Several people also posted their stories on the comments thread on the main story.[3]

What is it? | **What's *Next?*** | Summary

⬇ BUILD AN INTERACTIVE MAP WITH DATA

It's easy to build your own map mashup, with either actual code or a third-party service. If you are comfortable with HTML and want full control over your mashup, see https://developers.google.com/maps and sign up for a free Google Maps API key. The Developer's Guide on the site will walk you through the process for setting it up on your Web site.

If you don't want to mess with code, try one of the free online services that will build the map for you. For example, MapBuilder.net builds a map mashup as you enter locations with actual street addresses, one by one, and works with both Google and Yahoo maps. If you want to turn a spreadsheet

Credit: http://www.mapbuilder.net/

MapBuilder makes it easy to build custom maps for a Web site.

---

[3]Amy Gahran, "News Maps: Utah and Colorado," E-Media Tidbits, Poynter Online, February 25, 2009. www.poynter.org/column.asp?id=31&aid=138368.

into a map mashup, try ZeeMaps, which allows you to build a map from a list of addresses in industry-standard .csv (comma separated value) format, or MapAlist.com, which allows you to convert a Google spreadsheet into a Google Earth mashup for free.

Other services include UMapper, which allows you to create a map on Google, Bing or Yahoo and set privacy settings or embed it on any site, and Google's own My Maps. If you go to maps.google.com and click My Maps, you can customize and save your own map to share with others. You can add photos and draw lines for routes and publish your My Map on other Web sites.

▶ Think beyond single-use maps

Mashing up a Google or Yahoo map on a Web page is now a relatively old way of presenting news and information. More news organizations are discovering the power of building entire data ecosystems from geographically based journalism, data and user-submitted content. After all, if you live in the southeast neighborhood of your city, you want to see everything available on the Web that is happening in the southeast neighborhood—without visiting a dozen different Web pages. That's why some local newspapers have launched projects that display several types of news and information based on geography. So, instead of a single-use map mashup on the latest storm news and photos, a Web audience can visit a site such as The Cincinnati Enquirer's CinciNavigator and see data feeds and recent news stories based on location.

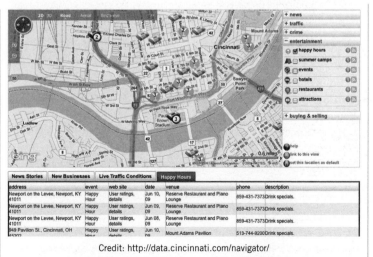

Credit: http://data.cincinnati.com/navigator/

CinciNavigator from The Cincinnati Enquirer.

The best of these implementations also allow the audience to contribute information to share with the neighborhoods, making these sites truly one-stop shopping for news and information tailored to geography.

"Avoid Google Maps fatigue," wrote Hilary Powell, who was part of a team of Northwestern University graduate students who studied the intersection of journalism and emerging location-based technologies in 2008. With Google Maps, Powell continued, you are limited by the interface and the inability to add more interactive features. The Google Maps API, however, gives you some of these capabilities, meaning that journalists should explore other options when using maps online.[4]

EveryBlock is arguably the best example of this. The site was founded by Adrian Holovaty, a computer science major in college who found his way to newspapers in Lawrence, Kan., and Atlanta before spending a couple of years innovating at The Washington Post. In 2007 he won a Knight News Challenge grant to build EveryBlock.

Holovaty sold the platform to MSNBC.com in 2009, but after NBC News took over, EveryBlock was shuttered in 2013. Comcast gave EveryBlock a new lease on life in 2014, however, and the site is now available in Chicago, Philadelphia, Houston, Boston and Denver.

The site's original mission of mapping all sorts of news and information, scraped from the Web by sophisticated algorithms, didn't account for the wave of social networking. Holovaty and his team retooled the site in 2011 and integrated community amid the postings of restaurant reviews, police blotter items, health inspections and links to news stories in traditional media and local blogs.

One of the community features added to the site was the ability to "thank" a neighbor, which is similar to "liking" someone's comment on a news story or blog post. In less than a year, users had thanked neighbors more than 100,000 times.

The power of EveryBlock, and its use of maps, is its geographic organization of information—and now community. Maps can be powerful information filters, and this is how they are used on EveryBlock. You are likely most interested in local news that is closest to you, and one of the easiest ways to present that information, and allow that filtering, is through maps. Ironically, the map as display is less intuitive, and EveryBlock has recognized this, demoting the map in its Web site layout to a small block on the side of the page.

---

[4]Hilary Powell, "Locative Journalism: Recommendations for Journalists, News Organizations and Media Companies," LoJoConnect, June 26, 2008. http://lojoconnect .com/2008/06/26/locative-journalism-recommendations-for-journalists-news-organizations-and-media-companies.

▶ Location-aware devices are changing the game

Displaying information, or even interacting with an audience, based on geography is a powerful new frontier for many local news organizations. Think about the basic structure of data for a news story: headline, byline, body, photograph, caption. Add latitude and longitude to the mix. Now you can display that news and information based on the geography that a Web user chooses in a traditional Web site presentation. But, more important, you can reach the people in the growing portion of the audience who carry GPS-enabled mobile phones, depending on where they happen to be.

"Simply put, location changes everything," Mathew Honan wrote in the January 2009 issue of Wired magazine. "This one input—our coordinates—has the potential to change all the outputs. Where we shop, who we talk to, what we read, what we search for, where we go—they all change once we merge location and the Web."[5]

Whether mobile or not, organizing information geographically opens up new possibilities for journalists to deliver news, information and even advertising tailored to neighborhoods, towns or regions.

But customizing news and information for this new, mobile audience isn't easy for many journalists. So-called locative technology, or location-based services, demands a different presentation because it's a different experience for the end user.

"We are accustomed to using linear interfaces, such as alphabetized directories and timelines, to organize and access information," Hilary Powell wrote on LoJoConnect, a blog run by Northwestern University graduate students. "But our experiences in the real, physical and non-digitized world are usually not linear. They're spatial, dynamic and intuitive. Locative technology has the power to capitalize on that instinct."

The Northwestern students concluded that it was past time to incorporate location-based storytelling into journalism, especially in light of the explosion of location-based services and devices that have hit critical mass in the past few years.[6]

[5]Mathew Honan, "I Am Here: One Man's Experiment With the Location-Aware Lifestyle," Wired, January 19, 2009. www.wired.com/gadgets/wireless/magazine/17-02/lp_guineapig?currentPage=all.

[6]Hilary Powell, "Locative Storytelling: Findings From Our Project," LoJoConnect, June 25, 2008. http://lojoconnect.com/2008/06/25/locative-storytelling-findings-from-our-project.

Credit: Photo courtesy
of Ryan Pitts

RYAN PITTS

▶ **SENIOR EDITOR FOR DIGITAL NEWS** |
The Spokesman-Review
@ryanpitts

NEWSROOM INNOVATOR

The best journalism isn't judged by form or medium, but by its effect on readers' lives. I can't think of a better goal than helping people understand where they live and giving them tools to make decisions, so it's exciting to see more newsrooms recognize the value of data on civic life. There's so much of it out there, on the other side of a FOIA, a screen scraper or, more and more often, just a simple download.

As a specialty, so-called computer-assisted reporting has been around for decades. But new tools that lower the technical barriers to entry, along with a real sense of collaboration in the journalism community, are making data journalism a mainstream discipline. This is great news. When we dive into a new data set, searching for patterns and following up with reporting, readers win.

Readers also win when we help them explore data on their own. That's my favorite part of data journalism, when we get to build something that not only exposes the big picture but also helps people focus on the details most relevant to their lives.

The 2010 Census release was a great opportunity to satisfy both those goals. We're talking about a massive amount of information; the database we use stores 671 distinct pieces of information for each of thousands of geographies, from counties to census tracts and plenty of areas in between. And that's just for one state.

We want people to see the scale of all these data, of course, and the census app we produced at The Spokesman-Review starts with a top-down look at Washington State. It's easy to see where population growth has taken place, and how age, gender, race and ethnicity have shifted. The statewide picture is a shared frame of reference for our readers.

But beyond that, each person has their own story to find, told by the places they care about most. My city, for instance, grew by 6.8 percent in the latest census, slower than most larger cities in the state. But Spokane County is 12.7 percent bigger, which tells me something about where nearby growth is taking place. And my kids' school district? Still mostly white, but definitely more diverse than it was a decade ago. Readers like me can use our census app to map facts like these, to figure out population density in voting districts or compare diversity across school districts. Every page invites exploration, with links to related places. And if I type in my address, one page tells me everything about exactly where I live.

One happy side effect of building this kind of site for readers: Our reporters also get a tool that makes it much easier to search for leads among the numbers. The same thing happens when a newsroom starts mapping crime reports, logging health inspections or tracking political contributions. That's some of the low-hanging fruit; there are countless data sets out there, just waiting to tell local stories.

This is the model we strive for in a data journalism project. The exciting part isn't dumping a bunch of numbers on a screen. It's uncovering the stories buried inside, adding context, and then helping readers make discoveries of their own.

[*Source:* Written by Ryan Pitts at the request of the author.]

★ BETTER LIFE, BETTER JOURNALISM

Online databases power the personal productivity tools, such as contact lists and online task lists, covered in the first part of this chapter and the examples of data-driven journalism in the second part. After you wrap your head around the power of databases, you'll open yourself up to a new world of possibility with regard to news and information.

"We still need people who are better writers than they are data-literate—but it's certainly more important now than it was," says Derek Willis of The New York Times. "That's because more data are available and being released in formats that weren't really available to journalists before. So, beat reporters should know how to obtain, analyze and write about data on their beats."

Everyone needs to leverage existing resources to get the most out of their data. Storing data electronically is a good place to start. Then convert, organize, update and enhance the data.

After you experience the power and ease of working with structured data, you will want to open yourself up to the possibilities of data-driven journalism.

GET GOING Checklist ✓

☐ Convert your contacts list to an electronic form. If your list is already electronic, organize, update and enhance it.

☐ Create a spreadsheet for something you want to track, such as job opportunities and contacts, reporting sources or the books, DVDs or video games you own.

☐ Convert the spreadsheet to a database using FileMaker, Google Docs, Access, Socrata, Zoho or Grubba.

☐ Build a map mashup for something in your life or a news story you are working on. Then publish the map to a Web site.

☐ Visit different sections of a news Web site and identify one story from each section that would have benefited from data or mapping.

CHAPTER 9

Building a Digital Audience for News

I f journalists produce great stories but no one reads them, how can news survive?

The traditional business model for journalism is in disarray. The distribution monopolies that publishers and broadcasters enjoyed for decades are crumbling. An informed discussion of journalism today must therefore include an awareness of new distribution models, efficiency and marketability.

Can marketing and analytics save journalism? Not on their own, of course. But we live in a world where the amount of content produced has increased exponentially, yet we still each have just two eyes, two ears and one mouth. Thus, journalism needs to find new benefits from new marketing strategies and measurement tactics.

This type of marketing is not advertising, or slogans, or logos. And this type of measurement isn't counting bylines for a performance review. Digital publishers need to establish effective publishing goals and be consistent in their pursuit of those goals. Quality content published in some significant quantity, and designed to be found easily in search engines and shared in social media, is a recipe for a successful digital publishing business.

In 2014, an internal report from The New York Times simply titled "Innovation" made its way around news industry circles. The report provided an exhaustive look at the state of the news media and where the Times stood in comparison to the new and existing players based on dozens of interviews with Times executives, staffers and industry experts outside the Times. Among its most important conclusions was that the organization was in dire need of finding new audiences.

"The New York Times is winning at journalism. Of all the challenges facing a media company in the digital age, producing great journalism is the hardest.

Our daily report is deep, broad, smart and engaging—and we've got a huge lead over the competition. At the same time, we are falling behind in a second critical area: the art and science of getting our journalism to readers."[1]

To build your audience online, you need to analyze what you publish, what your readers like and don't like, and then do more of what they like. You also need to make sure that your content, especially content your current readers have shown interest in, can be found by new audiences through search engines and shared through social media.

Data and analytics, whether counting page views and unique visits or total shares on social media, help drive decisions on where best to apply the news-gathering resources at most news organizations today.

"There are ways to use new platforms and tools as distribution channels as well as ways to create content and digital storytelling that take journalistic enterprising to new heights—an exciting prospect for the future of news and media," says Cory Haik, executive producer and senior editor for digital news at washingtonpost.com. "News organizations should consider success on both fronts when attempting to create new audiences. Experimenting and being out there early is important and should be taken seriously. Publishers should see where these efforts take them and act quickly to realign talent and production power to things that are working."

Editors might love multimedia and have staffs that are able to produce great video, but when they look at the audience numbers, they are forced to consider what they get back for that investment of time. In the business world, that's called ROI, or return on investment. It's a relatively new application in journalism, but one that comes with practicing journalism in the digital age.

The life cycle of publishing news has also changed dramatically. The competition for attention among the digital audience has forced journalists and news companies to adopt optimization techniques, which means changing headlines for better search engine optimization if stories are not doing well online and trying new angles and new platforms for promotion in social media.

"At The New York Times, far too often for writers and editors the story is done when you hit publish," said Paul Berry, who helped found The Huffington Post. "At Huffington Post, the article begins its life when you hit publish."[2]

---

[1] The New York Times, "Innovation," March 2014. www.scribd.com/doc/224608514/The-Full-New-York-Times-Innovation-Report#scribd.

[2] The New York Times, "Innovation."

Berry added that, at The Huffington Post, a story cannot be published unless it has a photo, a search headline, a tweet and a Facebook post. It's a smart approach, and one that news publishers everywhere have rushed to emulate.

Making smart business decisions based on data is critical to digital journalism today. This final chapter will get you started with the fundamentals of building an audience online:

- Content tracking
- Web analytics
- Search engine optimization
- Effective headline writing for the Web and social media
- Distribution and engagement through social media

The bottom line: For journalism to grow and be healthy, it needs a growing and healthy audience. And that job is no longer relegated to the circulation, research or marketing department.

As the Times'"Innovation" report summed it up: "More than ever, the hard work of growing our audience falls squarely on the newsroom."

What is it? What's Next? Summary

⁨⁇⁩ MEASURING JOURNALISM

As newsrooms have taken on publishing new forms of content—social media posts, blogs, video, breaking news updates, push notifications—to new platforms—e-mail, mobile apps, Twitter—new structures have been put in place. Management consultants will tell you that "what gets measured gets managed." In recent years some have also said, "What gets measured gets done."

"Smart digital journalists will spend time defining their audience and setting goals before picking up the tools," Haik says. "In some ways these are concepts that traditionally the publisher or business side of a media company considered before developing products. The editorial branch was created to meet that publisher framework. However, the success of everything in the current newsroom or digital publishing landscape—from a simple social media production on an investigative series to building a tablet app to creating an entirely new coverage area—should be thought of from a holistic perspective and tied to an audience strategy, which the newsroom is now helping to define."

Newsrooms now track and measure everything they do. Tom Chester, deputy managing editor at the News Sentinel in Knoxville, Tenn., begins each weekday with a stand-up meeting in the newsroom. The first item on the agenda each day is a detailed report of content published and traffic generated the previous day. "We track updates on all platforms: Web, mobile, e-mail," Chester said. "We started with almost nothing and now we're up to about 500 updates per week."

Chester added that in the first year of this tracking and measurement effort, the report was modified at least six times, demonstrating how adaptable a newsroom should be today. If the first assumption about what's important isn't quite right, make a change, try it out and keep moving. "Our goal is to measure metrics that impact our readers on all of our platforms and use those metrics to improve our content," Chester said.

If newsroom leaders had simply announced at a staff meeting the need for everyone to learn new skills and publish more frequently to more platforms, little progress would have been made. Instead, the print-centric newsroom—which published 3,000 videos from 2006 through 2009—put a structure in place to measure and manage the new content, and it was able to show significant progress and build on its successes.

Credit: Photo courtesy of the Knoxville News Sentinel

> *Tom Chester, news operations manager at the Knoxville News Sentinel, leads a morning meeting that begins with a detailed report of the previous day's performance.* <

Web, Mobile, Print Performance Report								
June 29-July 5, 2009	Mon	Tues	Wed	Thur	Fri	Sat	Sun	Totals
Web								
Unique visitors								
knoxnews.com/gvx.com								
Page views								
knoxnews.com/gvx.com								
knoxville.com								
Daily updates								
knoxnews.com								
knoxvillebiz.com								
pxtra/govolsxtra.com								
knoxville.com								
Hitwise Visits/Views								
knoxnews.com								
govolsxtra.com								
wbir.com								
Videos produced								
Weekly								
Blog views								
Monthly								
Comments								
Monthly								
Mobile								
Text Alerts								
Weekly								

Credit: News Sentinel

The Knoxville News Sentinel uses this spreadsheet format to track its content and audience.

Developing a culture and processes to track and measure your work product is essential to competing in this data-driven world. Traditional journalists may cringe at the idea that their artful storytelling or their dogged investigations can be "reduced" to a "work product," but nearly all digital publishers are building their businesses on the inventory of content produced, either by journalists or by other writers, bloggers or photographers. Producing that content on a regular schedule is vital to a functioning news business.

And without the business, there are no paychecks. This reality applies to mainstream news companies and independent journalism start-ups.

Track. Measure. Adapt. It's the way the Web works.

What is it? | **What's Next?** | Summary

⤓ TRACK ALL THAT YOU PUBLISH

"We track basically anything that is able to be tracked," says Jason Silverstein, senior vice president of digital product development at American City Business Journals in Charlotte, N.C.

Welcome to the new world. How many breaking news updates did you send last week? How many video stories did you publish last month? By percentage, how much did your online audience grow (or shrink) last year?

These questions, and dozens more, can be answered easily by sophisticated news operations and solo bloggers alike. Productivity, of course, is one of the key measurements for managers. But going beyond the basics and tracking content published is a smart business strategy.

Since this can be a time-consuming endeavor, start with only those areas you are focusing on as top priorities. And have a goal in mind: Do you want to increase the number of news updates posted each day? The only way to know if you are making progress toward your goal is to track your production.

▶ **What to track**

Baker's dozen plus one: Here is a starter list of content types that journalists and newsrooms could be tracking regularly:

Total news stories per day

News stories by topic or section (sports, business, local and so on)

Total blog posts per day (if these are different from news stories on the site)

Blog posts by specific blog

Slide shows per week

Video stories per week

Podcasts or other audio stories

News updates (if these are different from news stories on the site)

Breaking news e-mail alerts

Text message alerts or mobile push notifications

E-mail newsletters that are not sent automatically

Twitter, Facebook or other social network posts

Social media engagement and followers (to chart growth)

User-generated content (blog posts, photos, videos)

The easiest way to track this information is with a Web-based spreadsheet that many people can access, so the task of updating the information can be distributed (see chapter 8 for more information). Across the top, list the content types you already publish fairly regularly. Down the left side, list the dates. After a week's worth or month's worth of dates, insert a line that totals the amounts in each column for that week or month. Then copy and paste the format for that week or month for each time period going forward. Now the spreadsheet will do the math for you.

▶ How to set benchmarks

Compiling data on productivity without setting goals for either maintaining or improving the level of output is relatively pointless. The objective of tracking content is to create benchmarks that become the goals for a newsroom, or even a solo journalist, to aim for.

After you start tracking content, you will begin to get a more accurate sense of where to set your goals. Start with a simple number of stories, videos or blog posts to be produced per day or per week. These goals should evolve to include other measurements, including audience numbers, revenue and audience satisfaction metrics such as user registrations or e-mail newsletter and RSS feed subscriptions.

At Google, they call this process OKR, which stands for objectives and key results. Marissa Mayer, vice president of search product and user experience at Google, describes the OKRs as "incredibly measurable. Did we launch the product on time? Did we get the number of advertisers we wanted? Did we attain a certain level of user happiness?"[3]

If you still think revenue shouldn't be a factor in the content decisions journalists make, you should start looking for a time machine and go back a few decades. The reality of today's competitive landscape, what media expert Christopher Vollmer calls "digital Darwinism," demands that business needs and journalistic tactics work in concert.[4]

"The most important metrics I follow are revenue and unique users, often tracking the mix as revenue per unique user," Silverstein says. "Many

[3]Marissa Mayer, "Nine Lessons Learned About Creativity at Google," Stanford's Entrepreneurial Thought Leader Series, May 2006. http://ecorner.stanford.edu/authorMaterialInfo.html?author=205.

[4]Christopher Vollmer, "Digital Darwinism," Strategy + Business, May 11, 2009. www.strategy-business.com/resiliencereport/resilience/rr00069.

organizations would say unique users, which is very similar in that the goal is to have more unique people taking interest in your content. When the audience broadens, the opportunities to both display your content and find sales opportunities increase."

Establishing benchmarks and goals can be done only on a case-by-case basis. What works in one market may not make sense in another. And even within a particular Web site, some sections will have goals different from those of other sections. If you track pageviews to the local news section of a local newspaper Web site, for example, you can look backward to see what an average month produces and what the best and worst numbers are. Use this history to develop your estimates, and then determine where to set your goals for increasing the audience to that section.

By contrast, the progress of a relatively new section of a Web site, or a new blog, that doesn't have years of past performance will be more difficult to forecast. But you can use the performance of other sections or projects that are similar in scope as the basis for your estimates.

Don't set goals arbitrarily. Picking a number because it sounds good is not the same as making judgments based on historical data. If you expect your Web site to increase its traffic by 30 percent in the next six months, what specific initiatives are you launching that will propel that growth? Your audience, after all, is unlikely to grow just because you want it to.

And remember, goals should include more than just numbers of pageviews. Think about Google's Mayer and her OKRs: Are there new advertisers? Is the audience happy? Think broadly when setting goals, but use the traffic data and audience patterns to manage and measure the pursuit of those goals.

What is it? | **What's *Next?*** | Summary

⬇ TRACK YOUR AUDIENCE

After you know what you're publishing, you'll want to know what your audience is consuming.

At one time newsroom meetings were conducted in blissful ignorance of what, exactly, the audience was reading. Editors theorized about what the audience wanted, based on anecdotal feedback, phone calls, eventually e-mails and maybe letters to the editor. This echo chamber created assumptions that persisted through generations of journalists. It was common to hear editors assert at page-one meetings, "Readers don't like those stories. They like these stories."

But, when it came right down to it, those editors had no idea what they were talking about.

It's now standard practice for newsrooms to have large screens adorning the walls and hanging from the ceilings displaying current audience performance across Web, mobile and social media. New-media start-ups like Gawker, BuzzFeed and Vox Media were built from the ground up to include minute-by-minute analysis of audience data to help guide decisions and editorial activity.

Newspapers and TV news stations have transformed to adapt to this new competitive landscape.

▶ Use Web analytics software

> **DRILLING DOWN ▲▼**
>
> **Options for Analytics** You can choose among three possible sources of traffic-measuring tools, which are often referred to as "Web analytics":
>
> Commercial systems that charge monthly fees but allow real-time traffic reporting. Adobe Omniture is the industry standard. Chartbeat is a better option for small budgets and has grown to become an industry leader.
>
> Free programs that provide detailed traffic reporting but update only once every 24 hours (meaning you have to wait until tomorrow to see today's traffic). Google Analytics is the standard here and has improved its real-time results.
>
> Built-in tools offered by the content-management software or hosting service you're using.

Web analytics—the software and mechanisms to track Web site traffic—have changed all that. But it took years for many newsrooms to embrace the numbers coming from their Web sites and begin to use them in their editorial decision making.

Now Web services such as Omniture, Chartbeat and Google Analytics make it easy to track your Web site's performance with a Web-based dashboard panel. These services work by using bits of code you place on your Web pages, which feed traffic information to the tracking services on other servers.

You simply copy and paste a small piece of JavaScript code provided by the service into the HTML of every page on your site. The code keeps track of everyone who visits the page and sends the data it records over the Web to another Web site, where those results are tallied and displayed.

Google Analytics is a free Web-based tracking service that is practically as powerful as any commercial traffic service. It's quick and easy to set up and comes with an intuitive dashboard. Just sign up for an account, paste the code on your pages and visit the Google Analytics Web site anytime you want to check on your traffic (see www.google.com/analytics).

Thousands of Web sites use this free Google tool to track their visitors. It's easy to get started, and the administration screen is fairly intuitive and powerful—although it is tailored to Google AdWords customers, with emphasis on conversion rates and other customer metrics.

This is why Google offers the service for free. By using the data, Web site publishers can track which AdWords are driving the most traffic to their sites and will spend more money with Google to buy more AdWords. Thus, it's good business for Google to give away its Analytics.

Google isn't the only free option for Web analytics, and new players are coming onto the scene all the time. Other options to explore include Chartbeat and Clicky, which both offer low-cost services that will give you real-time tracking better than even Google offers.

Some content-management systems and blog platforms offer traffic-tracking tools as part of their administrative interfaces. Most of these services are limited and will probably only whet your appetite for more detailed information.

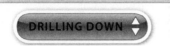

DRILLING DOWN

Just Add JavaScript Any service (such as Google Analytics) that relies on JavaScript code won't work if the visitor's browser blocks JavaScript. JavaScript is a simple programming language that adds interactive features to Web pages. It is used for everything from pop-up windows to buttons that change appearance when you roll over them with your cursor. It's rare but not impossible for hackers to use JavaScript code for malicious purposes, so most Web browsers offer their users the option to disable JavaScript support.

▶ Identify key data points

A robust traffic-reporting system will offer you a dizzying array of statistics and metrics to consider. It would be inefficient to try to keep track of all of them, so you need to decide which measurements are most important and will give you the best gauge of how your site is performing.

Generally, the best Web traffic measurements are pageviews, visits compared with unique visitors and engagement and referrers.

Credit: Google Analytics

→ *Google Analytics makes it easy to track your audience.* ←

Pageviews: This is the total of Web pages viewed in a given time period. If the Web site is supported with advertising, this is also directly related to the inventory the site has to offer prospective advertisers. It's also how content is ranked in terms of popularity. When Web sites provide lists of their most popular content, those lists are usually based on numbers of pageviews.

Visits and unique visitors compared: "Visits" refers to the number of times all visitors access a Web site. If you visit the site twice and I visit it three times, that's a total of five visits. But we would represent only two unique visitors. You can also use visits in conjunction with pageviews to determine the average number of pages viewed per visit (pageviews divided by visits).

Engagement and referrers: The amount of time spent on the site by each user will help you gauge the level of engagement for your Web site. Tracking referrers will help you learn where your traffic is coming from. Don't be surprised to see that Google and other search engines make up as much as one-third of this figure.

"When we analyze, we make sure to keep whatever metric is being reviewed in the context of other metrics," Silverstein says. "For example, one important editorial metric is pageviews. Yet pageviews can be misread easily without context.

"Taking the example further, if our editors see an article has a large amount of pageviews, that is considered more reaching than a 50-image slide show with the same amount of views. This is always proven by mixing unique users against the content, which gives the team context about the particular asset."

The search continues for the "killer metric" that will accurately and comprehensively reveal audience engagement. Pageviews and unique users can tell only part of the story. Some Web experts, for example, attribute significant pageview numbers to bad design, meaning visitors have to click on many pages just to find what they are looking for.

Most-viewed and most-e-mailed stories have influence on editorial planning meetings, as they should. But, as Silverstein notes, context and perspective are important when you use Web metrics to make journalistic decisions. Sensational stories involving crimes or celebrities will usually draw more pageviews. Professional and college sports coverage also does well on newspaper Web sites. The context is that the audience for coverage of sports and celebrities is larger than the audience for more local stories. If I'm a Chicago Cubs fan, for example, but I don't live in Chicago, I am still potential audience for the Chicago Tribune Web site. But I'm probably not going to read about the Chicago city council.

Click-driven metrics have been employed since the consumer Web hit the mainstream in the 1990s. Nowadays there is a push toward something more meaningful, what Chartbeat CEO Tony Haile calls the "Attention Web."

"The click had some unfortunate side effects. It flooded the web with spam, linkbait, painful design and tricks that treated users like lab rats. Where TV asked for your undivided attention, the web didn't care as long as you went click, click, click," Haile wrote on Time.com in 2014.

"Sites like the New York Times are redesigning themselves in ways that place less emphasis on the all-powerful click. New upstarts like Medium and Upworthy are eschewing pageviews and clicks in favor of developing their own attention-focused metrics. Native advertising, advertising designed to hold your attention rather than simply gain an impression, is growing at an incredible pace."[5]

Use traffic data to determine which projects are working, too. For example, Web analytics can help you to manage a new blog or a new section of a Web site. But if the traffic numbers are anemic, that doesn't necessarily mean you should pull the plug, especially if people are still excited about the idea behind the project.

---

[5]Tony Haile, "What You Think You Know About the Web Is Wrong," Time.com, March 9, 2014. http://time.com/12933/what-you-think-you-know-about-the-web-is-wrong.

News organizations have a tendency to plant lots of seeds but spend little time on the care and feeding of new sprouts. By analyzing traffic data and establishing benchmarks, you can more closely manage projects and improve them over time.

What is it?   *What's Next?*   Summary

◪ SEARCH ENGINE OPTIMIZATION (SEO)

How do you drive more audience to those good ideas everyone is excited about? Traditional marketing can take you only so far, so search engine optimization (SEO) and viral distribution through social media remain increasingly important.

To understand how to optimize your Web content so that it can be found by search engines, you must first gain an understanding of how search engines work.

▶ Understand search engines

Essentially, search engines perform three main functions:

Spiders and robots: These terms refer to small computer programs that are sent out by search engines such as Google and Bing to crawl the Internet and track and record the information found on Web pages. They are programmed to look for new pages or new information on existing pages and send back reports to their respective search engines for indexing.

Indexing: Larger, more powerful computer programs on the search engines' servers take the information sent from the spiders and robots and build large database files with references to all the content connected to the right links. This is the catalog of the Web that a search engine refers to when you perform a search.

Queries: When you type a keyword search into the home page of Google or Bing, you are making a query of that search engine's database. Additional computer programming takes your keywords and looks in the index for the most relevant results; then it returns and presents those results on Web pages for you to explore.

▶ SEO for journalists

Search engines rank the results of searches and present them on a series of Web pages, usually displaying 10 results per page. Google has become the dominant search engine during the past decade because of the algorithms it uses to establish relevance. Based on the peer-reviewed journal method found throughout academia, the Google algorithms give more importance to Web sites that other sites are linking to. Links from other sites are like endorsements. And the more credible (endorsed) a site is, the more credibility or authority it can give to another site by linking to it.

This phenomenon of credibility based on links has been referred to as "Google juice."

The vast majority of Web searchers do not venture past the first page of results, so having your Web site show up among the first 10 is a huge advantage if you are hoping to grow your audience. Many news sites, in fact, receive as much as two-thirds of their Web traffic from search engines, so improving the ranking of your pages in search engines is a smart strategy. And that's the goal behind SEO.

"What you need to understand is that the search engine has done all the hard work of collecting and analyzing web pages," Ken McGaffin wrote on Wordtracker.com. "BUT it only makes that information available when someone does a search by entering words in the search box and hitting return."[6]

Those words that people enter into a search engine are called "keywords," which is just a fancy way to describe the words that people use when searching for information online. The idea is, if you publish the most credible story on organic broccoli farming and someone enters the keywords "organic broccoli farming" into Google, the search engine will display a link to your story at the top of the first results page, driving more traffic to your site than to any other.

This concept raises some warnings for journalists. Some fear stepping out onto that slippery slope that can lead to journalism cheapened by the blatant insertion of popular keywords to get some added Google juice. Or, worse, editors and writers could start picking stories based on keywords in hopes of generating increased Web traffic.

---

[6]Ken McGaffin, "Keyword Basics Part 1: How Search Engines Work," Wordtracker, November 24, 2006. www.wordtracker.com/academy/keyword-basics-part-1-how-search-engines-work.

"This Boring Headline Is Written for Google" was the headline of a 2006 story by Steve Lohr in The New York Times about SEO and journalism.

"There are no algorithms for wit, irony, humor or stylish writing," Lohr wrote. "The software is a logical, sequential, left-brain reader, while humans are often right brain."[7]

It's really just the latest balancing act in efforts to make journalism interesting without allowing it to cross the line into the sensational. If journalists understand the basics of writing search engine–friendly headlines, they can drive more audience to their news and information without compromising any of their values.

What is it?   **What's *Next*?**   Summary

⬇ USE SEO TO GROW YOUR AUDIENCE

The importance of SEO, and its more commercial cousin SEM (search engine marketing), has led to the creation of a multimillion-dollar industry. Companies are available for hire to help you engineer your Web pages, and some even "guarantee" top placement in the big search engines for your site. But the reality is that plenty of information is available on the Web, and most Web publishers can do their own SEO—at least on a basic level.

At its core, the practice of SEO is simply a matter of putting the words on your Web pages that you think a prospective reader would type into a search engine while looking for an article on that subject. Some keywords are static, such as the title of your Web site and the description you create for your site. Other keywords are new to your site every time you publish a new piece of content.

Entire books have been written about the practice of SEO. But because you may not have the time or the inclination to take a deep dive into the topic, here is a quick guide to get you started.

▶ Grow audience with content and links

Content is king: Fortunately, the content factor is a big advantage for journalists in the SEO game. E-commerce and marketing Web sites struggle

9
CHAPTER

---

[7]Steve Lohr, "This Boring Headline Is Written for Google," The New York Times, April 9, 2006. www.nytimes.com/2006/04/09/weekinreview/0910hr.html.

DRILLING DOWN ▲▼

Search Engine Marketing   The SEM industry has exploded in the past 10 years and is filled with companies that will help other businesses buy text ads on search engines. Strategy is involved, since the ranking of the paid ads is determined by pay-per-click rates. Thus, the goal is to pay the lowest rate possible to get the highest ranking.

to publish quality content regularly to impress the search engines. But journalists? Hey, this is what we do.

Linking is queen: Tap into Web karma by linking out to as many sites as makes sense. This will increase your authority in many search engines and could lead to more Google juice if the sites you are linking to recognize it and return the favor.

Make sure you link between your pages, too. This is an easy way to increase the number of links to your pages and will also increase the usability of your site for your audience.

Make anything that is important a link off the home page, because search engines give greater value to those links.

Make sure your links make sense: See Drilling Down: Use Descriptive Links.

Title tags: The title tag appears at the top of a user's Web browser. Many content-management systems and blog platforms have the ability to display the headline from the story or blog post in the title tag. This is helpful, as search engines give a lot of credence to title tags. Search engines attach greater weight to the headline and the title tag on a Web page. That means headline writing is especially important for good SEO. It will be covered in a separate section.

HTML meta tags: If you select **View—Source** on a Web page, you will see the computer code that is behind the Web page. Near the top are some meta tags that provide information about the Web page even though this information doesn't actually display for the user. Web designers used to stuff this area with as many keywords as they could dream up in the hope that a search engine would give their pages credit for those words as content. Google and other search engines have changed their algorithms to account for this scheme, but putting a few relevant keywords in the meta description is still a good idea.

▶ Write effective Web headlines

Almost everyone writes headlines today. Even if you work for a newsroom that has a copyediting and headline-writing team, you will likely have a blog or publish other multimedia content that will need headlines, too. Even a post on Twitter requires concise, compelling language, just like a good headline.

Mac Slocum, the online managing editor for O'Reilly Publishing's Radar Web sites, points out, "You don't need to know the intricacies of indexing, but basic SEO is the conduit between an audience and content. It's not just a business initiative."[8]

DRILLING DOWN

Use Descriptive Links   Links help your visitors and search engines understand what your page or article is about. Therefore, they should not be generic, such as "click here" or "yesterday's article."

[*Source:* Patrick Beeson, former content manager, Scripps Interactive Newspapers Group.]

It is even more important for independent journalists who don't have the power of a big news brand and all that Google juice behind their stories.

On average, eight out of 10 people will read a headline, but only two out of 10 will read the rest of the piece. This is the secret to the power of the headline and why it so highly determines the effectiveness of the entire piece.[9]

Combine that with how important headlines are for search engines, and you can see how critical it is for a news site to put considerable thought and strategy into its headline writing.

▶▶ *Write for readers and robots*

Remember, you have two audiences online: readers and robots.

For readers: Web headlines have no friends.[10] The headline sits alone, without deck heads, photos or graphics, so it has to carry the entire load. Web headlines should be simple, literal and direct. They must motivate readers to move the mouse and click (or touch, if using a smartphone or tablet).

For robots: SEO means that if a headline contains search keywords that are also repeated in the text of the story (and elsewhere on the page), the story will acquire more Google juice and be returned higher on search pages.

---

[8]Amy Gahran, "How Much Should Journalists Know About SEO?" E-Media Tidbits, Poynter Online, March 13, 2009. www.poynter.org/column.asp?id=31&aid= 160037.

[9]Brian Clark, "How to Write Magnetic Headlines," Copyblogger, n.d. www.copyblogger .com/magnetic-headlines.

[10]Kathleen Cooper, presentation at an in-house workshop on writing headlines for the Web, The News Tribune, Tacoma, Wash.

▶ ▶ *Make good headlines better*

1. Keywords, keywords, keywords. Think about Journalism 101: who, what, where. This attracts both readers and robots. A sports headline must have the team name. A headline on a local story must have the city name. Write for readers with Google in mind.

When the Atlas foundry exploded in Tacoma in 2008, the headline in The News Tribune in Tacoma, Wash., the next day said, "Everything Shook, Then Went Black." It worked well . . . because it had friends, namely, a huge picture of black smoke and flames pouring from the building. Online, though, this headline doesn't tell the reader or the robot anything. The headline published on the newspaper's Web site, thenewstribune.com, was "Explosions Rock Tacoma's Nalley Valley."

2. Use conversational language. That makes the reader want to know more. Be direct, and focus on the unique.

Instead of "Council Votes to Raise Taxes," try "Get Ready to Pay More Property Taxes."

3. Don't be afraid to inject a little attitude. We must be fair and accurate, but that's no reason to be boring.

Look at all headlines as they appear without the context of the story. They should have something to engage potential readers, especially those who come across the headlines while conducting related searches.

Think about readers and robots when you are writing headlines. If you were Googling for information on a certain news story, what words would you use? Think of a handful of keywords; then use sound judgment to see how many of those keywords you can work into the headline without sacrificing its potential interest for readers.

What is it? | **What's *Next?*** | Summary

⬇ USE SOCIAL MEDIA AS DISTRIBUTION CHANNELS

If the top three priorities in real estate are location, location, location, then the top three priorities of Web publishing are distribution, distribution, distribution.

"The hardest part for me has been the realization that you don't automatically get an audience," said Janine Gibson, editor in chief of

The Guardian's Web site. "For someone with a print background, you're accustomed to the fact that if it makes the editor's cut—gets into the paper—you're going to find an audience. It's entirely the other way around as a digital journalist. The realization that you have to go find your audience—they're not going to just come and read it—has been transformative."[11]

Writers, bloggers and even the largest news companies have all learned how to offer their digital content through RSS feeds and e-mail newsletters and on mobile platforms. And we just discussed search, which is effectively like distributing content through Google and Yahoo and Bing. All are excellent methods of enabling visitors to find your content without visiting your Web site again and again.

What about reaching new audiences? That's what social networks and blogs are made for. They bring the benefit of new channels for distributing content in addition to cultivating a community for source development, transparency and credibility (as discussed in chapter 3).

The New York Times "Innovation" report focused on three areas for growing audience: discovery (how the journalism is packaged and distributed), promotion (calling attention to the journalism) and connection (creating a two-way relationship with readers that deepens their loyalty).

"Audience Development is the work of expanding our loyal and engaged audience. It is about getting more people to read more of our journalism."[12]

Loyalty is critical to audience growth, and social media platforms offer news organizations the unique ability to increase loyalty through engagement. This goes beyond simple distribution of content and attracting a "drive-by audience."

Many people believe that "if the news is important enough, it will find me." What makes this true more often than not is engagement. Facebook will show your content to more people the more engaging that content is. It's how the algorithm works. More Twitter users will find your news the more times it is retweeted and favorited. And then there is "dark social," which refers to links shared by e-mail, text message and other apps that are not easily trackable by Web analytics programs.

---

[11]The New York Times, "Innovation."

[12]The New York Times, "Innovation."

"Virtually every journalist today is closer to the tools of publishing the news than at any point since the hand-pulled press of colonial times," Derek Willis of The New York Times wrote on his blog in 2014. "We can push buttons and our words, images and graphics appear on the Web. A story's afterlife—what happens when it has been published—is something that we can revise and extend. These are hugely important changes; they alter what is possible for all of us."[13]

▶ Target specific channels

Here is a starter list of social media marketing channels that most—if not all—news media Web sites should be watching and participating in. Commenting and linking, when appropriate, are effective ways to get others to view, link to and comment on your journalism and become part of your community.

Blogs: Read blogs that focus on the same things you do. Contribute to the conversations you find on them, too.

YouTube, Flickr, etc.: Follow the channels and streams of people who post content that is related to what you cover. Link to interesting content from blogs or other pages on your site.

Twitter, Facebook, Google+, Pinterest, Instagram, etc.: More and more people are getting their news from social networks. Make sure they can get your news through these popular platforms, too. Create Facebook pages for specific sections or topics you cover. See chapter 2 for information on using Twitter and other microblogging services.

Digg, reddit, Fark, StumbleUpon, etc.: Social news and bookmarking sites can provide a significant short-term boost in traffic. Converting those new readers into an audience that is loyal is the challenge. "Digging" your own stories used to be ethically questionable for journalists. Not anymore.

---

[13]Derek Willis, "We're All Publishers Now," The Scoop, November 17, 2014. http://thescoop.org/archives/2014/11/17/were-all-publishers-now.

While it was once customary for a news organization to appoint one person or a small team to manage social media distribution efforts, that task has largely been distributed to everyone in the newsroom. For independent journalists or bloggers, it is also one more task. You can develop automated solutions that help, such as using Facebook applications to display your headlines and providing quick-click solutions on your Web pages to make it easy for your audience to help distribute your news, too.

▶ Increase social capital

It's important to understand the collateral benefits of social media distribution and participation. It goes beyond pageviews and unique users. A news organization can earn social capital—and thus become the trusted center for a community—by engaging in multiple channels.

Participating in social media forces you into really having that two-way conversation that journalists have talked about for years. Listening to your audience will bring huge benefits to your news gathering and news judgment, a form of product development that has never existed in journalism before.

"One of the benefits of having a digitally creative team working within the social and distribution landscape is the knowledge the team brings back to the content development cycle," Haik says. "There is no better time to create successful digital products that reach and develop audiences, as we are able to see our competitors in more full view, engage with our users and optimize/refactor on the fly to meet them where they are as platforms emerge."

Jumping into social media gives a news organization the opportunity to put a human face on the journalism it provides. Readers—"even the ones who hate you"—will engage with the people in a newsroom, while they might just shake their fists at an institution.

Building social capital is an increasingly important strategy for journalists and news companies. As public opinion regarding journalists and the news media continues to be skeptical, those who can find new ways to build bridges back to the communities they cover stand the best chance of increasing their audience.

Credit: Photo courtesy of
Marissa Nelson

MARISSA NELSON

▶ **SENIOR DIRECTOR,
DIGITAL MEDIA** | CBC
News & Centres
(@marissanelson)

As a digital journalist you not only need to be able to kick the ball—you also have to know where the goalposts are.

The only way to measure how well you're kicking and where the ever-changing digital goalposts are is by watching metrics—all the time.

One of the things that makes digital journalism exciting is not only do you need to create the content, you also have to figure out where the audience is, how you'll get your content in front of them and how you'll make it catch their eye.

The goalposts in digital media are always moving, so you have to adapt and change in order to keep scoring.

There are two broad kinds of digital audience—while it may sound polar, it's actually a spectrum. The first is what I call "snackers." These are people who don't know your brand, don't come because they were looking for your work or your organization's work—they come by chance. It could be from Google—they're looking for something specific. It's often driven by big breaking news. It could be because something goes viral, gets picked up by reddit or another site.

It could be also that they come via social—they see the content because someone else they know shared it. Snackers could also be called sampling audience—they're sampling your wares. With a big snackers audience, you'll be watching pageviews, referral rates from places like reddit or Google. When we see in a live-traffic metrics tool that a site like reddit is pushing a lot of traffic to our site, we'll quickly go in and add links, value-added content or other elements to try to make the audience stick around for a little longer. You'll tend to have a higher bounce rate, fewer pageviews per visit and visitor. But it's not bad—it's just a small window of opportunity to show these occasional audience members how great your work is.

At the other end of the spectrum are what I call "lovers." These are audience members who have a strong relationship with your work or your organization. They check you regularly. They come to see what you have published. You can create lovers by giving the audience what they want when they want it—solving key problems they face in their day, whether it's showing them how they can get around during a bad storm or explaining a complicated piece of legislation. You can also make sure investigative or enterprise work doesn't reach *only* your lovers—we plan search engine optimization as part of big projects to make sure we find snackers, too. The metrics that will show whether you've got lovers are high-engagement metrics—lots of pageviews per visit, many visits per unique visitor, higher time spent.

At CBC News, our managing editor, Brodie Fenlon, each morning surveys about 40 different sites to see what we need to be chasing on the snackers front. He watches "Canada" in Google Trends, the Canada reddit boards, what's trending on YouTube. He reviews yesterday's traffic and then around 6 a.m. sends a note to the whole operation. His "Search and story intel" notes are must-reads for everyone—not just digital staff. They set the stage for what we're going to chase, assess if we've kicked the ball in the right direction and whether we need to tweak how we're kicking so we do shoot toward the goalposts.

During big events when we know we'll get a lot of snackers, we try to deduce ways of keeping people on the site. If it's big breaking news, for instance, we'll run a live blog. We're hoping to increase time spent or visits per unique visitor—so people come back to us time and again during the big news event, not just once.

The basic goal is to grab people as snackers and convert them into lovers. But you also need to watch your metrics to know where on that spectrum your site sits—if you have lots of lovers, then the opportunity lies in attracting snackers, and vice versa. No matter where your site is on the spectrum, though, the ultimate goal is more lovers—more people who rely on your work day in and day out.

[*Source:* Written by Marissa Nelson at the request of the author.]

⚑ TRACK, MEASURE, DISTRIBUTE, ADAPT

The first rule in public speaking is to know your audience. It's the first rule of publishing news in the digital age, too. Learning how to track the data that all digital platforms compile on their visitors—and to track what you publish on your Web sites—isn't difficult. But it takes dedication and persistence to make what you learn from such tracking useful to your editorial and design decisions.

Measuring the content you publish and the audience that consumes it can also help you discover new stories and provide more context for your journalism.

Take the time to measure, analyze and adapt your coverage. In the digital age, these steps are critical to good journalism—and building a loyal audience.

"The most valuable audience is the one that comes back," wrote Haile, whose Chartbeat team looked at topics across a random sample of 2 billion pageviews generated by 580,000 articles on 2,000 sites for his Time.com article. "Savvy web natives like Say Media and Vox, as well as established players like the Financial Times, are driven by data more than tradition and are shaping their advertising strategy to optimize for experience and attention."[14]

Welcome to the new age of journalism, where ROI and optimization drive editorial decision making. Regardless of what new digital platforms are invented next, finding—and growing—an audience for journalism will always be a critical part of the job.

GET GOING Checklist ✔

☐ Visit different sections of a news Web site. Determine which section has the best headlines for readers and robots. Rewrite any headlines that need it.

☐ Pick three news Web sites as examples, and enter keywords into three different search engines that you would use if looking for those particular sites. For example, enter "new york news" and see where The New York Times appears in the hits you get.

☐ Pick one news Web site and see how it is using social media to distribute its news coverage. Note the differences between how the stories are presented on the main Web site and how they are presented on the different social networks.

---

[14]Haile, "What You Think You Know."

APPENDIX

Suggested Web Resources

This book comes with a caveat: It can't be updated on a daily or weekly basis. Technology—and the ways people use it—is changing every day. While the core concept of this volume is leveraging technology for better journalism and why it's important, there will always be something new out there.

Following is a list of blogs and Web sites that I used in writing this guidebook and that I frequent on a regular basis to keep in touch with what's next in journalism. Use your natural curiosity and journalistic instinct to sniff out the latest advancements to stay ahead.

These blogs and Web sites offer general information to students of journalism, whether you're in school or still learning about your craft.

General news about journalism innovation:

Journalism.co.uk: http://Journalism.co.uk

Nieman Journalism Lab: www.niemanlab.org

Poynter Online: www.poynter.org

News and commentary about the digital media revolution:

Alfred Hermida: www.reportr.net

CyberJournalist: http://cyberjournalist.net

DigiDave: www.digidave.org

GigaOm: www.gigaom.com/channel/media

Jeff Jarvis: www.BuzzMachine.com

Mashable: http://Mashable.com

Media Disruptus: http://steveouting.com

Mediapost: www.mediapost.com

MediaShift: www.pbs.org/mediashift

MediaShift Idea Lab: www.pbs.org/idealab

PressThink: http://pressthink.org

Reflections of a Newsosaur: http://newsosaur.blogspot.com

New skills, concepts for journalists:

Advancing the Story: http://advancingthestory.com

Interactive Narratives: www.interactivenarratives.org

Online Journalism Blog: http://onlinejournalismblog.com

The Scoop: http://blog.thescoop.org

TV Storytellers: www.tvnewsstorytellers.com

Organizations for online journalists:

Online News Association: www.journalists.org

Radio Television Digital News Association: www.rtdna.org

Society of Professional Journalists: www.spj.org

ABOUT THE AUTHOR

Mark Briggs (@markbriggs) is the author of "Journalism 2.0" and "Entrepreneurial Journalism" and maintains a widely read blog at www.journalism20.com/blog. He is a frequent speaker and presenter at journalism, media and technology conferences throughout the United States and overseas. He is currently the director of digital media at KING-TV in Seattle, and he previously served as assistant managing editor for Interactive News at The News Tribune in Tacoma, Wash., and as new-media director at The Herald in Everett, Wash. He earned journalism degrees from Gonzaga University and the University of North Carolina and was an adjunct professor at Seattle University from 2002 to 2006 and a Ford Fellow for Entrepreneurial Journalism at The Poynter Institute from 2010 to 2012.

INDEX

Pages references followed by (table) indicate a table; followed by (box) indicate a box.